Land Grabbing in Africa

T0300190

The sign that 'Africa is on Sale' has been appearing with regular frequency in major newspaper accounts across the world, indicating that large expanses of Africa's rich farmlands are being sold to transnational investors, usually on long-term leases, at a rate not seen in decades – indeed not since the colonial period.

Transnational and national economic actors from various business sectors (oil and auto, mining and forestry, food and chemical, bioenergy, etc.) are eagerly acquiring, or declaring their intention to acquire, large areas of land in Africa on which to build, maintain or extend large-scale extractive and agro-industrial enterprises to help secure their own food and energy needs into the future.

This book provides a critical appraisal of the growing phenomenon of land grabbing in Africa which has emerged to be a serious threat for the food security of millions of Africans and is undoubtedly one of the great challenges of our time for development on the continent. The case studies illustrate that African states are also complicit in this massive land grabbing by actively participating in isolated development while evicting and excluding the local communities. The case studies also reveal key features that characterise how the global land grab plays out in specific localities in Africa.

This book was published as a special issue of *African Identities*.

Fassil Demissie, PD.D is a faculty member in the Department of Public Policy, DePaul University, USA. He is currently the co-editor of *African and Black Diaspora: An International Journal* and is the author of *Colonial Architecture and Urbanism in Africa: Intertwined and Contested Histories* (Farnham: Ashgate, 2012) and *Postcolonial African Cities* (New York: Routledge, 2008).

Land Grabbing in Africa

The Race for Africa's Rich Farmland

Edited by
Fassil Demissie

Routledge
Taylor & Francis Group

LONDON AND NEW YORK

First published 2015 by Routledge

2 Park Square, Milton Park, Abingdon, Oxon OX14 4RN
711 Third Avenue, New York, NY 10017, USA

Routledge is an imprint of the Taylor & Francis Group, an informa business

First issued in paperback 2017

British Library Cataloguing in Publication Data
A catalogue record for this book is available from the British Library

ISBN 13: 978-1-138-84474-2 (hbk)
ISBN 13: 978-1-138-05693-0 (pbk)

Typeset in Times New Roman
by RefineCatch Limited, Bungay, Suffolk

Publisher's Note
The publisher accepts responsibility for any inconsistencies that may have
arisen during the conversion of this book from journal articles to book chapters,
namely the possible inclusion of journal terminology.

Disclaimer
Every effort has been made to contact copyright holders for their permission to
reprint material in this book. The publishers would be grateful to hear from any
copyright holder who is not here acknowledged and will undertake to rectify
any errors or omissions in future editions of this book.

Contents

Citation Information

The chapters in this book were originally published in *African Identities*, volume 12, issue 1 (February 2014). When citing this material, please use the original page numbering for each article, as follows:

Chapter 7

Land grab in new garb: Chinese special economic zones in Africa: The case of Mauritius
Honita Cowaloosur
African Identities, volume 12, issue 1 (February 2014) pp. 94–109

Chapter 8

Fixity, the discourse of efficiency, and enclosure in the Sahelian land 'reserve'
Erin Kitchell
African Identities, volume 12, issue 1 (February 2014) pp. 110–123

Chapter 9

Water resources and biofuel production after the fast-track land reform in Zimbabwe
Patience Mutopo and Manase Kudzai Chiweshe
African Identities, volume 12, issue 1 (February 2014) pp. 124–138

Please direct any queries you may have about the citations to
clsuk.permissions@cengage.com

The new scramble over Africa's farmland: an introduction

Introduction

> I'm convinced that farmland is going to be one of the best investments of our time. Eventually, of course, food prices will get high enough that the market probably will be flooded with supply through development of new land or technology or both, and the bull market will end. But that's a long ways away yet. (Soros, 2009)

During the first decade of the twenty-first century, more than 3 billion people, about half of the world's population, lived in urban areas for the first time in human history, outnumbering the number of people who lived in rural areas. Indeed, by 2050, this number is expected to increase to 10 billion people (Wolfgang, Sanderson, & Scherbov, 1997).[1] Most of the increase will take place in the impoverished cities of the Global South where many if not most people live in slums with income below the poverty line. At the height of the recent food price crisis in 2009, the Food and Agriculture Organization (FAO) announced that in order to meet the world's growing needs, food production would have to double by 2050, with the required increase mainly in developing countries, where the majority of the world's rural poor live and where 95% of the population increase during this period is expected to occur.[2]

This major demographic transition is taking place today, characterized by global crisis where climate change, peak oil and rising food prices have made food security and energy the primary political issue of our time in which,

> neoliberal land policies emerged within, and became an important aspect of, mainstream thinking and development policy agendas … and have been aggressively promoted by the World Bank and other international development institutions as the solution to persistent landlessness and poverty in the countryside of most developing countries. (Borras Jr., 2006)

As a result, we are witnessing a dramatic rise in the volume of cross-border large-scale land acquisition (land grabbing) in the Global South, in general, and Africa, in particular.

Transnational and national economic actors from various business sectors (oil and auto, mining and forestry, food and chemical, bioenergy, etc.) are eagerly acquiring, or declaring their intention to acquire large areas of land on which to build, maintain, or extend large-scale extractive and agro-industrial enterprises to help secure their own food and energy needs into the future.

In its study, the World Bank Report (2009) argued that vast areas of Africa's rich land is under-utilized and hence should be available for rapid commercial agricultural development considering the expected global population increase. The report suggests that Africa's under-utilized land extending from Guinea Savannah across most of the inland West Africa across the Horn, through much of Central Africa down to east coast of Mozambique, constitutes 'one of the world's largest underused land reserves' (World Bank, 2009, p. 2). Given that the world population is projected to reach 9 billion by 2040, the Bank believes that population growth would outstrip the world's ability to feed itself unless there are radical changes in agricultural production, particularly the commercialization of Africa's vast 'underused land reserve' to meet the growing international demand for food security. The Bank argues that large-scale agricultural investment when done right would directly support smallholder productivity and promote sustainable agricultural and rural development (World Bank, 2009, p. xiii). The Bank believes that the risks are not intrinsic to large-scale foreign investment and mega-projects, but rather rooted in the weak land market and governance as well as the prevailing culture of corruption and institutional breakdown which characterize the countries of the Global South, in general, and Africa, in particular. The Bank's Report reflects the ways in which old colonial powers once imagined Africa as a 'vast underused land reserve.' For example, Sir Charles Eliot, Commissioner of the East Africa Protectorate declared that,

> Nations and races derive their characteristics largely from their surroundings, but on the other hand, man reclaims disciplines and trains nature. The surface of Europe, Asia and North America has been submitted to this influence and discipline, but it has still to be applied to large parts of South America and Africa. (Matondi, Havnevik, & Beyene, 2011, p. 4)

Much of the contemporary discourse of land grabbing echoes this colonial imagination and offers a justification for much of the land grabbing in the continent today. In what appears to be a rationalization for land grab, Palmer (2005, p. 5) has catalogued a number of self-serving statements from officials of several African governments in support of land grab.

> Mozambique's Minister of Energy, Salvador Namburete, for example, stated that '36 million hectares of arable land could be used for biofuels without threatening food production, while another 41 million hectares of marginal land would be suitable for raising jatropha'; Zambia's Minister of Agriculture, Brian Chituwo, boasted 'we have well over 30 million hectares of land that is begging to be utilized'; while his counterpart in Ethiopia, Abeda Deressa, suggested that pastoralists displaced by land grabbing 'can just go somewhere else'. (Matondi et al., 2011, p. 5)

Indeed, as many studies have shown, the alleged empty or under-utilized land in Africa that is now being allocated to long-term leases or concessions to transnational and domestic investors is already occupied and used by 8 million small-scale African farmers, who supply most of the continent's food needs and produce 30% of its GDP. The World Bank places greater emphasis on the commercialization of Africa's 'marginal land' in order to increase the overall output of the agricultural sector. For example, Oliver de Scutter, UN Rapporteur for Right to Food, argues that the development of large-scale commercial agriculture will result in a type of farming that will have very little or no benefit in reducing poverty or improving the livelihoods of rural communities. In addition, this type of agricultural practice undermines local capacity for food production and exacerbates commercial pressure on land. As De Shutter cogently noted, land grabbing is a specific logic of capitalist development by commoditizing land and labor (de Schtter, 2011). Other scholars have also made similar critical arguments noting the intrinsic logic of land grabbing in the massive dispossessing of large numbers of rural people whose livelihood is tied to the land (Li, 2011, 66). A number of case studies drawn from various parts of Africa indicate the extent to which small-scale farmers have been displaced, pastoralists have lost their grazing rights, and rural people have lost access to critical common property resources (Hall, 2011, p. 3). As Palmer (2010, p. 2) has noted, the

> new concession hunters are on the march, seeking control over African land and water to augment food security back home, principally in the Persian Gulf and East Asia. They are finding willing local accomplices, only too eager to lease out vast tracts of land in return for derisory payments and illusory promises. As in colonial times, local people which are impacted are almost never consulted.

The scramble for Africa's rich farm land

At the beginning of the new millennium when Africa was slowly and precariously emerging from the full weight of Structural Adjustment Programs that had devastated the continent, a new and more ominous sign began to appear on the horizon in the form of 'land grabbing' which threatens the livelihood of millions of African peasant farmers that have not yet fully recovered from the destructive effects of agricultural policies pursued by African states under the advice and in response to directives of international financial institutions and donor countries.[3] The sign that 'Africa is on Sale' has been appearing with regular frequency in major newspaper accounts across the world, indicating that large amounts/expanses of Africa's rich farmlands are being sold to transnational investors, usually on long-term leases, at a rate not seen in decades – indeed not since the colonial period.[4]

Since the 2008 global food crisis, wealthy Middle Eastern states, such as Saudi Arabia and the United Arab Emirates, as well as investors from India and China, have been buying up vast areas of arable land across Africa to grow food to feed their burgeoning populations. In 2010 alone, up to 123.5 million acres of African land – double the size of Britain – have been snapped up or were being negotiated by governments or wealthy investors. Ethiopia alone has approved 815 foreign-financed agricultural projects since 2007.[5] The World Bank's study released in September 2010 identified 45 million hectares under negotiation for allocation during 2009 alone, of which 70% (about 32 million hectares) was in Africa (Deininger & Byerlee, 2011). This wave of large-scale land acquisitions is evidence of the magnitude of interest generated by a major global crisis that erupted with full force in 2008, which is fueling the dramatic rise in land acquisitions throughout Africa. Thus, 'today, there is momentum building behind the idea that long-term control of large landholdings beyond one's own national borders is necessary to supply the food and energy needed to sustain one's own population and society into the future ....' (Borras & Franco, 2010). At the same time, the demand for biofuel is also creating huge pressures for land investment as indicated by the expanding fuel initiatives already underway in a number of African countries.[6]

The huge increase in land deals across much of Africa stems from three interrelated and overlapping crises sometimes referred to as 'the triple-F-crisis'. In 2008, the world food crisis reached a new and unprecedented level, climbing to over 8% in just 18 months – which set the stage for the current land grab phenomenon as multinational companies, sovereign wealth funds (notably from Europe and Gulf States), private equity funds, and their financial institutions well as BRICS countries (Brazil, Russia, India, China, and South Africa) sought out farm deals. In addition, South Korea like other BRICS countries also entered the rush to acquire land in Africa to increase the country's food security.

At the height of the food crisis in June 2009, representatives from 200 financial and agribusiness firms gathered to discuss the lucrative agricultural investment in the Global South, in general, and Africa, in particular (Cotula et al., 2009, p. 4; von Braun & Meinzen-Dick, 2009). Later that same year, the UN International Fund for Agricultural Development (UNIFAD) and GRAIN – released reports detailing the extent of land grab in the Global South. The report released by GRAIN identified more than 100 land deals alone in 2008[7] while UNIFAD reported the purchase or lease of more than 6.2 million acres in Ethiopia, Ghana, Madagascar, Mali, and Sudan between 2004 and 2009 (Cotula et al., 2009, p. 42, Table 2.2). According to the study, about 2 million hectares of land across the four countries have been signed over to foreign investors. Table 1 provides a picture of the scale of land deals in Ethiopia, Ghana, and Mali between 2004 and 2009 as documented by UN's Food and Agricultural organizations and the IFAD and the International Institute for Environment and Development.

The rising and fluctuating oil prices, especially during the period 2007–2009, and the realization that the globe might have reached oil peak production created powerful incentives for transnational companies to seek an alternative source and hence the rush to acquire land in the Global South for the production of 'agrofuel' as the new plentiful source of green energy. This new source of energy, which was considered to ameliorate concerns without reducing economic growth, set the policy agenda in Europe and the USA and fueled massive investment in biofuel production in the Global South. The Inter-American Development Bank noted that 'The growth of biofuels will give the advantage to countries with long growing seasons, tropical climates, high precipitation levels, low labor costs, low land costs ... and the planning, human resources, and technological knowhow to take advantage of them.'[8] Another study argued that sub-Saharan Africa, Latin America, and East Asia can in the future provide more than half of all the required 'agrofuels', but only if 'the present inefficient and low-intensive agricultural management systems are replaced by 2050 by the best practice agricultural management systems and technologies' (Smeets, Faaij, & Lewandoski, 2004). Bringing this scenario to fruition is only possible by removing millions of small production farmers in Africa and replacing them with large-scale industrial agricultural plantations – the likes of which we have never seen before. For example, a study carried out by the Justiça Ambiental and União Nacional de Camponeses showed that in total, agrofuel investment companies in Mozambique applied for rights close to 5 million hectares in 2007 alone, which is one-seventh of the country's officially defined arable land (Matavel, 2010). Countries such as Tanzania and Senegal are also committing large sections of their arable land for biofuel production.

The phenomena of land grab in Africa must be considered within the broader context of neoliberal globalization in which Africa has emerged to be the focus of transnational actors who are buying or leasing Africa's rich farmlands for a variety of reasons. Over the past decade, economic liberalization, the globalization of transport and communications, and global demand for food, energy, and commodities have accelerated foreign investment in many parts of Africa – particularly in extractive industries and in agriculture for food and fuel (Carmody, 2011).

A study released by United Nations Conference on Trade and Development in 2007 about the flow of Foreign Direct Investment (FDI) indicated that the countries of Sub-Sahara absorbed well over US$ 22 billion in 2006 and US$ 17 billion in 2005. Although the distribution of FDI flows and stocks is highly uneven across the continent, the major share of the investments are concentrated in countries with important petroleum and mineral resources, such as Nigeria. But while investment flows to some countries have

Table 1. Land under investor claim in Ethiopia, Ghana, and Mali between 2004 and 2009 (approved projects only).

	Ethiopia	Ghana	Mali	Total
Total land area allocated	602,760	452,000	162,590	1,217,340
No. of projects approved (over 100 ha)	157	3[a]	7[a]	167[a]
Largest land allocation	150,000	400,000	100,000	
Total investment commitments (US$)	78,563,023[a]	30,000,000	291,988,688[a]	400,551,711[a]

Source: Adopted from country studies. Cotula et al. (2009).
[a] Denotes incomplete data.

stagnated (e.g. Cameroon), countries such as Ethiopia, Ghana, Mozambique, Sudan, Tanzania, and Zambia, that received little foreign investment until the early 1990s, now host sizeable stocks of foreign investment.[9] Although the global financial crisis and the slow recovery rate may affect the flow of capital to Africa, increased investment in land for food and biofuel security in Africa will continue in the years to come.

Three major factors shape this phenomenon. First, food price spikes of 2007/2008 showed just how vulnerable food-importing nations are to fluctuations in global commodity markets. The skyrocketing cost of stable grains and edible oils triggered riots across the Global South particularly in the improvised cities where many people spend up to 75% of their meager incomes on food. There were an unprecedented number of protests and 'food riots' in the global cities of the South between 2007 and the end of 2008. Demonstrations, marches and rallies in more than 25 countries in Africa, Asia, the Middle East, the Americas, and the Caribbean highlighted the social and economic consequences of dramatically increased food prices which plunged hundreds of millions of people globally into hunger and starvation, from which most have not fully recovered.[10] The rising agricultural commodity prices and uncertainties in global food prices, supply shortage, and the general volatility plaguing global good imports, led a number of countries including Gulf States and several East Asian countries to re-evaluate their strategies; they sought to secure land and water elsewhere to use for agriculture, essentially turning to 'offshore' food production in the Global South to increase their food security.

Second, rising and fluctuating oil prices in the period 2007–2009 and the realization that the world has reached peak oil production have created powerful incentives for companies to acquire land for the production of 'agrofuel' or 'biofuel' crops. Foremost among these feedstocks are jatropha, palm oil, maize, soya for biodiesel, and sugarcane for bioethanol. Compounding the rush toward biofuel are policies in European Union's target of 10% renewable content in its fuel stocks by 2020. Globally, the World Bank found that 12% of land deals in 2009 was for biofuel production, while the international Land Coalition's (ILC) more updated figures put the figure higher at 44%. While there are substantial regional variations, East and Southern Africa have emerged to be the 'new Middle East of biofuel' production.[11] Third is the meltdown in international financial markets beginning in 2008 and the subsequent recession first in the Global North led investors to perceive those markets volatile and highly risky. Many sought to invest in the more tangible asset such as farmland, where the promise of rising demand for food and fuel would make this a secure investment in an increasingly unpredictable global system.

This special issue of *African Identities* hopes to provide a critical appraisal of the growing phenomenon of land grabbing in Africa. Far from being a technical issue associated 'good governance' as the World Bank claims, the problem of land grabbing by transnational corporation and states is a serious threat for food security of millions of Africans and is undoubtedly one of the great challenges of our time for development on the continent. As the case studies in the following pages indicate, African states are also complicit in the massive land grabbing by actively participating in isolated development while excluding the local communities. The case studies also reveal key features that characterize how the global land grab plays out in specific localities in Africa.

Notes

1. However, the population of sub-Saharan Africa will double putting new light to the present land grab in the continent.
2. FAO. Hunger on the rise due to soaring food princes, 2 July 2008.

3. Financial players include pension funds, sovereign wealth, and rich individuals (collectively referred as investors).
4. According to one recent report, there are about 45 new private equity funds that are planning to invest an estimated $2 billion in the [agricultural] sector across the continent, in the next three to five years, 'African farms lure overseas investment' (*Business Report*, 31 August 2010, http://www.busrep.co.za/general/print_article.php?fArticleId=5627527&fSectionId=561& fSetId=662). See also, 'Is agriculture the next big investment thing?' (*The Guardian*, 24 July 2010, http://www.guardian.co.uk/money/2010/jul/24/agriculture next-biginvestment/print).
5. 'Ethiopia: thousands driven out in land grab' (*Business News*, 18 January 2012, http://www.upi.com/Business_News/Energy-Resources/2012/01/18/Ethiopia-Thousands-driven-out-in-land-grab/UPI-60071326912191/#ixzz2ttXmp2qF).
6. GRAINS, http://farmlandgrab.org/8122 (Cited in ABN, 2009).
7. GRAIN (October 2008, p. 11), referencing 'Seized! *GRAIN* Briefing Annex: The 2008 Land Grabbers for Food and Financial Security'. Policy Brief 13. April 2009.
8. 'A Blueprint for Green Energy in the Americas', Prepared for the inter-America Development Bank by Garten Rothkopf. (Cited in GRAIN, July 2007).
9. UNCTD, Export Performance Following Trade Liberalization: Some Patterns and Policy Perspective, 2008.
10. In 2009, the World Bank responded to the food crisis which erupted in the Global South with short-term 'band aid' of assistance with food purchases for poor countries and for the poor within those countries by enlargement of the World Bank's Global Food Crisis Response Program to $2 billion in April 2009.
11. Recognizing the effects of fossil fuel on the environment, especially the production of carbon dioxide gas which contributes to the greenhouse effect, biofuel has emerged as a potential alternative throughout the world. In Africa, although jatropha (*Jatropha curcas*) is not indigenous to Africa, large-scale production by peasant farmers will have adverse impact on local food security. A Report by Dutch consultancy firm Ecofys claims that European demand for biofuels is not to blame for 'land grabbing' in poorer countries and implies that 'land grabbing' has been exaggerated, and concludes that the demand for biofuels has not been a major driver of land acquisition. See http://www.ecofys.com/en/news/report-virtually-no-biofuels-on-the-eu-market-come-from-grabbed-land/. A separate report published in 2011 found that biofuels accounted for 63% of land acquired in Africa since 2005. See George C. Schoneveld, The anatomy of large-scale farmland http://www.cifor.org/publications/pdf_files/WPapers/WP85Schoneveld.pd.

References

ABN. (2009). *Biochar land grabbing: The impacts on Africa: A briefing paper*. The African Biodiversity Network, Bio Fuel Watch, and The Gaia Foundation.
Borras, S. Jr. (2006). The underlying assumptions, theory, and practice of neoliberal land policies. In P. Rosset, R. Patel, & M. Courville (Eds.), *Promised land: Competing visions of agrarian reform* (p. 99). Oakland, CA: Food First Books.
Borras, S., & Franco, J. (2010). From threat to opportunity? Problems with the idea of a 'code of conduct' for land-grabbing. *Yale Human Rights and Development L.J.*, *13*, 507–523.
Carmody, P. (2011). *The new scramble for Africa*. London: Polity Press.
Cotula, L., et al. (2009). *Land grab or development opportunity? Agricultural investment and international land deals in Africa*. Food and Agricultural Organization of the United Nations, International Fund for Agricultural Development (UNIFAD) and International Institute for Environment and Development (INEDF).
de Schtter, O. (2011, March). *Agroecology and the right to food*. Report presented at the 16th session of the United Nations Human Rights Council [A/HRC/16/49].
Deininger, K., & Byerlee, D. (2011). *Rising global interest in farmland: Can it yield sustainable and equitable benefits?* Washington, DC: World Bank.
GRAIN. (2007). *Stop the agrofuel crazy!* Retrieved from http://www.grain.org/article/entries/597-stop-the-agrofuel-craze
GRAIN. (2008). *SEIZED! The 2008 land grab for food and financial security!* GRAIN Briefing, Barcelona.

Hall, R. (2011). *Land grabbing in Africa and the new politics of food*. Policy Brief 42. Future Agriculture.

Li, T. M. (2011). Centering labor in the land grab debate. *Journal of Peasant Studies, 38*, 281–299.

Matavel, D. R. N. (2010). *Jatrophal! A socio-economic pitfall for Mosambique*. Justical Ambiettal (JS) and e Uniao Natiional de Camponeses (UNAC).

Matondi, P. B., Havnevik, K., & Beyene, A. (2011). *Biofuels, land grabbing and food security in Africa*. London: Zed Books.

Palmer, Colin (2010). Would Cecil Rhodes would have signed a code of contact: Reflections on global land grabbing and land rights in Africa, past and present. *African studies association of the UK, Biennial Conference*. Oxford, 16–19 September 2010.

Smeets, E., Faaij, A., & Lewandoski, I. (2004). *A quick scan of global bio-energy potentials to 2050: Analysis of the regional availability of bio-mass resources for export in relations to underlying factor*. Utrecht: Copernicus Institute, Utrecht University. NWS-E-2004-19.

Soros, G. (2009). *The new farm owners: Corporate investors lead the rush for control over overseas farmland*. GRAINS. Retrieved from http://www.grain.org/es/article/entries/4389-the-new-farm-owners-corporate-investors-lead-the-rush-for-control-over-overseas-farmland

von Braun, J., & Meinzen-Dick, R. (2009). *'Land grabbing' by foreign investors in developing countries: Ricks and opportunities*. Washington, DC: International Food Policy Research Institute. Policy Brief 13.

Wolfgang, L., Sanderson, W., & Scherbov, S. (1997). Doubling of world population unlikely. *Nature, 387*, 803–804.

World Bank. (2009). *Awakening Africa's sleeping giant: Prospect for commercial agriculture in the Guinea Savannah zone and beyond*. Washington, DC: Author.

Fassil Demissie

Department of Public Policy, DePaul University, Chicago, IL, USA

Geopolitical drivers of foreign investment in African land and water resources

Antoinette G. Sebastian[a] and Jeroen F. Warner[b]

[a]Independent Researcher and Scholar; [b]Disaster Studies, Social Sciences Group, Wageningen University, Wageningen, The Netherlands

Resource grabs, particularly land and water, can be a proxy for geopolitical influence. As such, 'grabs' become intertwined in international power relations and the competing collective goals and state priorities of economic development, poverty elimination, ecosystem management, energy, self-sufficiency, and food supply stability. African land has become the most appealing and vulnerable to acquisition. In this article we will analyze external investor actions in Africa by South Africa to explain how regional and global geopolitics are fostering a 'new' scramble for natural resources on the African continent. This south–south geopolitical concern examines South Africa's investment in the Democratic Republic of Congo and Lesotho. We argue that 'grabbing' is important, but often it is not the foremost factor in south–south relations and, as such, is an inadequate basis for exploring the role of domestic capital and government investment corporations. We contend that grabbing is not only about food, finances, energy, or even water itself, but also about geopolitical influence. Land and water resource acquisition become intertwined in international power relations and the competing goals of state priorities. This article uses an International Relations framework to analyze these complex relationships, spheres of influence, and asymmetries. Its central argument is that countries with limited arable land 'securitize' (B. Buzan, O. Waever, & J. de Wilde [Eds.], 1998, *Security: A framework for analysis*, Hemel Hempstead: Harvester Wheatsheaf) their food supply and seek ways to increase the supply of food and sources of 'virtual' water by targeting 'easy targets' for resource imperialism, like weak states.

Introduction

Since 2008, the focus on land grabs has come under heavy scrutiny. Investor states perceive investment in agricultural land, and consequently the related water resources, as not only an answer to augmenting their domestic food security but also a way to secure water resources. Also, agro-investments on the part of financial institutions, brokers, and hedge fund managers offer profit-making opportunities to investors and encourage the commodification of land at the global level. At the same time, selling land to foreigners can be a prickly affair. This is an especially sensitive issue in Africa where the 'shadow of the past' (Sebastian, 2008), i.e., the history of colonialism and warfare, mostly resulted in powerful European states 'grabbing' land (and other resources). This 'shadow' makes such deals more complicated than mere real estate deals.

Despite this history, Africa is 'open' for investment. African states have been aggressively seeking investors beyond their borders (foreign direct investment [FDI]).

Where they have not, external actors are courting African states. However, this courtship offers little to explain the geopolitics; as noted by Baldwin (1979), the conversion of 'land power' into 'political power' is rarely straightforward. In this analysis, land and water grabs are useful 'hooks' for drawing out the complex power relationships and geopolitics behind international water interdependencies (Warner, Sebastian, & Empinotti, 2012), and the globalization nexus of freshwater and food security. Furthermore, as emphasized in our definitions of land and water grabs below, these resource grabs are not new behavior.

Countries with plentiful land, water, and mineral resources that lack the knowledge to capitalize or use them to the state's advantage may find it difficult to convert them into power. The absence of capital and expertise may result from prolonged conflict, weak and noncompetitive domestic educational systems, and postindependence structural programs that have saddled countries with debt repayment. These absences may also be the result of corrupt, kleptocratic leadership exploiting resources that provide local elites with wealth and political power at the domestic level, leading to a misdistribution of wealth, and a lack of investment in modernization and development.[2]

This article links the fraught discussion of 'land grabs' (the large-scale acquisition of land in developing, economically and politically weak countries through FDI by powerful, developed, economically robust, but water-stressed, nations) to the larger issue of the globalization of water security and geopolitics. Literature on land and water grab is concerned with institutional and legal implications, or assessing socioeconomic developmental impacts. We argue that access to resources is both a means and an end. As a means, it may serve ulterior power objectives, explaining 'the exploitation of foreign natural resources and the international redistribution of its benefits' (Palo, Uusivuori, & Mery, 2001). In so doing, this discussion illustrates why a water or land grab may not be primarily about food, forestry, or even water itself, but about geopolitical influence. We illustrate this geopolitical concern with the examples of South Africa's investment on the African continent: in Lesotho, the Republic of Congo (Congo), and the Democratic Republic of Congo (DRC). South Africa, a regionally hegemonic power (Turton & Earle, 2005), is semiarid and always actively engaged in managing and securing water resources. Two of its recent investments, in Congo and DRC, suggest that it is seeking control of both physical and virtual water. This highlights water as a political good and a lever for wielding power (cf. Donahue & Johnston, 1998).

We use the 'grab' debate to highlight the importance of water, power, and geopolitics. We focus on the case of South Africa to discuss power asymmetries: spheres of influence; national, regional, and international actors vying for influence and position; and multinational private and national private interests in the context of state interests.

We also reassert the importance of state behavior. While both the liberal and critical traditions in international/relations background the role of states, the public sector seems to have reasserted itself after the global food-price peaks of 2007–2008 and 2011 with a variety of 'security mercantilism' (McMichael, 2011). Many of the more aggressive foreign state investors are those facing real and potential arable land and water shortages at home, e.g., China, India, South Africa, Saudi Arabia, Egypt, and Korea. However, since each of those nations is undergoing internal and global political change and rapid economic growth, their 'potential' shortage offers only a partial explanation (speculation and/or assuring long-term productive capacity) for these dynamics.

We chose to focus on South Africa because:

(1) this is an African country, not an 'outsider', and is expected by the global North and others to be the exception, the success story on the Continent, to somehow

avoid many of the labels – corruption, inept government, cronyism – applied to other African nations;

(2) it's access strategy, we will argue, is about more than access to resources; it is about the enhancement of its geopolitical influence in Africa; and

(3) this is a (reluctant) regional hegemon and hydro-hegemon (Zeitoun & Warner, 2006), and has used its technical prowess across multiple sectors in the past as a means to secure, advance, and retain its dominant Continental position.

Borras and Franco (2010) define the global land grab as 'a catch-all framework to describe and analyse the current explosion of (trans) national commercial land transactions related to the production and scale of food and biofuels'. Others define a land grab as 'taking possession of and/or controlling a scale of land for commercial or industrial agricultural production, which is disproportionate in size in comparison to the average land holding in the region'.[3] Food and Agricultural Organization (FAO) reports (Cotula, Vermeulen, Leonard, & Keeley, 2009) discuss land grabs in the context of land deals and consider the emphasis on land grabs by some media only part of the overall equation. We argue that land grabs represent one aspect of calculated FDI strategies and general investment 'opportunities' for state and nonstate actors usually at the invitation of the investee country and, are central to geopolitics. We submit, further, that land grabs and related water reappropriation are routinely initiated by states wanting to achieve some 'higher' purpose, dam construction, flood control, infrastructure development, irrigation schemes, etc., as part of their economic development strategy. *Water grabs* (and reappropriation) by states occur when one state initiates an upstream activity that reduces downstream flows, establishes policies or engages in practices that assure states beyond its borders will undertake projects likely to capture, redirect, or appropriates a significant amount of water for activities for which water resources are not currently being used. Water grabbing includes dams paid for and constructed in one state for hydropower export well beyond its borders across multiple states as well. They occur whenever water is moved or transferred, via pipeline, inter basin transfer schemes, or other diversionary means from where it is located to support activities in another location, or when water has been reappropriated/taken from its originating location somewhere else in support of nonfreshwater ecosystem activity. As such, the Lesotho Highlands water project (LHWP) and South African and other international financial support for dam construction of the Great Inga in the DRC constitute water grabs using our criteria.

Fierce demand, willing suppliers

Like humans, crops have very specific water requirements. Irrigation, for the purposes of this article, is one example of a 'water grab' scenario, as it diverts surface water from one location to another, from multiple users to a single purpose user, and, in many places may include groundwater withdrawals. In all instances, water use and demand is inextricably linked to food production and, as a consequence, food security.

Water serves many masters and, as repeated often, water is the essential component of the very existence of life. On a global scale, food and agricultural production consumes an estimated 70% of all water use (through rainfall and irrigation). Land grabbing for food justified by the world food crisis is undertaken by combinations of development agencies (World Bank, FAO, investment banks [Goldman Sachs], funds [Carlyle Group], and philanthropists [Soros, Gates Foundation]), and was sanctioned by the World Food Summit of 2008 (McMichael, 2011).

In Africa, the epicenter of FDI, these transactions are occurring at high rates because of the following:

(1) The perception that not only is there an abundance of available water and land, but that it is either underutilized or vacant;
(2) Untapped availability and opportunity;
(3) Willingness on the part of political leadership to aggressively invite FDI or create 'open for business' opportunities to incentivize investment;
(4) Inadequate land-property rights or tenure systems, or weak and unclear laws and institutional frameworks, including the absence of enforcement protocols for existing or customary land tenure systems;
(5) Lack of transparency, documentation, monitoring, or government accountability, or the state's insistence (by constitution or political leadership) that it has sole and exclusive ownership rights and control of all natural and mineral resources and is therefore not obligated to recognize 'stakeholders' or customary or traditional practices (Deininger et al., 2011; Sharife, 2009; Shepard & Mittal, 2009).

Arguably, many of the states where this type of FDI is occurring are weak states, like Mozambique, Ethiopia, and Zambia. Others have recently evolved from long-term conflicts, e.g., the DRC. Several are trying to retire outstanding foreign debt (IMF or other international financial institution loans). Even where host-country governments have codified progressive laws and procedures designed to protect local rights, their enforcement is likely weak or nonexistent (Cotula et al., 2009; Kugelman & Levenstein, 2009; Oakland Institute, 2011).

What does a hegemon want? The geopolitical perspective

To reproduce and secure itself, a sovereign state needs resources, control of territory, and a tax base. If resources are scarce, it needs to project its power beyond its borders to gain access to these resources. In an arid or semiarid region such as the Southern African Development Community (SADC) region, scarce water is one of the key constraints. Regional hegemony is a possible way out. Being a regional superpower carries considerable burdens, but it also enables that state to write or bend the rules to its advantage. An ideological strategy seeking to unite under the same agenda (e.g., 'Africa's resurgence/ renaissance') can be the foundation of such an ideational strategy (Griggs, 1997).

In water-scarce countries, like South Africa, water is easily 'securitized'. Water continues to be invoked by South Africa and its neighbors as a national survival issue (Davidsen, 2006; Jacobs, 2007; Turton, 2010). As Donahue and Johnston (1998) have noted, state apparatuses use water and its perceived scarcity to expand their bureaucratic power. They protect companies they deem essential to furthering those goals. Geopolitical influence is obviously related to access to strategic resources. A *hegemonic* power is also very much concerned by peace and stability, so that markets and institutions can continue to operate. This is why hegemonic powers often prove willing to shoulder disproportionate burdens and go to any length to guarantee regional stability. This is as true of the USA on a global scale as it is of South Africa on a regional scale, as South Africa outranks everyone else on the continent, not just in a material, hard-power sense (with its relatively small but state-of-the-art military) but also in the ideological sense (Furlong, 2006), buttressed by knowledge and technology, wealth, and symbolic power (Bourdieu, 1991). Hegemony is close to what Keohane (1984) refers to as 'legitimate domination', which is not so much domination, but leadership. The follower country makes it easy by willingly internalizing the norms and principles established by the hegemon (see also Monyae, 2012). Hegemony rests on assent and may even be actively courted (cf. Wesselink, Warner, & Kok, 2012). In fact, investee states may actively seek out investors.

To get what it wants, a hegemon, however, needs a hegemonic project. A hegemonic project or comprehensive concept of control is shaped, and continuously reshaped, in a process of struggle, compromise, and readjustment, resulting in 'a succession of negotiated settlements, of concessions to the rigidities and dynamics of structures as well as the political possibilities of the moment' (Drainville, 1994, p. 116). It is about fostering a relatively stable and widely accepted order based on an 'intersubjective sharing of behavioural expectations' (Cox, 1989, p. 829). In line with that literature, we perceive multiple lines of 'attack' with increasing degrees of directness: (1) direct material foreign investment, (2) shaping the rules of the game (treaties, agreements, or communities promoting access, and (3) using soft power: ideology (e.g., Ubuntu and Pan-Africanism).

South Africa has followed the prescriptions of the West, opening its market-based economy to trade. But it has struggled. The high unemployment rate, persistent inequality, poverty, crime, social unrest, growing corruption, graft, and calls for nationalization of private mining companies and privately owned farmland continue to plague one of the continent's richest nations. The country's divisive history continues to cast its shadow (Sebastian, 2008); domestic intra- and interracial struggles and national debate by the ruling African National Congress (ANC) party pushed for the nationalization[4] and transfer of privately owned farmland has led to an exodus of white commercial farmers to countries as nearby as Mozambique, and as far afield as DRC and even Georgia in Eastern Europe.[5]

Despite these internal struggles, South Africa '... now seems poised to dominate the continent that once shunned its products and leaders' (Swarns, 2002). Former President Thabo Mbeki, speaking in Parliament (on 18 February 2003) attempted to assure South Africa's immediate neighbors 'and the peoples of the rest of Africa that the Government (RSA) had no great "power pretentions" and would not impose its will on any independent country' (Daniel, Naidoo, & Naidu, 2003). The irony is that South Africa's past and present behavior indicates a different reality, a 'shadow of the past' that is not easily erased (Sebastian, 2008): historically, it aggressively pursued regional economic and territorial dominance over several of its neighbors and has had considerable success capturing water and influence beyond its borders since. During the apartheid era, among its many other strategies, South Africa achieved much of its power through labor and transportation arrangements with its bordering countries. It has had a long history of covert and overt regional intervention and alignment with colonial rulers, such as aiding the Portuguese in the wars of independence in Mozambique and Angola during the apartheid era. Not only has South Africa backed factions in domestic struggles in Sub-Saharan Africa (Vehnämäki, 2002), it is also a key large-scale agricultural investor on a continent where large-scale farming is rare (Kugelman & Levenstein, 2009). Sebastian (2008) argues that history aligns power and shapes identity by framing the language of politics and power. In that way the 'shadow of the past' has positioned South Africa as a powerful hegemon.

South Africa's postapartheid expansion has been anything but covert. South Africa already dominates the continent's economy. With peace in Angola and the DRC, the South Africanization of the region is likely to expand. Even now, there are many examples of South Africa influence. South Africa businesses are running the national railroad in Cameroon, the national electricity company in Tanzania, managing major city airports in seven African capitals (Daniel et al., 2003), and engaged in retail expansion (Shoprites Checkers stores) in Nigeria, Egypt, Zambia, and elsewhere in Africa (Miller, Nel, & Hampwaye, 2008). South Africa has controlling shares in Telecom[6] Lesotho, with whom it has a long-standing relationship due to the LHWP,[7] which provides water to Gauteng Province. In addition to cell phone service, South Africa corporations (and parastatals) are managing power plants and building roads, bridges, and hydroelectric power facilities throughout the region and continent. It controls *and* manages a gas pipeline between offshore Mozambique and South Africa, as well as numerous banks, hotels, breweries, groceries, and department stores. One of South Africa's foremost investors is Eskom – wholly owned by the South Africa government,[8] which provides 95% of the electricity used in South Africa and 45% of all the electricity used in Africa (Figure 1).[9]

With its extensive economic reach, South Africa is a regional and continental economic and 'knowledge' hegemon. It has knowledge, expertise, and capacity, all of which enables South Africa to expand its reach and compete as a significant power capable of shaping Africa's geopolitics. In this context, South Africa has power in part because it declares it has such power, but importantly because other states have 'recognized' the symbolic (Bourdieu, 1991) and real power of South Africa. In this case, the DRC, as well as others, have accepted and recognized that some of the power South Africa exercises and exports are their knowledge, technology, and capital. In return, rather than exhibiting overt physical force, something it *is* capable of, South Africa uses its 'symbolic power' to gain influence, which it can then use to generate real power.

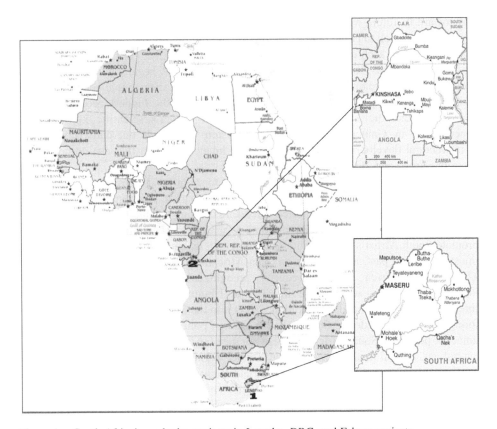

Figure 1.   South Africa's geohydro projects in Lesotho, DRC, and Eskom projects.
■ African countries with secured (and/bid) Eskom projects.
* Map Source: Central Intelligence Agency *The World Factbook* at https://www.cia.gov/library/publications/the-world-factbook/geos/lt.html
** Map Source: Central Intelligence Agency *TheWorld Factbook* at https://www.cia.gov/library/publications/the-world-factbook/geos/cg.html

In its postapartheid state, South Africa has struggled to continue and advance further toward African hegemony. Schoeman (2003) identifies South Africa as an 'emerging power' or 'emerging middle power'. South Africa recognizes itself as an integral part of the African continent. South Africa acknowledges its national interest as intrinsically linked to Africa's stability, unity, prosperity, and security. This philosophy translates into an International Relations approach that acknowledges that it is in South Africa's national interest to promote and support the positive development of other African nations.[10] We will explore this further using a closer examination of the geopolitics of South Africa and its postapartheid relationship with the DRC.

Under the leadership of SADC and in particular South Africa, the Southern African Hydropolitical Complex[11] (SAHPC) has provided the crucial function of not only linking riparian states in a series of interstate arrangements, but has demonstrated to a greater extent that 'water issues have become drivers of international relations in their own right' (Turton & Earle, 2005, p. 15). Among the economically advanced and stable countries in the SADC region, South Africa is a 'pivotal' riparian in 'pivotal basins' (Turton & Earle, 2005). The Orange, Limpopo, and Incomati rivers, all critical to South Africa, are either near or are facing closure.[12] If it was just about the water, South Africa's desalination program (South Africa Department of Water Affairs and Forestry, 2004) would go a long way toward its future water security.[13] South Africa, however, has used its capacity and hegemonic position to project its power beyond its borders and has a long history of doing so. LHWP is one such example.

South Africa has, so far, opted to be a 'friendly giant'. A hegemonic power does not need to be aggressive to be a hegemon. Thus, South Africa is hegemonic not only in terms of 'hard power' but also 'soft power': economic (it is the biggest economy on the continent), scientific knowledge (roughly 80% of Africa's scientific knowledge is concentrated in Gauteng), stable political system (although one-party dominated), infrastructural development, all coupled with a financial system that can compete with those in Europe and North America.

Hegemons have (to a degree) the wherewithal to set or bend the rules and as the most competitive power they tend to be in favor of the free market. The domestic liberal values that Furlong (2006) claims are exported abroad are certainly visible. South Africa refers to their foreign policy approach as its 'diplomacy of Ubuntu'. Ubuntu diplomacy strives to promote South Africa's national interest, strengthen its national identity and address the injustices of the past, and focuses on 'Pan-Africanism and South–South solidarity'.[14] Thus, South Africa national security recognizes that 'interconnectedness and interdependency', as well as the infusion of Ubuntu (South Africa Department of International Relations and Cooperation, 2011) into the South African identity shapes its foreign policy. In so doing, South Africa's foreign policy has a critical role in meeting domestic priorities. South Africa's strategy for meeting its growing demand for electricity, natural gas, and oil is one such example (Daniel & Lutchman, 2006).

Currently, South Africa coal-generated electricity (90%) and nuclear reactors (7%) provide the majority of its power needs through its public utility Eskom,[15] which provides 95% of electricity used in South Africa, and approximately 45% of that used in Africa. South Africa, however, acknowledges the increasing demand on a strained coal-based power supply system *and* the necessity to diversify to include one that includes oil, natural gas, and hydro-powered electricity. To accomplish this, South Africa is engaged in joint ventures in other national utility companies, in Botswana, Angola, and Namibia, designed not only to fulfill South Africa's national power supply but also to continue the interrelationship of meeting national interests (reliable energy) and reinforce its foreign policy under the framework of Ubuntu, as demonstrated 'by collaboration, cooperation, and partnership' (AllAfrica Online, 2012). Recent actions on the part of South Africa, through its state-owned public utility Eskom reaffirm this policy. When the Mozambique Hidroelectrica de Cahora Bassa (HCB) dam operation, which supplies electricity to South Africa, ceased to operate as a result of a broken reactor Eskom supplied a replacement and transported it to HCB.[16] To enlarge and secure its gas and oil exploration and supply, South Africa, through PetroSA, has wide-ranging arrangements in several African countries, including Gabon, Namibia, Equatorial Guinea, the Central African Republic, and Swaziland. In addition to the joint ventures for African oil and natural gas markets, South Africa continues to focus on the Grand Inga as the vital element in securing its long-term objective of ensuring self-sufficiency in electricity (Daniel & Lutchman, 2006).

South Africa's interest in the DRC is long-standing and will intensify as its status as a continental hegemon and power broker grows – if past actions are testament. Indeed, when war erupted in the DRC in 1996, the very popular and respected then-President Nelson Mandela attempted to assist the peace process by bringing Mobutu and Laurent Kabila together. Mandela is credited with negotiating Mobutu's departure into exile (Kabemba, 2007). Arguably, it was South Africa's principal mediating role in what would be known as the Inter-Congolese Dialogue in 2003 which positioned it as a prime ally and regional actor in the DRC's gradual but steady progress toward peace, stability, and democratization. The end of the civil conflict in the DRC created an opportunity to normalize regional and international relations.

More recently, however, South Africa's involvement with the politics in the DRC is suspect (Sturman, 2011). South Africa printed and delivered the ballots for the recent DRC presidential election. In addition, at the DRC's electoral commission, the Commission Electorale Nationale Indépendante (CENI), the South African National Defence Force (SANDF) assisted with logistics – delivery of ballots to voting locations throughout the country, as well as other tasks. As a result, rumors circulated that many of the ballots had been marked in advance, all of which aided Kabila's win (Nossiter, 2011; Sturman, 2011).

South Africa has contributed peacekeeping troops, millions of rand,[17] and years of diplomacy in trying to bring stability to the eastern DRC, and in particular the Ituri province which borders on Uganda with Lake Albert in-between. Ituri has both gold and oil that are not easily accessible or extracted, especially without political stability and security. This involvement was not solely based on a moral duty to share South Africa's peace dividend with Africa – President Jacob Zuma and others have said that it was in South Africa's economic interest to 'stabilize the Great Lakes region'.[18] As both are members of SADC, trade and other political relations between South Africa and the DRC should be expected. So while the relationship between DRC and RSA is being mutually exploited, the trade balance between the two is decidedly in South Africa's favor. Outside of SADC, to date, there are 32 bilateral agreements between South Africa and the DRC.

Then, there is the *water* – the Congo River – as well as an abundance of other resources and potential markets for South Africa, which cannot be overlooked or easily disaggregated from its interest in a stable peaceful neighbor in the DRC. Even in the absence of a 'peaceful' DRC, South African corporations and business interests were commercially involved in 'extraction' activities during both the 1996 and the 1998 wars.

These deals, regimes and agreements involve 'real' ('blue') water (Woodhouse & Ganho, 2011). More significant would seem to be the 'virtual' ('green') water: the water contained in the root zones of arable land (Allen, 1998) . These resources, like the Congo and the deals with the DRC, take South Africa further afield. However, it is not only South

African government negotiating but other South African entities as well. Chief among them are controlled in part or wholly state-owned companies ('parastatals'), like Eskom and, importantly, commercial farmers' union organizations.

In 2010, the commercial farmers' union association, Agri South Africa[19] (AgriSA) was engaged in land acquisition negotiations with the governments of 22 African countries (Hall, 2011). Li (2011) suggests that these deals are for purposes other than food production and what is being grabbed extends to land, to water, and other natural resources along with the labor necessary to exploit these. Toward that end, Li argues that acquiring land is part of a wider business strategy to extend South African value chains and include not only farmers but also a 'wide range of private and public sector actors in South Africa and in "host" countries' (Li, 2011).

The most significant concluded deal negotiated by AgriSA is with the Republic of Congo (Hall, 2011), which interestingly enough, imports 95% of its food requirements. The deal-agreement between the Congo government and AgriSA *gives* South African commercial farmers an initial 200,000 hectares of former state farms, the associated farmland, and places another 10 million hectares of arable land under the control of AgriSA farmer members.

There are both push and pull factors. AgriSA has emphasized the 'push', i.e., concerns about increased government regulation, taxation, and most of all, the threat of land expropriation designed to address land restitution, redistribution, and tenure reform – all postapartheid policies. In addition, AgriSA cites water constraints, its growing scarcity, low profitability, and land degradation[20]. Among the 'pull' factors are the favorable terms being offered by the 'host' country, which in this case is the Republic of Congo.[21] Such deals often do not result in benefits for the small farmers, traditional land holders, women, the environment, or a country's development in a larger or more immediate manner, as documented by the Oakland Institute (2011), Shepard and Mittal (2009), Bailey (2011), Aarts (2009), and GRAIN (2010). The lack of transparency for land deals makes collecting empirical evidence difficult, thus analysis on land investments problematic and challenging to characterize. Many deals are conducted in secrecy and lack transparency. Nonetheless, numerous reports and existing literature identify the negative implications of these deals. In the case of the Guba District in Ethiopia, a land deal increased competition for limited water resources and threatened the water supply for the areas small farmers and villages. Mozambique, Ethiopia, and the DRC are experiencing deforestation, loss of biodiversity and wildlife resources, along with displacement of small farmers and villages and a disproportionate adverse social and economic impact on women (Cotula, et al, 2009; Dessie & Christiansson, 2008; von Braun & Meinzen-Dick, 2009). Diminishing access to local food production resources as a result, many land deals fail to increase food security (Daniel & Mittal, 2009). A Global Land Project (GLP) Report (2010) concluded the motivation of investments in Ethiopia and Madagascar was biofuel (i.e., energy crops of jatropha, corn, and sugarcane) production, not food (Friis & Reemberg, 2010).[22] In fact, while '(t)he spectre of a hungry world is being used to push the agenda for industrial agriculture … in reality, the majority of the land is used for producing animal feed and agro-fuels, as well as land speculation, rather than food crops' (Henriques, 2011).

AgriSA's land acquisition is interesting because it is a neither a governmental organization nor strictly a private 'investment' organization. It appears to function without direct governmental oversight, but such a conclusion is misleading. Consistent with South Africa national policy to export South Africa's agricultural skills and technology and business expansion, the government of South Africa has updated and signed bilateral agreements and investment treaties with many of the same countries in negotiations with

AgriSA. Recently, AgriSA has been offered an estimated 10 million hectares for development by the Republic of Congo. Furthermore, when asked, Andre Botha, president of AgriGauteng, a division of AgriSA, cited among the reasons for Congo was '... to assist the government of South Africa to fulfill the expectations of the world in stabilizing the African continent through the exchange of skills and technology' (Sharife, 2010). South Africa has also entered into 'land deals' with the DRC involving approximately 8 million hectares.[23]

For South Africa, one dividend from DRC investments and political agreements is access to clean, cost-effective energy, vis-à-vis its water. South Africa's industrial, commercial, domestic, and international growth and development depends upon this. Provided the funding can be arranged, it would appear that South Africa is now poised to capitalize on the 'blue' and 'green' waterpower of the Congo River. Achieving this would be an even greater indicator of South Africa's ability to expand itself regionally, economically, and socially.

South Africa's multinationals, its capital, technology, and expertise have been and continue to be significant in expanding its reach among African countries. Both during and postapartheid, South Africa has established a strong claim to the regional space of southern Africa (Miller et al., 2008). Still, the South Africa narrative is flawed, as the policy of Ubuntu is not reflected in its internal politics of class, race relations, debates around the nationalization of land and mining industries, and the increasing level of corruption among the country's political elite. Nonetheless, South Africa has embraced its hegemonic position in part through providing technical assistance, knowledge, and capital for fixed investments like the Grand Inga, roads, and rail.

In the long run, those with the greatest need of the basics; electricity, food security, water and sanitation, jobs, and education may derive some benefit, but the evidence suggests that the state (South Africa) and business interests come first. As evidenced by the signing of the 2004 General Cooperation agreement of the DRC-RSA (Republic of South Africa), relations have been formalized. The Agreement established a Bi-National Commission (BNC), which recently (September 2013) resulted in a South Africa-organized 43 businessperson delegation to visit the DRC, under the leadership of South Africa's Deputy Minister of Trade and Industry. She noted:

'... [the] DRC is a strategic country for South Africa, with a domestic market estimated at 75 million and bordered by nine countries with a potential market of 200 million consumers and it presents the largest market for South African products and services in Sub-Saharan Africa.'[24] Another signed agreement concerns the RSA and Mozambique. It's a parliament to parliament 5-year Memorandum of Understanding (MOU).[25] Not including the transboundary water agreements or those involving water and the environment more generally, South Africa has either initiated or signed multiple formal bi-national (bi-lateral) and several multinational agreements with many African states. Only two have been mentioned.

From an International (IR) perspective many (Neumann, 1992; Nolte, 2010; Osterud, 1988) would agree that South Africa is a recognizable regional great power. It is a state which is (1) geographically part of the delineated region; (2) able to stand-up against a coalition of other states in its region; (3) decidedly influential in regional affairs and governance; (4) connected to the region culturally, economically, and politically; (5) provides leadership to states within the region, engenders regional stability, both militarily and politically, and creates and seeks economic development and trade stimulus. As noted previously, South African foreign policy and regional hegemony and leadership is exhibited in its diplomatic and military engagements to stabilize African areas in conflict, including Angola, Burundi, Lesotho, Kenya, Mozambique, Sierra Leone, Sudan, and, to a lesser extent, Zimbabwe (Habib, 2009). Along with Nigeria's Obasanjo, South Africa, under Mbeki, was central to the creation of the African Union, and then later with Senegal's Abdoulaye Wade, the three engineered [the] New Partnership for Africa's Development (NEPAD). With consistent insistence, South Africa is a leading voice in the effort to popularize the African agenda in the international community (Gelb, 2001) and used its chair role in the UN Security Council to prioritize African conflicts and solutions. Active in more than 20 countries, and second only to China, South Africa leads in Continental investment across various economic sectors, including mining, energy, manufacturing, telecommunications, and research and development (Daniel et al., 2003). All of South Africa's parastatals, e.g., Eskom, PetroSA, and its state-owned Industrial Development Corporation are actively expanding their economic investment footprint on the African Continent (Daniel et al., 2003).[26]

The expansionist politics of South Africa have not transpired without debate – domestically, regionally, and continentally. The nonmilitaristic regional hegemonic leadership and political and socioeconomic vision of security, stability, and economic and human development has been met with some skepticism. Criticism was leveled in South Africa's actions when it engaged in Lesotho (1998 Boleas Operation), and again, when it (under Mbeki) failed to intervene or forcefully condemn Mugabe's actions in Zimbabwe. However, it is important to remember that South Africa's contemporary foreign policy and regional geopolitics cannot be separated totally from its past apartheid state ('shadow of the past') or its postapartheid democratic transition. ANC's struggle for independence in South Africa shared similar struggles with the anticolonial transitions that had occurred in other African states: states that supported and provided succor to antiapartheid nationalists. In the absence of long protracted civil wars or internecine conflicts characterized by other African nations in their postcolonial stages, the economically viable apartheid South Africa state was better positioned as a postapartheid state. As a consequence, it is that shared anticolonial, antiapartheid history that enables these second-generational black African nationalist leaders, like Mbeki or Zuma, to exercise regional power – despite having been seen sharing an anticolonial agenda: a commitment to racial equality, economic and human development, ending poverty, and modernizing African states. It is in this sense that the Ubuntu foreign policy vision links South Africa's national interests with those in neighboring states and the reverse. As these examples illustrate, through its actions we observe South Africa advantage its position as both a continental hegemon and regional power through direct material investment; shaping the rules of the game (treaties, bilateral agreements, continent-wide intuitions) and communities; promoting access and entrepreneurship; and using soft power (Ubuntu) to rebuild, restructure, and redevelop a modern Africa – state-by-state and deal-by-deal..)

FDI in land, natural resources, or in farms, is nothing new, it is the scale that is new. For a would-be hegemonic power like South Africa, the persistent question is how best to use its material force ('hard' power: technology, AgriSA, parastatals, capital, etc.) and 'soft', ideational power (the attraction of success; persuasion; ideology) (Nye, 1990) to make its allies fulfill its own needs. The fact that regional neighbors so keenly ply their wares at cut-rate prices only facilitates South African hegemonic needs being met. Mostly due to the manner and location of these transactions, attention-grabbing terms are being used to bring awareness to the deals, investment practices, and social and environmental impacts. The negative perception of this behavior, i.e., the powerful taking advantage of weaker states or one's former colony has a long history.[27] South Africa's Ubuntu diplomacy is one attempt to resist that history.

The evidence indicates that it is very much an 'investors' market. Still, from a geopolitical perspective, investee states also stand to gain. One way is an infusion of capital essential to development, technology, knowledge, and capital that can be used to pay off debt. Then there is, of course, the potentially lucrative financial benefit for the personal accounts of the political elite. Another and important gain is being the 'power' and having control of the investee state. Investee states have become important actors; their new status not only increases their power but also enables alliance frameworks, not only with states with which they share a watershed but also regionally and internationally. This results in structural and financial interdependencies, which in turn induces investee states to cooperate, even when it is they who have invited the investor.

Conclusion

This article examined the geopolitical dimensions of land and water grabs in Africa. There is significant competition for African investment and trade among key global and African hegemonic contenders, undertaken in part by state-controlled or state-run 'private-sector' companies. Looking beyond direct water and energy interests, we examined the water geopolitics of South Africa, showing how a powerful country is engaged in two-level water geopolitics – domestic (nation-building) and international (hegemonic) relations – and advantageously negotiating 'deals' in their foreign policy interests. South Africa's hegemonic strategy centers on securing economic interests to support (and protect) a growing powerful hegemon: itself.

'Water grabbing' investor state engaged in cross-boundary 'transfers' of either real or virtual waters may resort to political tactics to help assure favorable conditions. To protect its interests, South Africa may devise multiple means to assure its ability to influence DRC politics, resource decisions, and land use. For example, South Africa's *assistance* during the DRC's recent presidential elections could be seen as one means of securing its influence. For South Africa, keeping Kabila in power eliminates the need to engage with a new group of politicians who may be less predisposed to doing business the 'old' way.

South Africa's foray into the DRC is being shaped by:

(1) the physical dimensions of water – real water – as a process capable of being converted into a profit-making enterprise, direct benefit – financial return and economic benefit;
(2) indirect water, i.e., energy (as is the case with the Grand Inga Dam);
(3) virtual water, *vis*-à-vis agricultural production and export to South Africa; and
(4) political power by way of influence in local and regional politics much like it has done in the *recent* past (the last 15 years or so).

Water has real power beyond economics; its perceived scarcity or abundance influences the behavior of states. How states choose to exercise their response, either collectively or independently determines how water is securitized. Table 1 offers an interpretive conclusion of each of these factors.

The real or perceived availability of water is also a factor. The perception of water vulnerability prompts states to prioritize securing water for their future. Increasingly, water security is a central factor in the politics of both the investor and investee country. Turton (2010) even argues that the economic development of the entire SADC region is defined by the availability of water – not just its control but also the development of hydraulic infrastructure necessary to improve water security.

South Africa has successfully expanded its retail and commercial interests throughout Africa and is aggressively engaged in the export of its technology and knowledge, both of which will influence how investee states make decisions: invest within their borders; cooperate with South Africa, especially in the future; and engage in policy and cross-border negotiations. With an eye on Security Council membership, South Africa,

Table 1. South Africa water investment and geostrategic objectives.

Level of proximity	Action	Ulterior geostrategic objective	Relationship
Direct water access	LHWP + Orange-Senqu River treaty	Control of Lesotho Government and protect water supply for Gauteng Province, South Africa	Stop/start relationship, sometimes heavy handed. Investment courted by recipient state
Indirect water access	Eskom investment in Inga mega dam (DRC)	Stabilizing region	Investment courted
Virtual water access	South Africa major FDI in DRC land	Food and water security	Investment courted

seemingly, wants it all: to be the dominant African hegemon and a global player. As such, it will resort to direct, indirect, and virtual water access as one means of accomplishing its goals. To return to one of our initial questions: what does a hegemon want? Achille Mbembe[28] (quoted in Moore, 2001 p. 914) noted that South Africa's 'virtual frontier stretches from the Cape to Katanga. That is closer than ever to Rhodes' ancient desire to reach Cairo …' In other words: the world stage.

Notes

2. The exploitation of resources and associated power by political leadership at the state level (e.g., Angola, Equatorial Guinea), when accompanied by the *select* or misdistribution of wealth derived from the exploitation of those resources, like oil, is often characterized as a resource curse. On the resource curse and land grab, see, e.g., Sharife (2009) and Sparks (2011).
3. http://www.grain.org/article/entries/4227-it-s-time-to-outlaw-land-grabbing-not-to-make-it-responsible.
4. Nationalization of mining companies is also part of the debate. Despite statements from President Zuma that nationalization of mining companies was 'not government policy', many who support such a position, including the Confederation of South African Trade Unions (a key ANC ally) insist that the nationalization of both land and mining companies offers the best solution to South Africa's economic and social problems, high unemployment, persistent poverty, etc. Nationalization of either land or mining companies, or both, could have a chilling effect on FDI.
5. It would seem that the white farmer exodus from South Africa is motivated by several factors having to do with personal security and safety, land redistribution, existing and future water availability, less inconvenience (uncertainty), lower costs of operation amounts to greater profit margins. Many skilled whites, not just farmers, are leaving South Africa – mostly due to crime but also because of affirmative action, increasing corruption, and possible government nationalization (Johnson, 2009).
6. Telecom is the leading cell phone provider for service in Nigeria, Uganda, Tanzania, Swaziland, Rwanda, and Cameroon.
7. LHWP dates to the 1970s when the Joint Technical Committee between Lesotho and South Africa was created to identify options for providing South Africa with bulk quantities of water from the upper reaches of the Orange-Senqu River in Lesotho.
8. Established in 1923, Eskom is South Africa's electricity public utility. South Africa and DRC signed an MOU that gives South Africa's ESKOM and the DRC's national utility Société nationale d'électricité (SNEL) the lead for implementation and management of the Grand Inga, largest and fourth in a series of dams.
9. http://www.eskom.co.za/OurCompany/CompanyInformation/Pages/Company_Information.aspx

10. South Africa's unique approach to global issues has found expression in the concept of Ubuntu. According to the State's White paper, 'These concepts inform our particular approach to diplomacy and shape our vision of a better world for all. Its evolving international engagement is based on two central tenets: Pan-Africanism and South-South solidarity. South Africa recognizes itself as an integral part of the African continent and therefore understands its national interest as being intrinsically linked to Africa's stability, unity, and prosperity. This philosophy translates into an approach to international relations that recognizes that it is in our [South Africa] national interest to promote and support the positive development of others' (http://www.info.gov.za/view/DownloadFileAction?id=149749). Ubuntu diplomacy has been adopted as a central element of South Africa's foreign policy framework. Cilliers and Handy (2011, p. 63) argue, '... despite the rhetoric about links between foreign policy and national interests'. They assert further, under President Zuma it has not been adequately defined since the administration has failed to articulate how their realization impacts the conduct of external affairs, its implementation remains unclear, is considered ill-defined and only a vaguely explained term.

11. A hydro-security complex is defined as those states that are geographically part owners and technically users of the rivers and as a consequence, consider the river as a major security issue (Schultz, 1995).

12. Basin closure is described as a river with no utilizable outflow of water and when all the available water has been allocated to some productive activity with no more water left to be allocated. See Svendsen, Murray-Rust, Harmancioğlu, & Alpaslan (2001, p. 184), and also see Molle (2006).

13. NWRS specifically includes desalination, but gives a higher priority to importing water from the Zambezi River, augmenting rainfall through cloud seeding, shipping water from large rivers, and towed icebergs. Many other countries have desalination plants and plans as part of water resources plans and security – Saudi Arabia has over 30 plants, which supply 70% of its water.

14. See note 9.

15. Eskom is wholly owned by the South African government, as is PetroSA, South Africa's national oil company. Parastatals, a common term of use in South Africa, to characterize companies wholly owned or controlled by the government. Another frequently used term is state-owned entities.

16. In July 2012, by road, Eskom sent a replacement reactor to Cahora Bassa for HCB, the dam operating company, to assure repair and continued capacity to send full power to South Africa.

17. Rand refers to South Africa's currency (ZAR).

18. See Sturman (2011). Kathryn Sturman, Head of the Governance of Africa's Resources Programme, South African Institute of International Affairs. See also Landsberg and van Wyk (2012, p. 500).

19. AgriSA was formed in 1904 as the South African Agricultural Union (SAAU) when it represented only white farmers. In 1999, a newly deracialized association of farmers was formed. The chief negotiator for AgriSA is Theo de Jager, Deputy President. There is another group, the Transvaal Agricultural Union (TAU) of South Africa whose members are white farmers only, and allegedly, represent an agenda that seeks to 'escape black rule'. TAU has sought land acquisition through negotiations with the government of Georgia (former USSR) as a 'new' location for white farmers who want to leave South Africa altogether. Hall (2011) argues, importantly, that the 'trek' of TAU members from South Africa is complex, and '*should not be interpreted narrowly*' (author's emphasis) in terms of disaffected Afrikaner farmers 'fleeing' one regime to establish a new order elsewhere.

20. While 13% of South Africa's land can be used for crop production, only 22% of this is high-potential arable land. The other areas are limited by the availability of water, uneven rainfall, and drought. Half of South Africa's water is used for agriculture (http://www.southafrica.info/business/economy/sectors/agricultural-sector.htm#ixzz1gC9NnAA7).

21. Multiple studies highlight the various 'incentives' made to attract investors, including, among other things, no taxation; land cost considerably less than US$ 1.00 or the equivalent of $0.50 per hectare; and no infrastructure requirements, other than those necessary for crop production. In many instances, even the hiring of local labor is not a requirement. Many deals negotiated with China involve imported Chinese labor.

22. Of the 26 land deals in Ethiopia, 15 were for biofuels, and in Madagascar, of the 24 deals, 16 were for biofuels and 3 industrial productions (Friis & Reemberg, 2010, p. 13).
23. See note 21. At the time of publication (2010), the South Africa had confirmed six major deals with DRC involving approximately 8 million hectares (Friis & Reemberg, 2010).
24. South Africa Foreign Policy Initiative (SAFPI) 11 September 2013, online report, "DRC: RSA investment and trade initiative" at http://www.safpi.org/news/article/2013/drc-rsa-investment-and-trade-initiative.
25. South Africa: National Assembly signs Cooperation Agreement with Mozambique's Legislature, 2013 (AllAfrica News Stories at http://allafrica.com/stories/201309111059.html).
26. Government subsidized and supported both South African corporate and state-owned economic involvement extends to over 22 countries as far north as Egypt, in small neighboring states of Swaziland, Zambia, and Lesotho, and as strategically important as Nigeria (Daniel et al., 2003).
27. European nations first established farming plantations in their colonies, and then again in their ex-colonies, sometimes referred to as 'banana republics'. In the 1990s, English, French, and US water utilities aggressively sought access to markets in the global South, where a privatization wave was in full swing. Supported by export credits, the Western companies built dams, and distribution infrastructures and offering services where the receiving countries' state companies were perceived as underperforming. However, the flurry of direct investment was accompanied by corruption scandals. Other scandals include the privatization of Jakarta's water, and Cochabamba (the US-Bolivian joint venture Aguas de Tunari in the famous 'Cochabamba water war' of 2000, see, e.g., Bakker, 2008) and conflict over Coca Cola's water grab in India.
28. Achille Mbembe is a senior researcher at the Witwatersrand Institute for Social and Economic Research (WISER) and professor at the University of Witwatersrand, Johannesburg, South Africa.

Notes on contributors

Antoinette G. Sebastian, PhD, is an independent researcher who works on international (transboundary) water politics, conflict and cooperation, and land use and water issues. She lectures at the University of Maryland and has extensive professional experience in environmental policy and analysis, and urban development.

Jeroen F. Warner, PhD, is an Assistant Professor of Disaster Studies, Wageningen University, the Netherlands. He has written extensively on the politics of flooding, water resources, and is editor of *Multi-Stakeholder Platforms for Integrated Catchment Management* and co-editor of *The Politics of Water*.

References

Aarts, V. (2009). *Unraveling the land grab: How to protect the livelihoods of the poor?* The Hague, The Netherlands: Oxfam Novib.
AllAfrica Online. (2012). *South Africa: Cabinet approves amended white paper on foreign policy.* Retrieved 6 December from http://allafrica.com/stories/201212061272.html
Allen, T. (1998). Watersheds and problemsheds: Explaining the absence of armed conflict over water in the Middle East. *Middle East Review of International Affairs, 2,* 49–51. Retrieved from http://www.gloria-center.org/meria/1998/03/allan.pdf
Bailey, R. (2011). Growing a better future: Food justice in a resource-constrained world. *Oxfam GB.* Oxford: Oxfam International.
Bakker, K. (2008). The ambiguity of community: Debating alternatives to private- sector provision of urban water supply. *Water Alternatives, 1,* 236–252.
Baldwin, D. A. (1979). Power analysis and world politics: New trends versus old tendencies. *World Politics, 31,* 161–194.
Borras, S., & Franco, J. (2010). *Towards a broader view of the politics of global land grab: Rethinking land issues, reframing resistance* (Working Paper Series edited by ICAS). Retrieved from http://www.tni.org/sites/www.tni.org/files/Borras%20Franco%20Politics%20of%20Land%20Grab%20v3.pdf

Bourdieu, P. (1991). *Language and symbolic power (G. Raymond & M. Adamson, Trans.) (J. B. Thompson, Ed.)*. Cambridge, MA: Polity Press.

Cilliers, J., & Handy, P. (2011). South Africa as a regional power: Multiple audiences, one foreign policy? *ISPI: Quaderni di Relazioni Internazionali, 14*. EGEA, 56–68. Retrieved from http://www.ispionline.it/it/documents/QRI14_cilliers_handy.pdf

Cotula, L., Vermeulen, S., Leonard, R., & Keeley, J. (2009). *Land grab or development opportunity? Agricultural investment and international land deals in Africa*. London: International Fund for Agricultural Development (IFAD). Retrieved from ftp://ftp.fao.org/docrep/fao/011/ak241e/ak241e00.pdf

Cox, R. (1989). Middlepowermanship, Japan, and future world order. *International Journal, 44*, 823–862.

Daniel, J., & Lutchman, J. (2006). South Africa in Africa: Scrambling for energy. In S. Buhlungo, J. Daniel, & R. Southall (Eds.), *State of the nation: South Africa, 2005–2006* (pp. 508–532). Cape Town: Human Sciences Research Council (HSRC) Press.

Daniel, S., & Mittal, A. (2009). *The great land grab: Rush for the world's farmland threatens food security for the poor*. Oakland, CA: The Oakland Institute. Retrieved from http://www.oaklandinstitute.org/sites/oaklandinstitute.org/files/LandGrab_final_web.pdf

Daniel, J., Naidoo, V., & Naidu, S. (2003). The South Africans have arrived: Post-apartheid corporate expansion into Africa. In J. Daniel, A. Habib, & R. Southall (Eds.), *State of the nation: South Africa, 2003–2004* (pp. 368–391). Cape Town: Human Sciences Research Council (HSRC).

Davidsen, P. A. (2006). (Masters thesis). University of Bergen, Bergen, Norway *The making and umaking of the politics of exceptionality: Studying processes of securitization an desecuritzation in the Orange and Okavango river basins*.

Deininger, K., Byerlee, D., Lindsay, J., Norton, A., Selod, H., & Stickler, M. (2011). *Rising global interest in farmland: Can it yield sustainable and equitable benefits?* Washington, DC. Retrieved from http://siteresources.worldbank.org/INTARD/Resources/ESW_Sept7_final_final.pdf The World Bank (International Bank for Reconstruction and Development).

Dessie, G., & Christiansson, C. (2008). Forest decline and its causes in the south-central rift valley of Ethiopia: Human impact over a one hundred year perspective. *Ambio, 37*, 263–271.

Donahue, J. M., & Johnston, B. R. (Eds.). (1998). *Water, culture, & power, local struggles in global context*. Washington, DC: Island Press.

Drainville, A. (1994). International political economy in the age of open Marxism. *Review of International Political Economy, 1*(1), 105–132.

Friis, C., & Reemberg, A. (2010). *Land grab in Africa: emerging land system drivers in a teleconnected world*. [The Global Land Project (GLP) Report No. 1.] Copenhagen: GLP-IPO. Retrieved from http://www.globallandproject.org/arquivos/GLP_report_01.pdf

Furlong, K. (2006). Hidden theories, troubled waters: International relations, the 'territorial trap', and the Southern African Development Community's transboundary waters. *Political Geography, 25*, 438–458.

Gelb, S. (2001). *South Africa's role and importance in Africa and for the development of African agenda*. Johannesburg: EDGE Institute.

GRAIN. (2010). *World Bank report on land grabbing: Beyond the smoke and mirrors*. Retrieved from GRAIN: http://www.grain.org/article/entries/4021-world-bank-report-on-land-grabbing-beyond-the-smoke-and-mirrors

Griggs, R. (1997). The boundaries of an African renaissance. *Boundary & Security Bulletin, 5*, 64–68.

Habib, A. (2009). South Africa's foreign policy: Hegemonic aspirations, neoliberal orientations and global transformation. *South African Journal of International Affairs, 16*, 143–159. Retrieved from http://dx.doi.org/10.1080/10220460903265857

Hall, R. (2011). *The many faces of the investor rush in Southern Africa: Towards a typology of commercial land deals* (Working Paper Series No. 2 edited by ICAS).

Henriques, G. (2011, February 12). Stop the local land grab. *The Guardian*.

Jacobs, I. (2007). *Taking water hostage. The impact of global environmental norms on joint water resource management in the Orange and the Nile basins*. In Conference on Adaptive and Integrated Water Management (CAIWA), Basel, Switzerland.

Johnson, S. (2009, February 13). Fleeing from South Africa. *Newsweek Magazine*.

Kabemba, C. (2007). South Africa in the DRC: Renaissance or neo-imperialism? In S. Buhlungu, J. Daniel, & R. Southall (Eds.), *State of the nation: South Africa 2007* (pp. 533–551). Cape Town: Human Sciences Research Council (HSRC).

Keohane, R. (1984). *After hegemony: cooperation and discord in the world political economy.* Princeton, NJ: Princeton University Press.

Kugelman, M., & Levenstein, S. L. (Eds.). (2009). *Land grab: The race for the world's farmland.* Washington, DC: Woodrow Wilson Center.

Landsberg, C., & van Wyk, J. (2012). *South African foreign policy review*, Vol 1. Pretoria: Africa Institute of South Africa and the Institute for Global Dialogue.

Li, T. M. (2011). Centering labour in the land grab debate. *Journal of Peasant Studies, 38*, 281–298.

McMichael, P. (2011). *Implications of the global land grab for international relations.* Paper presented at the International Studies Association Conference. Montreal.

Miller, D., Nel, E., & Hampwaye, G. (2008). Malls in Zambia: racialised retail expansion and South African foreign investors in Zambia. *African Sociological Review, 12*(1), 35–54.

Molle, F. (2006). *Why enough is never enough: The societal determinants of river basin closure.* Paper presented for the World Water Week 2006, Stockholm, 20–26 August, SIWI.

Monyae, D. (2012). The evolving 'doctrine' of multilateralism in South Africa's foreign policy (Chapter 7). In C. Landsberg & J. van Wyk (Eds.), *South Africa foreign policy review*, Vol 1. Pretoria: Africa Institute of South Africa and the Institute for Global Dialogue.

Moore, D. (2001). Neoliberal globalisation and the triple crisis of 'modernisation' in Africa: Zimbabwe, the Democratic Republic of the Congo and South Africa. *Third World Quarterly, 22*, 909–929.

Neumann, I. B. (1992). *Regions in international relations theory: The case for a region-building approach.* Oslo: Norwegian Institute of International Affairs.

Nolte, D. (2010). How to compare regional powers: Analytical concepts and research topics. *Review of International Studies, 36*, 881–901.

Nossiter, A. (2011, December 9). Congo leader is declared winner in disputed vote. *New York Times.*

Nye, J. S. Jr (1990). Soft power. *Foreign Policy, 80*, 153–171.

Oakland Institute. (2011). *Understanding land investment deals in Africa. Country Report: Mozambique.* Oakland, CA. Retrieved from http://www.oaklandinstitute.org/land-deals-africa/mozambique Author.

Osterud, O. (1988). The uses and abuses of geopolitics. *Journal of Peace Research, 25*, 191–199.

Palo, M., Uusivuori, J., & Mery, G. (Eds.). (2001). *World forests, markets and policies, Vol. 3.* Dordrecht: Kluwer.

Schoeman, M. (2003). South Africa as an emerging middle power: 1994-2003. In J. Daniel, A. Habib, & R. Southall (Eds.), *State of the nation: South Africa, 2003–2004* (pp. 349–367). Cape Town: Human Sciences Research Council (HSRC).

Schultz, M. (1995). Turkey, Syria and Iraq. A hydropolitical complex. In L. Ohlsson (Ed.), *Hydropolitics* (pp. 91–122). London: Zed Books.

Sebastian, A. G. (2008). *Transboundary water politics: Conflict, cooperation, and shadows of the past in the Okavango and Orange river basins of Southern Africa* (PhD dissertation). University of Maryland, College Park, MD.

Sharife, K. (2009, November 26). Land grabs: Africa's new 'resource curse'? *Pambazuka News*, p. 459.

Sharife, K. (2010). The South Africa-Congo concession: Exploitation or salvation? *Pembazuka News*. Issue 464. Retrieved from http://pambazuka.org/en/category/features/61251

Shepard, D., & Mittal, A. (2009). *The great land grab: Rush for world's farmland threatens food security for the poor.* Oakland, CA: Oakland Institute.

South Africa Department of International Relations and Cooperation. (2011). *Building a better world: The diplomacy of Ubuntu.* White paper on South Africa's foreign policy, Final Draft 13 May. Retrieved from http://www.info.gov.za/view/DownloadFileAction?id=149749

South Africa Department of Water Affairs and Forestry. (2004). *National Water Resource Strategy.* Retrieved from: http://www.dwaf.gov.za/Documents/Policies/NWRS/Default.htm

Sparks, D. (2011). India and China's growing economic involvement in Sub-Saharan Africa. *Journal of African Studies and Development, 3*, 65–75.

Sturman, K. (2011, February 15). Political intrigue undermines investments in the DRC. *Mail & Guardian.* Retrieved from http://mg.co.za/article/2011-02-15-political-intrigue-undermines-investments-in-the-drc

Svendsen, M., Murray-Rust, D. H., Harmancioğlu, N., & Alpaslan, N. (2001). Governing closing basins: The case of the Gediz river in Turkey. In C. L. Abernethy (Ed.), *Intersectoral management of river basins* (pp. 183–214). Colombo: International Water Management Institute (IWMI).

Swarns, R. (2002, February 17). Awe and unease as South Africa stretches out. *New York Times*.

Turton, A. R. (2010). *New thinking on the governance of water and river basins in Africa: Lessons from the SADC region*. Cape Town: South African Institute of International Affairs (SAIIA).

Turton, A. R., & Earle, A. (2005). Post-apartheid institutional development in selected Southern African international river basins. In C. Gopalakrishnan, C. Tortajada, & A. K. Biswas (Eds.), *Water institutions: Policies, performance and prospects* (pp. 154–168). Berlin: Springer.

Vehnämäki, M. (2002). Diamonds and warlords: The geography of war in the Democratic Republic of Congo and Sierra Leone. *Nordic Journal of African Studies, 11*(1), 48–72.

von Braun, J., & Meinzen-Dick, R. (2009). *Land grabbing by foreign investors in developing countries: Risks and opportunities*. IFPRI Policy Brief 13, International Food Policy Research Institute (IFPRI), 2020 Vision Initiative, Washington, DC.

Warner, J., Sebastian, A., & Empinotti, V. (2012). Claiming (back) the land: The geopolitics of Egyptian and South African land and water grabs. In J. A. Allan, M. Keulertz, S. Sojamo, & J. Warner (Eds.), *Handbook of land and water grabs in Africa. Foreign Direct Investment and Water Security* (pp. 224–243). Oxford: Routledge.

Wesselink, A., Warner, J., & Kok, M. (2012). You gain some funding, you lose some freedom: The ironies of flood protection in Limburg (The Netherlands). *Environmental Science and Policy, 30*, 113–125. doi: 10.1016/j.envsci.2012.10.018.

Woodhouse, P., & Ganho, A. S. (2011). *Is water the hidden agenda of agricultural land acquisition in Sub-Saharan Africa?*. Paper presented at Global land grabbing conference organised by the Land Deal Politics Initiative (LDPI), University of Sussex.

Zeitoun, M., & Warner, J. (2006). Hydro-hegemony-A framework for analysis of transboundary water conflicts. *Water and Policy, 8*, 435–460.

The perils of development from above: land deals in Ethiopia

Dessalegn Rahmato

Forum for Social Studies, Addis Ababa, Ethiopia

The paper examines Ethiopia's program of large-scale land investments with special emphasis on the rapid expansion of these investments between 2008 and 2011 when huge tracts of agricultural land were leased out to foreign and domestic investors over a short period of time. It is estimated that the total land ceded to investors from the mid-1990s to the end of 2011 may be in the order of 3.00–3.5 million hectares. I shall present a discussion of the program in the context of the government's grand strategy of state-led development, followed by an examination of the serious difficulties the program is presently facing. State-led development is characterized by emphasis on large-scale public investment and huge public debt which has damaging implications for people's livelihoods and has led to a non-inclusive and skewed growth path. Land investment, it is argued, is one among a number of public sector initiatives meant to enhance the country's export market and contribute to the growing demand for state accumulation. The real needs of the country on the other hand are poverty reduction and food security which the program does not address to any significant degree. It is further argued that the problems faced by the program are not solely caused by poor governance and lack of capacity but raise questions of policy choice and democratic decision-making. State-led development enhances the power of the state and exacerbates the vulnerabilities of small producers in the rural areas whose lands are increasingly being threatened by expropriation.

Abbreviations: AISD, Agricultural Investment Support Directorate; CSA, Central Statistical Agency; DI, Development Initiatives (Nairobi); EOC, Ethiopian Orthodox Church; EPA, Environmental Protection Authority; FAO, Food and Agricultural Organization; FDRE, Federal Democratic Republic of Ethiopia; GTP, growth and transformation plan; Ha, hectare(s); HRW, Human Rights Watch; IMF, International Monetary Fund; MOARD, Ministry of Agriculture and Rural Development; MOA, Ministry of Agriculture; MOFED, Ministry of Finance and Economic Development; MOPED, Ministry of Planning and Economic Development; OI, Oakland Institute; SNNP, Southern Nations, Nationalities and Peoples; USD, United States Dollar(s)

Introduction

My purpose in this paper was to examine Ethiopia's program of large-scale land investments, particularly those involving the transfer of extensive stretches of land to foreign investors between 2008 and 2011. The scale of the land transfers and the low land prices were unprecedented and aroused serious concerns among citizens and civil society groups in the country. This dramatic land rush was driven by the government which thought it would benefit by what it considered to be golden opportunities opened up by the global food price and food supply crisis of 2007/2008, and at the same time African countries in the region, which were also scrambling to attract foreign capital. The government believed that Ethiopia had better resources to offer and what was required was to steal a march on its competitors, by offering an attractive package of concessionary terms to lure foreign investors, particularly from the emerging economic power houses of East Asia and the capital-rich but food-poor countries of the Middle East.[1] Land transfers to investors had been going on for over a decade prior to the period in question, but at that time the pace of expansion was slow; the investors were almost always domestic ones, and the plots leased were relatively small in size (Dessalegn, 2011 for details).

There is no consensus on the definition of the phenomenon we are concerned with, nor is there a common terminology to refer to it – terms such as 'land grabbing,' 'land deals,' 'land acquisitions' and, sometimes, 'land rushes' are widely employed in the literature as well as by international advocacy organizations campaigning against it.[2] What we are dealing with in this work is the makings of a property and production regime in which rights over large-scale rural resources are transferred to private individuals, corporate or sovereign business interests, allowing them to engage in mechanized farming for the purpose of producing agricultural goods either for the international market or for economies far removed from the local communities where the investment is based. In either case, local communities receive very little benefit. What has been 'grabbed' is not just land but also water, forest, and biodiversity resources, most of which are claimed or customarily used by, or are important to the livelihoods of peasant farmers, herders, and other small rural producers.

While it is too early to call for a postmortem at the moment, it is quite evident that the program is facing severe difficulties, which I believe are harbingers of an evolving crisis from which it is unlikely to emerge in a sound state. As we shall see later in this work, the immediate causes of its predicament are diverse: they include agricultural, financial, and environmental factors as well as growing opposition from local communities regarding the loss of their land and other resources. It was evident from the beginning that the program and its hasty execution carried the seeds of its own contradiction, but I shall argue that at another level, the crisis looming over it is a product of the strategy of development from above and the 'ideology' of state-led development.

In what follows, I shall first present a brief discussion of the land investment program in the context of the government's grand strategy of state-led development, and this will be followed by an examination of the serious difficulties the program is presently facing, showing why these difficulties are not a passing phenomena but in fact harbingers of a deeper crisis. In the final section, I shall suggest that the answer to the question, what needs to be done – a question that, in many different forms, has aroused strong debate in the literature and among different interest groups – does not lie in adopting or tinkering with the 'code of conduct' approach favored by the World Bank and its partner organizations, but rather in thinking through democratic alternatives that empower local communities and lead to the sustainable use of the land and resources in question for the greater good of these communities.

Land deals and state accumulation

A brief note on some features of rural Ethiopia is necessary to put the discussion that follows in context.[3] As a result of complex historical processes as well as high population growth and increasing resource degradation over the years, shortage of arable land is acute in most of the countryside. In the cereal farming complex of the northern highlands, per capita family holdings are less than one hectare, while in the *enset* culture complex in the south of the country [in Southern Nations, Nationalities and Peoples (SNNP) in particular], a family that works half a hectare is considered fortunate. Agriculture is dominated by hard working peasant cultivators, but rural society has often been plagued by severe food shortages, catastrophic famines, and endemic hunger since the 1950s. As recently as 2002/2003, there was widespread starvation in many parts of the country affecting more than 13 million rural people, and it required large inflows of international food aid to avert a tragedy on the scale of the famine of 1985/1986 when hundreds of thousands of peasants and pastoralists perished in the worst tragedy in the country's history. Malnutrition is endemic in the countryside as well as in the urban areas, and diseases associated with poor nutrition and scarcity of clean water are common. In 2009, over 22% of the rural population was dependent on a combination of emergency food aid and safety net programs financed by Western countries and international agencies. While the number of people seeking emergency food assistance has decreased since then, nearly eight million rural people continue to be supported by donor financed safety net programs.[4] On the other hand, there has been a fairly high rate of economic growth in the last 10 years and improvements in health services have been registered, nevertheless this has not made a significant impact on *real* rural poverty nor has it helped to ensure food security to a great number of farming households.

Extent of transfers

Land leasing to private investors was in progress in many parts of the country long before the new global land rush was under way. Indeed, one of the first acts of the present government soon after establishing itself in power in 1991, after the overthrow of the military regime (the *Derg*), was to open up opportunities for agricultural investment by providing private interests access to farm land which was not available to them under the economic policy of the Derg. We can distinguish three phases of the land investment program under the present regime. The first phase covers the period from the mid-1990s to 2000 when the size of land transferred was relatively small, less than 500 ha, and the investors were almost exclusively domestic businesses and individuals. The second phase extends from 2001 to 2007 – a period in which the government's investment proclamation of 2002, providing generous incentives and sweeteners to foreign investment was issued, and the horticultural sector registered a boom in exports of cut flowers to European and other markets. The floriculture business, in particular, which acquired fertile crop land in peri-urban areas and near transport corridors at the expense of peasant farmers, became the darling of decision-makers and was given a free hand and a good deal of support to expand and flourish (Melese & Helmsing, 2010). The size of land leased out was small to medium scale, but while the majority of the land transfers was made to domestic investors, the period saw growing interest by foreign investors as well as investors from the Ethiopian Diaspora. During the first and second phases, the great majority of investors held the land idle because many simply did not have the resources to put the land to use, and some used it for purposes for which it was not approved (Ministry of Agriculture and Rural Development [MOARD], 2009b).

The third phase, from 2008 to 2011 was a period of unprecedented land rush by foreign companies attracted by the country's investment climate, and when the government became particularly keen to promote the production of agricultural and agro-industrial goods for the export market. The first 3 years, in particular, witnessed what may be described as mega-land deals, in which the government ceded huge stretches of land measuring 25,000–50,000 ha, and in one case, 100,000 ha to foreign investors. The lands were to be used to grow three categories of crops: food crops for export, notably rice, oil seeds, soya, and maize; biofuel crops such as palm oil, *Jatropha curcas*, and castor beans;

and industrial crops, especially, sugar cane and cotton.[5] It was also in this period that an ambitious plan for public sector investment in sugar production was launched requiring huge land allocations in various parts of the country. The rental fees for agricultural land are astonishingly low, perhaps one of the lowest in the world: in most parts of the country, investors pay less than 10 USD for a hectare of land per year. Indeed, land rents are so low that many foreign investors apply for more land than they can possibly manage (Dessalegn, 2011 for details).

The government has made highly exaggerated claims of the availability of *unused* land suitable for all kinds of crops that can be given out to investors without risking the livelihoods of small farmers. The country's 'investment potential' has, at various times, been put at 10 million hectares or more (MOARD, 2008; *Reporter* interview). Accurate figures of the extent of land transferred over all phases of the program or in any one of them are not available. Such is the poor state of record keeping that even in cases of individual transfers the size of the land registered is an estimate and not an accurate measure, and what is entered in the records is different from what appears on the ground. Government officials occasionally admit that the figures they put out in official documents are based on estimates derived from satellite imagery or aerial photographs, in most cases not supported by surveys on the ground.[6]

In 2008, the government designated the Federal Ministry of Agriculture and Rural Development (MOARD) as a lead agency for large-scale land deals with foreign and local investors. The Ministry's responsibility included preparing information and other technical inputs to attract investors, signing contracts with and transferring lands to those eligible and undertaking follow-up and oversight. Environmental protection authority's responsibility in regard to environmental impact assessment and oversight, vested in it by law (Federal Democratic Republic of Ethiopia [FDRE], 2002b), was transferred to MOARD in 2009 by means of an exchange of letters and a memorandum of understanding between the two agencies, even though MOARD did not have the technical and institutional capacity to carry out the duties involved. MOARD was to receive and administer all consolidated investment lands measuring 5000 ha or more from the *Killils*.[7] These lands were to be put into what was called a Federal land bank to be accessed by investors through MOARD. This decision deprived the *Killils* some of the powers vested in them by the 1995 Constitution with respect to land administration, and some *Killil* authorities were initially reluctant to comply. While all aspects of the land deals were to be concluded by and through MOARD, the income from the transactions, namely land rent, income tax, and other payments were to be utilized for the benefit of the *Killils* concerned. This change of procedure and division of responsibility was formally endorsed by a directive issued by the Council of Ministers in early 2010 (FDRE, 2010). The *Killils* were to continue to allocate land to investors as they had done prior to this decision, but the lands in question were those measuring less than 5000 ha and not part of the land they had submitted to the Federal land bank. Some *Killils* were said to possess enormous land potential, and the transfer of some of it to the Federal land bank was not seen as depriving them of the power of making land deals themselves. Thus BeniShangul, for example, is estimated to have as much as 1.4 million hectares potentially available for investors, Gambella 1.2 million, SNNP 500,000, and Oromia 1.7 million (MOARD, 2008, 2009b). These lands were subsequently transferred to the Federal land bank in 2009.

The growth and transformation plan (GTP), which was launched in the last quarter of 2010c and expected to run to 2015, has set ambitious targets for the expansion and development of sugar production in the country. At present, the country has four medium-sized sugar factories but what they produce is not sufficient to meet domestic demand. The goal at the end of the plan period is not only to fully cover domestic needs but also to export 1.2 million tons of sugar earning 662 million USD per year. To meet this goal, the plan calls for the expansion of the existing facilities as well as the establishment of eight new large factories with a combined plantation area of over 200,000 ha (Ministry of Finance and Economic Development [MOFED], 2010b). For this purpose, the government established the Sugar Corporation in October 2010, a semi-autonomous body with a substantial annual budget which replaced the earlier Ethiopian Sugar Development Agency. The Corporation has embarked on a massive construction and land acquisition program in SNNP, Amhara, Tigrai, and Afar *Killils*. According to information recently posted on its website, it is constructing 12 new large-scale factories of which 7 are in the south Omo valley of SNNP with a total land area of 175,000 ha, 3 in TanaBeles (western Amhara) with 44,000 ha, and 1 in Wolkait (northeast Tigrai) with 75,000 ha.[8] It is also responsible for the Kessem sugar factory (which has a 21,000 ha plantation) and Tendaho (50,000 ha) in Afar in the Awash valley, which have been under construction since 2005 but are still unfinished.

In 2012, the Corporation acquired, through purchase, the property of a Pakistani company which had leased 28,000 ha of land to establish a sugar enterprise in the ArjoDidessa valley in Oromia, western Ethiopia. The company was unable to proceed with the project and decided to pull out transferring all its assets to the Corporation. The ArjoDidessa sugar project now owns over 72,000 ha of land on which the Corporation is building a dam on the Didessa river, a major tributary of the Nile, which is expected to inundate about 13,000 ha of land and to displace many thousand peasant farmers, though the exact number is not clearly known.[9] The Corporation thus controls under its new projects launched since 2010 a total land area of over 437,000 ha on which it is undertaking dam building, irrigation canal construction, construction of housing for laborers and staff, and planting of cane sugar for the factories. Some of the land under development in south Omo, its largest project so far, lies well within the boundary of the Omo National Park, one of the two important wildlife parks in the area established over four decades ago. The government body responsible for managing the country's parks and nature reserves, the Ethiopian Wildlife Conservation Agency, is aware of the encroachment but has kept silent about it (Dessalegn, 2011; Ensermu, Negusu, & Tadesse, 2009).

All the new projects will involve the displacement of pastoralists, agro-pastoralists and peasant cultivators from their land, and pose a risk to their livelihoods. The massive project in the Omo valley, for example, may displace 50–70 thousand people or more, according to reports in the local press, though other sources put the figure much higher (see below). While accurate figures are not available, the TanaBeles, Wolkait in Tigrai, and ArjoDidessa projects have displaced tens of thousands of peasant farmers from their land (Ethiopian Orthodox Church [EOC], 2012; *Reporter*, 8 April 2012, and 25 March 2013). The Corporation says all displaced people, including pastoralists in the Awash and south Omo valleys will be resettled in purpose-built villages, and provided irrigated land for their livelihood. It claims that the new projects will provide employment for over 162,000 people. Critics of the Corporation, not least international advocacy groups, argue, however, that the project in the lower Omo threatens the unique ecosystem of the valley, and has been accompanied by large-scale human rights abuses, forcing indigenous people from their ancestral lands, using violence and arbitrary arrests to do so. It is argued that the lives of between 200,000 and 500,000 people are endangered as a consequence of their displacement as well as severe disruptions to their livelihoods. A recent article in *Bloomberg News* reports that indigenous people who were interviewed were very unhappy with the loss of their land and water resources and were fearful that the project will eventually put at risk their livelihoods and the future of their communities.[10] The Corporation has so far declined to allow journalists, researchers, and other independent observers to visit the project area to gather information or undertake research.[11]

How much land has actually been transferred to investors over the three phases of the investment program may not be accurately known. One of the earliest documents released by MOARD (2009a) shows that in the period between 1996 and the end of 2008, some 8000 applications for land were approved by the *Killils* with the total land committed measuring over three million hectares. Other sources give different figures though for different time periods. The World Bank (2010), for example, puts the total land transferred to investors in Ethiopia between 2004 and 2008 at 1.2 million hectares. Recently, in the interview noted above, the senior official at the Agricultural Investment Support Directorate (AISD) of Ministry of Agriculture (MOA), which until recently was responsible for managing the land investment program, suggested a rough estimate of 2.2 million hectares as the total land leased out to investors up to the present, but stressed that this estimate was not based on any reliable measurement. Furthermore, the GTP has set a target of 3.3 million hectares of land to be transferred to investors in the 5-year periodMOFED, (2010a). On the other hand, recent figures posted on MOA's website indicate that between 2008 and 2012, some 500,000 hectares of land were leased out to investors both by MOARD and the *Killils*.[12] All in all, taking into account the figures given, I estimate that the total land ceded to investors from the mid-1990s to 2012 may be in the order of 3.00–3.5 million hectares. Looking ahead, it now looks highly unlikely that the government's target of leasing out an additional 3.3 million hectares to investors in the period up to 2015 will be met.

What was ceded and to whom?

What kind of land was transferred and were these lands indeed unused as the government claims? The wide diversity of lands leased out to investors, both private and public, include crop land, pasture and rangeland, woodland and forest as well as wetlands. Moreover, as we found out during our field work in 2010, lands in designated national parks, protected areas, and wildlife habitats have also been given out, posing a serious threat to the country's ecological and biodiversity resources. A critical resource that has been given away almost free but which is often not mentioned in the land deals discourse is *water*. Indeed, the term *land deals* should be replaced by land and water deals because the two often go together. All these resources are vital to the livelihood of peasants, herders and small producers in the rural areas, and the claim by the government that they are unused is not supported by the reality on the ground.

There is finally the matter of population relocation in Gambella and BeniShangul, two *Killils* that have been the main target of large-scale land deals. The *Killil* governments are responsible for the implementation of the resettlement program (or villagization as it is sometimes called) but have been supported by the Federal government in the form of special budget allocations. They deny that the program is connected in any way with the land deals but the timing of the program (at the end of 2010), and the fact that the people relocated were living in areas close to where investors had been allocated land suggests that there is certainly a strong link. Village residents living close to the land leased to a Saudi-financed rice project called Saudi Star in Gambella that we interviewed in 2010 told us that they were convinced they were being moved to enable Saudi Star, which had requested for additional land, to expand its rice project (Dessalegn, 2011). Human Rights

Watch (HRW) claims, in its report on Gambella, that people were forcibly relocated and there was a high degree of human rights abuses (Human Rights Watch [HRW], 2012a).

The dominant actors in the land rush in Ethiopia are not transnational companies based in the West, as was the case in the past, but new players from Asia and the Middle East, of which the most prominent have been Indian investors. Indian capital is by far the largest both in terms of the number of investors involved and the extent of farm land acquired. Some of the biggest acquisitions have been made by Indian firms; the following is a sample of the largest beneficiaries: Karuturi, a company based in Bangalore, India, was initially given 300,000 ha of land in Gambella, but this was subsequently reduced to 100,000 ha; it has also leased 11,000 ha in Bako Tibee*woreda* in Oromia. Emami Biotech acquired 80,000 ha in Oromia for biofuel crops; Shamporji, a subsidiary of the giant Indian conglomerate, Tata Group, received 50,000 ha in BeniShangul also for biofuel crops; BHO leased 27,000 ha in Gambella for rice and sesame seeds; and Ruchi Soya was ceded 25,000 ha also in Gambella to grow soya and palm oil for export. At the end of 2011, there were about 25–30 Indian agricultural investors holding among them between 450,000 and 500,000 ha of land in various parts of the country. In view of the dominance of Indian capital, the land rush of 2008–2011 may well be described as the Indian Scramble for Ethiopia. Other investors worthy of note include Saudi Arabia, the Gulf countries, and Malaysia.[13]

State accumulation and development from above

We need to pause here and ask: what was the central objective behind the land investment program, and what specifically did the government expect the country to benefit by it? The government's economic policy formulated in the mid-1990s, called Agriculture Development-Led Industrialization (ADLI), placed high hopes on agriculture, making it the engine of economic growth, and small-holder farming as the dynamic force within it (Ministry of Planning and Economic Development [MOPED], 1994). For the next 10 years or so, peasant farming, which was and remains the dominant occupation for the rural population, received increased extension services and new technologies such as modern inputs and high yield seeds (Kassahun, 2012). Despite the fact that rural society was frequently battered by severe environmental stresses, and, occasionally, catastrophic disasters, and despite doubts among expert opinion as to whether ADLI was capable of delivering growth, the importance given to smallholder production was welcomed by many, including civil society and development practitioners. However, by the turn of the new millennium, there was a shift in government thinking away from the earlier emphasis, and by the middle of the first decade of the millennium family farming was no longer the darling of decision-makers. Instead, large-scale land investment was seen as one among several initiatives to bring about not just growth but 'growth and transformation,' which was to be achieved by a substantial inflow of foreign investment. In an influential policy-framing document first issued in Amharic in 2001 and translated into English in 2003, the government argued that foreign capital in agriculture would serve as a catalyst in the transformation of the rural economy, driving the inevitable shift from subsistence farming to large-scale commercial agriculture (MOFED, 2003, p. 52). The document went on to emphasize that while there would be no discrimination against domestic investment, the focus of attention should be on attracting foreign investors because they are better endowed with investment capital, technology, and market expertise (MOFED, 2003, p. 52). This turn toward large-scale agriculture driven by foreign capital was made real by several institutional reforms such as the 2002/2003 investment laws, greater openness to foreign investment, beginning with the floriculture sector and culminating in the accelerated land leases in 2008 and after. Along with its transformative role, land investment was also expected to enable the country to expand and broaden its exports of agricultural commodities, and increase its foreign earnings. Other benefits included creating employment opportunities, construction of social assets such as health facilities, schools, and access to clean water for local communities, and opportunities for technology transfer to the rural areas.[14]

The land deals in Ethiopia were driven by the state: the state has been the sole actor all through the various stages of the land 'grabbing' process, from the initial task of publicity and investor attraction to the final stage of allocation of specific farm plots. This is an important point to bear in mind, one that perhaps sets the country apart from others in Africa and elsewhere. Another way of putting it is that it is the state that has been the real land grabber with foreign and domestic investors willing beneficiaries. This land grab has been made possible by the system of land tenure in place in the country which gives the state rights of legal ownership and land users rights of usufruct only, subject to expropriation and displacement at any time. The implementation of the land certification program in the last 10 years has provided land users with an increased sense of assurance but by no means full security of tenure (Dessalegn, 2009). Land transfers have occurred despite the program and peasants with title certificates have been expropriated for various reasons including private and public investment projects. That rights of ownership are vested in the state has given public authorities considerable power over land users and rural communities. The leasing out of large tracts of land to investors in a process based on the exclusion of the local people and their communities further reinforces state power leaving small land users greatly weakened and increasingly vulnerable.

As mentioned earlier, an important aim of the land investment program has been to contribute to state accumulation which in turn was meant to serve the ambitious goals of state-led capitalist development. This economic model, state developmentalism, if we may call it that, which evolved as government policy at the turn of the millennium, has the following characteristics: (a) development is based on heavy public sector investments on a variety of projects, some of which are aimed eventually at gaining export earnings; (b) state investment relies on heavy public borrowing from domestic financial institutions; (c) this has placed serious impediments on the activities of the private sector not least because it has been crowded out of the credit market with much less space for growth; and (d) this has led to a skewed and non-inclusive growth path measured in terms of access to resources, markets, and opportunities as well as in terms of the regional balance (International Monetary Fund [IMF], 2012). Equally important is the fact that decision-making is also not inclusive because all major economic decisions are made by the power elite and do not include public consultation nor participation by stakeholders. The state is the dominant actor in the economy in terms of investment and asset ownership (not least rural land), as well as a significant player in the production of goods and services.

There are a number of medium to large enterprises still under public control, the largest of which, the Metals and Engineering Corporation, a giant engineering and construction conglomerate established under the Ministry of Defense, has become the sole contractor for massive government construction projects such as dams, irrigation schemes, factories, and other large-scale public undertakings. At the end of 2012, the government established the Chemical Industries Corporation under the Ministry of Industry with a budget of over 1 billion USD. This Corporation was given the mandate to establish and run enterprises producing a range of chemical products, fertilizers, and cement for the export and domestic market. To this list must be added a number of businesses and investments controlled by four to five quasi-government organizations attached to the ethnic-based ruling parties of the major *Killils* in the country. While a number of public enterprises inherited from the previous Derg regime, of which some were loss making and a few others in state of decline, had been transferred to the private sector, the state's commanding role in the economy has not been diminished in any way. On the contrary, the large-scale investment it has undertaken over the last 10 years, and its long standing control of such key sectors as telecommunications, power, shipping and air transport, banking, and insurance continue to reinforce its dominant position.

The GTP, the centerpiece of the state-led development strategy, which was launched without meaningful public consultation or serious debate in Parliament, provides a dominant role for the state and only a junior role for non-state actors. A criticism of some of the country's international partners is that the state has embarked on far too many mega investment projects, some of which have not been judiciously prioritized nor based on a sound financial basis. The Renaissance Dam on the Nile, for instance, is estimated to cost 10% of the country's GDP (IMF, 2012). The World Bank (2013) cautiously points to the need for sound public investment management, but management shortfalls, frequently reported in the local press, remain a persistent problem at a number of projects, not least the Gibe dams, and a good number of the Sugar Corporation's enterprises which have failed to meet their completion targets causing costs to spiral. The strategy is also fuelling inflation, which is hitting the poor very hard, and constraining private financial institutions. The annual inflation rate has remained in double digits for the better part of the decade, and in 2010 and 2011, food inflation had soared well over 50% (Central Statistical Agency [CSA], 2005–2012), squeezing the living standards of most income groups but particularly those in the lower income brackets. While government data suggest that there has been a reduction in the number of people living below the poverty line in recent years, the same data indicate that there has been an increase in the severity of poverty in the same period, which means that the poor are worse off in 2012 than they were in 2005 (CSA, 2012). On the other hand, government expenditure on education has been commendably high over the decade, nevertheless, the largest share of public expenditure did not go to those sectors that support poverty reduction (excluding education), but went instead to national defense, public debt, and public order and security. Expenditure on health is below the target set by the Abuja Declaration, which requires African governments to spend at least 15% of their public budget allocations on health (Development Initiatives [DI], 2013, pp. 14–18). The GTP in fact cannot be said to be particularly pro-poor: it gives only a passing glace at the problem of food security and has only a few things to say about long-term efforts at ending hunger and malnutrition, the country's enduring problem.

In brief, state-led development has meant giving the state a dominant role and promoting growth through public investment financed through heavy domestic borrowing. There are risks associated with the choice of investments and this, according to the International Monetary Fund (IMF), includes the build-up of a heavy and unsustainable public debt burden, making a number of public enterprises and banks highly vulnerable, and causing a significant draw-down of the country's foreign reserves creating severe difficulties for private businesses and investments. The IMF argues that growth in the years ahead is expected to decelerate due, it believes, to the limited opportunities for the private sector which has been hampered not just by limited access to credit but also by restrictive regulations and the worsening business climate (IMF, 2012). The World Bank also expects the growth rate to slow down but gives different reasons for it (World Bank, 2013). According to IMF's analysis, the relatively high growth rate achieved so far has been due in part to large-scale public investments and not primarily because of significant productivity growth.

At the same time, state-led development has had significant implications for the political realm as well. The country is effectively a one-party state and political power is concentrated at the top. State developmentalism combined with the non-inclusive land investment program has contributed to greater elite power concentration and state hegemony. We have already mentioned earlier the transfer of the power of the *Killils* to the Federal MOA with regard to land administration. The years 2008 and 2009 saw a spate of anti-democratic and almost draconian laws issued restricting the freedom of the press, crippling the activities of civil society organizations, and creating fear and uncertainty among citizens due to the increased powers given to security and law enforcement agencies in connection with the prevention of terrorist act (FDRE, 2008, 2009a, 2009b).

The emerging crisis of land investments

The rush to acquire land in the period under discussion has not been accompanied by a similar move to utilize the land. Indeed, it became evident shortly after the investment program was launched aggressively in 2008 that the program had attracted not only commercial farming interests but speculators as well. A few years into the program, nearly a dozen foreign investors that had acquired large estates for biofuel crops in BeniShangul, Oromia and SNNP terminated their leases and pulled out, citing financial difficulties and doubts about the profitability of the business scheme, and alleging that the global recession had made biofuel production a less attractive investment. Since then, other foreign investors, including several from India with large leases, have also withdrawn for various reasons including shortage of capital, lack of support from the government, and conflicts with local officials and communities.[15]

Moreover, a serious concern of the government in the last 2 years has been the low utilization of land by investors. A major assessment of land investment projects in the country for the period from the 1990s to the end of 2011, undertaken for United Nations Development Programme (UNDP) and MOA by an international consultant (UNDP, 2012), shows that by the end of 2011 only a small percentage of investors had undertaken farm activities on their land. The assessment report provides evidence for a catalogue of failings and incompetence inclusive of the following: poor performance by investment projects, of high rates of underutilization of land, low levels of farm expertise, and low levels of productivity. It found that among the 112 sample investors selected for case study, the rate of land utilization among those with leases greater than 10,000 ha was 1%, and those with 3000 ha or more was 9%. Overall, the finding was that the average domestic and foreign investors were farming 11% and 8%, respectively, of the land that is registered in their names (p. vii). In other words, 89% and 91%, respectively, of leased land was idle. What is more revealing is the finding regarding agricultural performance. The assessment found that average yield figures for similar crops grown in the same region and under the same climatic conditions showed that investors had a *much lower rate of performance than peasant farmers* for 80% of the crop yield comparisons (p. 89). Moreover, comparison of domestic and foreign investors revealed two important facts that are worthy of note. First, regarding project implementation, domestic investors were found to be better than their foreign counterparts in converting leased land into farm land by a wide margin. Second, regarding productivity, yield figures for seven crops grown by both kinds of investors showed that except for cotton, domestic investors had a higher level of productivity for all other crops, namely coffee, maize, rice, sesame, sorghum, and soya (p. 103). These findings must have come as an embarrassment to government officials who had frequently argued that foreign investors have much better advantages than domestic investors not only in terms of access to capital and technology, but also in terms of land-use efficiency and agricultural performance.

The view in the government at present is that while the investment program has performed below expectations, there is still hope that proper and centralized management and supervision by a public agency can improve matters and enable the program to achieve its objectives (Ministry of Agriculture [MOA], 2013). The real verdict, I believe, is that the program is on the verge of a crisis and the technocratic remedy proposed for its recovery seriously underestimates the severity of the difficulties it is facing. To begin with, because of the urgency created by the 2008 global food crisis and the haste with which investors rushed to 'grab' land in 'uncharted territories,' many investors were saddled with a host of problems for which they were ill prepared and which they were not able to easily overcome. In many instances, proper land and environmental impact assessment was not undertaken before land deals were concluded; the UNDP report notes that 84% of investors had not used any environmental impact assessment document (p. 50). In a number of cases, project staff lack farming expertise, employ poor land management practices, and have limited, if any, knowledge of the specific agro-ecological conditions of the localities concerned. The UNDP document for instance notes that crop failures due to water-logging and flooding, which had damaged crops in a number of projects, should have been predictable and avoidable with proper on-farm water management. The following quote from a recent news report is indicative of the lack of knowledge of local conditions which a good discussion with the surrounding communities would have helped to overcome:

> Eighty percent of the Bangalore-based company's land in the southwestern Gambella region is on a flood plain, meaning its 100,000-hectare (247,100-acre) concession is inundated by the Baro River for as much as seven months of the year, according to Managing Director Ramakrishna Karuturi. The company was unaware of the extent of the flooding when it leased the land, he said.[16]

To give another example: Karuturi's other farm in Bako, some 250 km west of Addis Ababa, which we investigated for an earlier study, was flooded during its first year and the maiden maize crop was badly damaged as a result. It was evident that the damage could have been prevented if the project's senior staff, all of whom were from India, had employed simple protection measures which local farmers often used. Peasants we interviewed near the project were scornful of the farming methods used by the management (Dessalegn, 2011).

Second, there is also the matter of governance of large-scale investments by local and Federal authorities. Governance was not only inadequate and poor but also irresponsible: the authorities had placed too much confidence on foreign investors to do the right thing because it was believed they had better access to capital and technology and were thus better farmers. Moreover, it was clear from the beginning that both at the Federal level and lower levels, from the *Killil* to the local *kebelle*, there was a severe deficit of governance capacity: competent staff, expertise, technical equipment, planning, and preparedness were all lacking (MOARD, 2009b; *Reporter* interview, 2013; UNDP, 2012). An even more serious flaw has been the non-inclusive and non-transparent manner in which the investment program was undertaken from the beginning in the 1990s to the present. The government has been unwilling to invite public dialogue on the program and has employed a top-down and undemocratic approach in which decisions are made at the top and passed down to local officials to implement. A significant shortcoming, one that is an important contributing factor to the emerging crisis, has been the failure to consult the most important stakeholders in the whole program, namely peasant farmers, herders, and their communities. The government has proceeded to implement the program without their participation or consent and without even informing them. On many occasions, peasants and herders learned of the transfer of land in their community to an investor only when the investor appeared on the scene, together with local officials, to claim his land (Dessalegn, 2011).

Third, the reactions of local communities to the expropriation of their land and deprivation of their ancestral rights, and the security concerns this is raising, especially in Gambella, need to be taken into account. Sporadic protest and agitation by local communities in opposition to the land deals have occurred in a number of rural areas, and in several cases protest action has had an impact on investor performance. The form of protest has varied from angry complaints made to local authorities by groups of peasants, low level activism, and violent protest. The following are examples from several areas where large-scale land transfers have been made. In 2012, there were two violent incidents in Gambella causing loss of life and serious injuries to people and property. While the perpetrators did not give any statement indicating their reasons for the attacks, opposition to the investment program and the large inflow of outsiders into the area cannot be ruled out as important factors. In the first incident, which took place in March of that year, a bus carrying students and heading to Gambella city was attacked by gunmen and, according to authorities, 19 people were killed and many others were injured. In the second incident, in April, gunmen attacked a Saudi Star worksite in Abobo*woreda* where men were working on a water diversion scheme in which four Ethiopian staff and one Pakistani were killed. The perpetrators in both cases were said by the authorities to be from a secessionist group called the Gambella Nilotic Union Movement; some of them were apprehended a few months later across the border in South Sudan (*Reporter*, 2012, various issues).

Other dissident groups, not least among the Gambellan Diaspora, have also made strong criticism of the investment program in the *Killil*. A different kind of protest has occurred to the west of the *Killil* in Godere*woreda*, which is noted for its forest cover and lush vegetation. The Godere forest has been designated as 1 of the 58 protected forests in the country, and the people living here depend on forest resources for their livelihood and have protected the forest since time immemorial. In 2010, a large stretch of the forest, 5000 ha of it, was leased to an Indian investor called Verdanta Harvest against strong protest not only by the local communities but also by the President of the country (see Dessalegn, 2011; Zelalem, 2009). It turned out that Verdanta Harvest (part of a large Indian company called Lucky Group), which was given the land to establish a tea plantation, had a different agenda: it was reported by the local authorities that it was engaged in the timber trade and was harvesting the wood from the forest for that purpose. In October 2013, an unidentified group of people set fire to the company's property destroying and damaging machinery, fuel, vehicles, and buildings. The authorities sent a police force and arrested several people said to be responsible for the arson and also set up an investigating committee.[17]

Other violent protests have occurred in the ArjoDidessa valley where the Pakistani-held plantation was torched by irate peasants who were resentful of losing their land. According to press reports, the fire that was started by unidentified individuals, most probably by angry peasants in the community, was said to have raged for 3 days destroying plantation property and causing severe damage to crops (*Reporter*, 22 February 2012). In 2010, peasants in Bako Tibee*woreda* in western Oromia, where we did field work, took part in a violent agitation against a domestic investor who had recently received 3000 ha of land. Informants told us that the peasants were angry because they considered the land to belong to the community and had been used for generations for grazing, for access to water, and as a venue for traditional social and religious services. Our informants said the authorities had to call in the Federal police to quell the disturbances. The projects under construction by the Sugar Corporation have also been put under pressure by strong reaction in the south Omo valley, in Wolkait in Tigrai as well as in Tendaho in the Awash valley. There is not much information about activism on the part of the indigenous communities in south Omo but the project is guarded by a large detachment of armed troops, and international advocacy organizations have reported a number of arrests of people suspected of being opposed to the project and agitating against it (HRW, 2012b; Oakland Institute [OI], 2013). In Wolkait, there was serious agitation by a large number of priests and community people because the construction of the dam was said to threaten the integrity of an ancient monastery located nearby. The agitation appears to have calmed down because of assurances given by the project, though according to the report prepared by the Ethiopian Orthodox Church (EOC), three of the churches closely linked with the monastery will be inundated. The report criticizes the Corporation for not consulting with the clergy and the community before launching project activities (EOC, 2012). One of the reasons behind the long delay in the completion of the Tendaho project has been persistent dispute with the surrounding pastoralist communities which are concerned the project will deprive them access to their customary sources of pasture and water.

There were also what Scott (1985) has called 'everyday forms of resistance,' such as driving cattle to graze inside investor plantations, damaging crops and plantation property, or stealing plantation assets. Examples of such activities have appeared in the local press from time to time (*Reporter*, 31 October 2012). At the time of our visit to Bako in 2010, Karuturi's farm was partially fenced with barbed wire and there were guards on duty carrying automatic rifles. Asked about the armed guards, peasants interviewed said it was to deter people from breaching the fence and grazing their livestock inside the farm which had happened several times in the past. It is not uncommon to see armed guards protecting investor projects elsewhere in the country; in some instances, armed men stand guard over heavy farm machinery out in the field for fear of attacks against them.

In 2012, MOA temporarily suspended land allocations pending a review of the program, the outcome of which was a series of new 'reform' measures and institutional changes. A new body, the Agricultural Investment Land Administration Agency, which incorporates the AISD, was set up in June 2013 tasked with the responsibility of improving program governance. Some of its duties include undertaking proper land assessment, setting up strict guidelines for land allocations, closely monitoring investment projects, and ensuring investors employ environmentally sustainable agricultural practices. The Agency will be responsible for managing all lands leased to investors both by the *Killils* and the Federal MOA as well as land transferred to the Federal land bank (MOA, 2013). This enhanced power by a Federal Agency will certainly further erode the authority of the *Killils* regarding land administration. It is evident that the *Killils* will now have hardly any role in land investment which has become the sole preserve of the Agency. The Agency is also charged with administering the Agricultural Economy Zones, to be set up in 2013 with an initial land fund of 285,000 ha spread over several *Killils*. The government is to provide basic infrastructure in the Zones and lease the land to investors for a much higher rent than previously. The reforms also call for scaling down the amount of land allotted to new investors who will now be offered, initially, 500 ha (or even less), though this could be raised up to a maximum of 3000 ha under certain circumstances. The UNDP assessment report noted above recommended the establishment of a cap on leases in each *Killil* at a level shown to be most efficient in terms of investor land use, advising a maximum limit of 2000 ha. There are also plans to establish some sort of criteria for determining land use efficiency which will be followed by land repossessions (in whole or in part) from investors who fail to meet the criteria. The AISD and *Killil* authorities had already revoked the leases of a number of foreign investors (in BeniShangul, Gambella, and Oromia) on account of failing to use the land they had acquired and breach of contract (FDRE, 2013; MOA, 2013; *Reporter interview, 8 September 2013*; UNDP, 2012).

The conclusion to be drawn from all this is that the country's land investment program, launched in the 1990s but more vigorously pursued with the participation of foreign capital in the last 6 years, has been a failure, and all the indications are that it is unlikely to achieve its major objectives in the years ahead. The assessment commissioned for UNDP and MOA does not provide a comprehensive picture of the investment program, focusing mainly on investor performance, land use efficiency, and related issues. The broader questions of the program's impact on the environment, whether or not there is a role for democratic governance, and the choice of large-scale agriculture driven by foreign capital as a vehicle for sustainable development have not been given due consideration, and the remedy that is proposed focuses essentially on technocratic change and improvements in investor management.

What is to be done?

The wave of land acquisitions in Africa and elsewhere, in the past 5–6 years, has elicited varied reactions and concerns from a wide diversity of regional and international organizations, advocacy groups, development practitioners, and the academic and research communities. Some of these reactions have been strong. The African Union Commission, for example, expressed deep concern over what it called the 'new scramble for Africa' – an apparent reference to the historical Scramble for Africa when the continent was carved up among a small number of European colonial powers in the nineteenth century (African Union Commission [AUC], 2009). The Eastern Africa Farmers Federation, in its Entebbe Declaration of 2010, was highly critical of foreign land grabbing, declaring that securing the land rights of small farmers, pastoralists, and fisher folk remains the best option not only for addressing hunger and poverty but also for wealth creation (Eastern Africa Farmers Federation [EAFF], 2010). The response of such advocacy groups as GRAIN, HRW, and the Oakland Institute (OI) has been equally robust: they have claimed that these acquisitions are unjust and have been accompanied by human rights abuses and heightened the vulnerability of small producers in most of the host countries.

Closer to home, long before the global outcry about land grabbing, Ethiopian civil society organizations, notably environmental advocacy groups, had expressed serious concern about the ecological and economic impact of the land rush taking place in the country in 2007 and 2008. They were particularly concerned about the program of 'agrofuel development' pursued by the government, and the large stretches of land being ceded, without adequate environmental safeguards, to foreign companies claiming to help the country achieve energy security (Ensermu, et al., 2009; MELCA Mahiber, 2008; Tibebwa & Negusu, 2008). They saw and pointed to the dangers hanging over critical natural resources and wildlife in a number of national parks and protected areas which were being threatened by investor encroachment. They raised the alarm when, for example, land in a protected area in southeastern Ethiopia which was the habitat of a unique species of elephant found only there was given to a German company growing castor beans for biofuel. Similar concern was expressed when lands in SNNP which were part of or very close to Omo and Mago national parks, and forest land in Gambella were offered to investors. These concerns are still valid today.

On the other hand, international organizations such as the World Bank (2010), Food and Agricultural Organization (FAO, 2010), and others have adopted a conciliatory approach, arguing that in the best of circumstances land investments could lead to a 'win-win situation' in which all parties concerned, not least governments, local communities and investors, could benefit. The World Bank (2010) in particular has maintained that African countries have considerable 'underutilized' land but they lack the requisite capital and technology to develop it and hence must attract foreign investment. It accepts, however, that these governments lack adequate capacity for sound and effective investment governance and to help them make up this deficit and create a win–win situation the Bank, along with its other partners, has proposed what is known as the principles of responsible agricultural investment. These principles call on governments to establish clear laws on tenure security and to respect these laws, conduct land deals in a transparent manner, and ensure that investment governance includes measures for environmental protection and sustainable land management. Businesses are required to be guided by widely accepted norms of corporate social responsibility and self-regulation. All these measures, however, are to be put into practice on a voluntary basis (World Bank, 2010).

This 'code of conduct' approach, if we may call it that, has been widely criticized.[18] Critics have argued that the underlying assumptions are flawed and unrealistic. The approach does not question whether there are other viable options to large-scale land investments, or indeed whether such investments are desirable. It merely recommends that all parties concerned should follow best practices and be governed by mutually beneficial regulations. Many of the countries where land grabbing has occurred do not have good credentials regarding democratic governance and respect for the law. They often lack a strong and independent judiciary, and small producers and the poor in general do not believe they can get justice or a fair hearing for their grievances. An additional factor in Ethiopia is that civil society and advocacy groups which would have played an important role in raising awareness and supporting the demands of small producers have been seriously crippled by a recent law (FDRE, 2009a). To expect investors, such as those that have leased land in this country, to voluntarily adopt self-regulation and corporate social responsibility is unrealistic. The farm projects set up here or elsewhere in Africa are capitalist enterprises whose sole aim is to make profit for their owners in a short period of time. In many instances, investors will be driven by a 'get-the-maxim-profit-quick' approach because of uncertainties regarding political stability in the host country and concerns having to do with volatility in the global agricultural and financial markets. These pressures will, in all likelihood, drive many to employ environmentally unsustainable land management methods and to refrain from long-term economic or social investments.

Some critics have gone further and questioned whether large-scale land investment is a viable option or desirable for countries dominated by small holders and family-based farming systems. One such critic is De Schutter (2011) who has argued that giving away large tracts of land has immense opportunity costs because it will lead to a type of farming which will have less poverty reduction impacts compared to revitalizing small farmers, and will direct agriculture toward the export market, thus increasing the country's vulnerability to price shocks. Moreover, the experience of countries such as India and China in the recent past, countries with predominantly family-based farming systems, is instructive. These countries were able to register high rates of agricultural productivity and meet domestic demand for food and other agricultural goods without foreign capital or without shifting to large-scale farming systems. India's successful green revolution which enabled the country to attain self-sufficiency in many food crops and to become a net exporter of rice was based on strong public sector support to its small and medium farmers through a variety of targeted programs. Similarly, China's agricultural breakthrough in the 1980s came, thanks to land tenure reforms and the implementation of what was called the household responsibility system, which transferred responsibility for land management from the commune, which was inefficient and wasteful, to the individual household (see Quizon, 2013).

In our case, the real criticism of the land investment program must focus, not merely on issues of inadequate governance and lack of management capacity, but rather on fundamental issues of policy choice and principle. As was noted earlier, state-led development is inherently undemocratic, eschewing consultation and public dialogue in the decision-making process and attributing almost divine omniscience to the state elite. Among the fundamental democratic principles that the investment program has flouted with detrimental effects are the following: (a) the right of local communities to have an *informed say* in matters having to do with the utilization and disposal of land and other natural resources in their locality; (b) the right of *informed consent* by communities without which: (i) local natural resources cannot be ceded away to outsiders, and (ii) community residents cannot be moved from their ancestral lands. Other significant limitations have been the lack of transparency in program design and management, blind faith in what decision-makers thought was the transformative power of large-scale farming and foreign capital, and the failure to incorporate the goals of food security and poverty reduction as important objectives of the program. It is quite evident that the new policy review and the changes initiated as a result have not provided any improvements in this regard.

The choice made by decision-makers to promote land deals and entice foreign capital to promote agricultural development has been counter-productive. The assumption held by decision-makers that agricultural transformation would be achieved through the instrumentality of foreign capital is proving illusory, and, if not seriously reconsidered in the light of the current experience, will cause immeasurable damage in the long run. The more judicious policy option would be to invest in a program of what I wish to call *internally driven agrarian transformation.* Such a program would involve, among other things, not only channeling greater resources into modernizing smallholder agriculture, but also, importantly, encouraging, through a variety of support mechanisms, the growth and development of resident *farmer-investors* from among the peasantry and other land users. The goal would be to enable such farmer-investors to operate large-scale farms so that they can play an important role in the modernization of agriculture. There are already a good number of dynamic and entrepreneurial peasant farmers in the rural areas, but they face, at present, a host of financial, institutional, and technical road blocks inhibiting their efforts and the chances for progress. Enabling these farmers to grow and become investors will take time but it is an investment worth the effort and the resources expended in the medium to long term. Such farmer-investors have the advantage of extensive practical knowledge of farming and local conditions combined with respect for the environment and natural resources. These farmers live in the rural areas among their own communities and are more likely to be more eco-friendly and more responsible in their enterprise than external investors. What indigenous farmers lack in access to capital and technology, which can be remedied without too much difficulty by prudent and timely financial and technical support, can be compensated by their greater practical know-how, social responsibility, and sense of accountability.

Notes

1. Documents posted on MOARD's website in 2008/2009 spoke of competition with other African countries, but were full of high expectations from foreign land investment. All early MOARD documents have since been removed.
2. Much of the debate on land grabbing has been conducted in the pages of the *Journal of Peasant Studies*; see the special collection in Vol. 39, Nos. 3 and 4, 2012. Advocacy groups that have been highly critical of Ethiopia's land deals include GRAIN, HRW, and the OI.
3. This section is based in part on the findings of field work and interviews carried out in 2010 for an earlier study (Dessalegn, 2011). See also Fouad (2012), Lavers (2012), and Cotula, Vermeulen, Leonard, and Keely (2009) has some discussion on Ethiopia.
4. On food security, see the recent collection of papers in Dessalegn, Pankhurst, and van Uffelen (2013); on land and landownership, see Dessalegn (2009).
5. See Dessalegn (2011). Other works include Lavers (2012) and Malik (2012).
6. Interview with Bizualem Bekele, coordinator at the Agricultural Investment Support Directorate, MOA, in *Reporter*, 8 September 2013. MOARD is previous name of MOA. UNDP (2012) gives much higher figures.
7. Under the Federal system the country is divided into nine major ethnic-based administrative units called *Killils* in Amharic (rendered as Region in English, but I prefer the Amharic term). The lowest unit is the *kebele* (equivalent to a sub-district), and above it is the *woreda* (district).
8. http://www.etsugar.gov.et Accessed November 2013. Information posted earlier, in 2011, but since removed, provides different figures.
9. According to press reports, it may be 100,000 or more (*Reporter*, 8 April 2012, and 13 January 2013); the Corporation's website provides the most minimal information and no word on displacements.
10. The higher figure is in HRW (2012b), the lower in OI (2011, 2013). William Davison, 'Development, rights, and restrictions in Ethiopian's South Omo,' 16 September 2013.
11. A rare exception is the recent paper by Tewolde and Fana (2013), which was based on field work in one of the Corporation's sites in SNNP; the paper raises concerns about conflicts and 'cultural invasion' by outsiders.
12. See http://www.moa.gov.et
13. Based on MOA and MOARD websites, and local press reports (*Reporter* and *Fortune*). Some of the companies have since pulled out.
14. For the purposes of this work, I shall use the terms 'development from above' and 'state-led development' to mean more or less the same thing.
15. *Reporter*, 22 April 2012, Ministry of Mines quoted in *Reporter*, 27 May 2012; *Fortune*, 8 April 2012; *The Hindu*, 1 June 2013 and 5 November 2013.
16. William Davison, Ethiopia's push to lure farm investment falters on flood plains, *Bloomberg News*, 25 November 2013.
17. Both the arson attack and the Gambella authorities complaints against Verdanta are covered in *Reporter*, 28 October and 11 December 2013; also in the Indian paper, *The Hindu*, 5 November 2013.
18. See Borras and Franco (2010), De Schutter (2011), and White, Borras, Hall, Scoones, and Wolford (2012) for the criticism.

References

African Union Commission. (2009). *Framework and guidelines on land policy in Africa*. Addis Ababa: African Development Bank and Economic Commission for Africa.

Melese, A., & Helmsing, A. H. J. (2010). Endogenisation or enclave formation? The development of the Ethiopian cut flower industry. *Journal of Modern African Studies, 48*, 35–66.

Borras, S. M. Jr., & Franco, J. (2010). *Towards a broader view of the politics of global land grab. Rethinking land issues, reframing resistance*. ICAS Working Paper Series No. 001. Initiatives in

Critical Agrarian Studies, Land Deals Politics Institute and Transnational Institute. Accessed by web search.

Central Statistical Agency. (2005–2012). *Consumer price index reports*. Addis Ababa: Author.

Central Statistical Agency. (2012, December). *The 2010/2011 Ethiopian households consumption – Expenditure (HCE) survey*. Statistical report. Addis Ababa.

Cotula, L., Vermeulen, S., Leonard, R., & Keely, J. (2009). *Land grab or development opportunity? Agricultural investment and international land deals in Africa*. London: International Institute for Environment and Development.

De Schutter, O. (2011). How not to think of land-grabbing: Three critiques of large-scale investments in Farmland. *Journal of Peasant Studies*, *32*, 249–279.

Dessalegn, R. (2009). *The peasant and the state: Studies in agrarian change in Ethiopia 1950s– 2000s*. Addis Ababa: Addis Ababa University Press.

Dessalegn, R. (2011). *Land to investors: Large-scale land transfers in Ethiopia*. Addis Ababa: Forum for Social Studies.

Dessalegn, R., Pankhurst, A., & van Uffelen, J.-G. (Eds.). (2013). Food security, safety nets and social protection in Ethiopia. Addis Ababa: Forum for Social Studies.

Development Initiatives. (2013, February). *Ethiopia. resources for poverty eradication: A background paper*. Africa Hub, Nairobi: Peace Nganwa.

Eastern Africa Farmers Federation. (2010). *The entebbe declaration on large foreign land acquisitions*. Retrieved 2012, from http://www.eaff.org

EnsermuKelbessa, NegusuAklilu & Tadesse Woldemariam (Eds.). (2009). *Agrofuel development in Ethiopia: Findings of an assessment*. Addis Ababa: Forum for Environment.

Ethiopian Orthodox Church. (2012). *Report of the dispute between Waldiba Monastery and Wolkait sugar project*. Addis Ababa: Mahibere Kidusan.

Federal Democratic Republic of Ethiopia. (2008, December 4). *Freedom of the mass media and access to information proclamation*. (Proclamation No. 590). Addis Ababa: Negarit Gazeta.

Federal Democratic Republic of Ethiopia. (2009a, February). *Proclamation to provide for the registration and regulation of charities and societies*. (Proclamation No. 621). Addis Ababa: Negarit Gazeta.

Federal Democratic Republic of Ethiopia. (2009b, August). *Anti-terrorism proclamation*. (Proclamation No. 652). Addis Ababa: Negarit Gazeta.

Federal Democratic Republic of Ethiopia. (2010, March). *Council of ministers directive regarding the administration of agricultural investment land*. Addis Ababa, [Unpublished].

Federal Democratic Republic of Ethiopia. (2002a, July). *Re-enactment of the investment proclamation*. (Proclamation No. 280). Addis Ababa: Negarit Gazeta.

Federal Democratic Republic of Ethiopia. (2002b, December). *Environmental impact assessment proclamation*. (Proclamation No. 299). Addis Ababa: Federal Negarit Gazeta.

Federal Democratic Republic of Ethiopia. (2013, March 4). *Council of ministers regulation to establish the Ethiopian agricultural investment land administration agency*. (Council of Ministers Regulation No. 283/2013) Addis Ababa: Federal Negarit Gazette.

Food and Agricultural Organization. (2010, September 20–22). *Eastern and Anglophone Western Africa regional assessment: FAO voluntary guidelines on responsible governance of tenure of land and other natural resources*. Addis Ababa.

Fortune. (2012–2013). English language business weekly, various issues.

Fouad, M. (2012). Power and property: Commercialization, enclosures, and the transformation of agrarian relations in Ethiopia. *Journal of Peasant Studies*, *39*, 81–104.

GRAIN. (2010–2012). Land grab threaten annual. Retrieved 2012, from http://www.grain.org

Human Rights Watch. (2012a). "Waiting here for death": Forced displacement and "villagization" in Ethiopia's Gambella region. Retrieved 2012, from http://www.hrw.org

Human Rights Watch. (2012b). "What will happen if hunger comes". Abuses against indigenous peoples of Ethiopia's lower Omo valley. Retrieved 2012, from http://www.hrw.org

International Monetary Fund. (2012, August 27). *The federal democratic Republic of Ethiopia: Staff report for 2012 article IV consultation*. Washington, DC.

Journal of Peasant Studies. (2011 and 2012). Various issues in volumes 38 and 39.

Kassahun, B. (2012). *The political economy of agricultural extension in Ethiopia: Economic growth and political control*. Working Paper 042, Future Agricultures, University of Sussex, Brighton.

Lavers, T. (2012). "Land grab" as development strategy? The political economy of agricultural investment in Ethiopia. *Journal of Peasant Studies*, *39*, 105–132.

Malik, F. (2012). Power and property: Commercialization, enclosures, and the transformation of agrarian relations in Ethiopia. *Journal of Peasant Studies, 39,* 81–104.

MELCA Mahiber. (2008, September). *Rapid assessment of biofuels development status in Ethiopia and proceedings of the national workshop on environmental impact assessment and biofuels.* Addis Ababa.

Ministry of Agriculture. (2012). Retrieved 2012, from http://www.moa.gov.et, Addis Ababa.

Ministry of Agriculture. (2013, August). *Agricultural investment land administration agency implementation manual [Amharic].* Addis Ababa: Draft.

Ministry of Agriculture and Rural Development. (2008, November). *Agricultural investment potential of Ethiopia.* Addis Ababa.

Ministry of Agriculture and Rural Development. (2009a). *List of investment projects in agriculture sector from July 1992–February 6, 2009 (compiled from Killil investment data).* Addis Ababa.

Ministry of Agriculture and Rural Development. (2009b, June). *Planned system for administration of investment land [Amharic].* Addis Ababa.

Ministry of Agriculture and Rural Development. (2010). Retrieved 2010, from http://www.moard. gov.et, Addis Ababa.

Ministry of Finance and Economic Development. (2003, April). *Rural development policy and strategies.* Addis Ababa.

Ministry of Finance and Economic Development. (2010a). Updated 2nd PASDEP Agric. Sec. Plan (2003–2007) [2011–2015]. PDF file.

Ministry of Finance and Economic Development. (2010b). PASDEP – 2011 Plan. Final. PDF file.

Ministry of Finance and Economic Development. (2010c). *Growth and transformation plan (GTP) 2010/11–2014/15.* Addis Ababa: Draft.

Ministry of Planning and Economic Development. (1994, June). *Agricultural development led industrialization. A development strategy for the future.* Addis Ababa.

Oakland Institute (OI). (2010). Mismanagement in agriculture. The role of the international finance corporation in global land grabs. Retrieved 2011, from http://www.oaklandinstitute.org

Oakland Institute. (2011). Understanding land investment deals in Africa. Country report: Ethiopia. Retrieved 2011, from http://www.oaklandinstitute.org

Oakland Institute. (2013). Omo: Local tribes under threat. A field report from the Omo valley, Ethiopia. Retrieved 2013, from http://www.oaklandinstitute.org

Quizon, A. B. (2013). *Land governance in Asia. Understanding the debates on land tenure rights and land reforms in the Asian context.* Series No. 3 Rome: International Land Coalition.

Reporter. (2012 and 2013). Twice weekly independent Amharic newspaper. Various issues for these years.

Reporter. (2013, September, 8.). *Interview with AtoBizualemBekele, coordinator, agricultural investment support directorate in MOA [Amharic].* Addis Ababa.

Scott, J. C. (1985). *Weapons of the weak: Everyday forms of peasant resistance.* New Haven, CT: Yale University Press.

Tewolde, W., & Fana, G. (2013). *Socio-political and conflict implications of sugar development in SalamagoWereda, Ethiopia.* (Unpublished paper), Addis Ababa.

Tibebwa, H., & Negusu, A. (Eds.). (2008). *Agrofuel development in Ethiopia: Rhetoric, reality and recommendations.* Addis Ababa: Forum for Environment.

UNDP. (2012, May–June). *An assessment of factors affecting the performance of Ethiopian commercial farmers. Report of mission for UNDP-Ethiopia*; May–June 2012. Ceredigion: AA International Ltd.

White, B., Borras, S. M. Jr., Hall, R., Scoones, I., & Wolford, W. (2012). The new enclosures: Critical perspectives on corporate land deals. *Journal of Peasant Studies, 39,* 619–647.

World Bank. (2010, September). *Rising global interest in farmland. Can it yield sustainable and equitable benefits?* Washington, D.C.

World Bank. (2013, June). *Ethiopia economic update II: Laying the foundations for achieving middle income status.* Washington, DC.

Zelalem, T. (2009). Godare forest and possible impacts of its conversion to oil palm plantation. In Ensermu Kelbessa, Negusu Aklilu, & Tadesse Woldemariam (Eds.), *Agrofuel development in Ethiopia: Findings of an assessment* (pp. 133–151). Addis Ababa: Forum for Environment.

Forest investments and channels of contestation in highland Ethiopia

Kathleen Guillozet

Department of Forest Ecosystems and Society, Oregon State University, Corvallis, OR, USA

Increasing demands for forest products and services in forest-limited places such as Ethiopia necessitate deeper consideration of the social, political, ecological and economic institutions that underpin forest access. Given the key role that forests play in rural livelihoods, access limitations associated with emerging agricultural and forest-based foreign land investments have significant implications for communities located at the forest-farm interface. While private investment in Ethiopian forests is limited, a lack of citizen empowerment and transparent information inhibits local communities and advocates from effectively monitoring and protecting resource rights. This paper describes the tenure systems surrounding forests in Ethiopia today and examines two aspects of emerging forest investments in Ethiopia and highlights spaces within them for social transformation that might lead to more equitable benefit sharing. First, it describes the absence of a uniform definition of forestland, and a lack of clear institutional authority and information transparency surrounding land deals affecting forests. Second, it illustrates constraints to local citizen participation in decision-making.

Introduction

The phenomenon of land grabbing has received significant critical attention in recent years, as evidenced by several special themed issues in the Journal of Peasant Studies (2011 and 2013), Water Alternatives (2012), Globalizations (2013) and this issue of African Identities. Researchers identify land and water scarcity as a primary driver of foreign investment in the global South (e.g. Deininger et al., 2011; Rice, 2009). Zoomers (2010) emphasizes additional contemporary processes including increased foreign demand for non-food crops (especially biofuels), conservation, ecosystem services, tourism and land purchases by retirees and Diaspora. Among the chief concerns associated with land grabs are their deleterious impacts on the rights, resources and livelihoods of marginalized rural smallholders (Borras, Hall, Scoones, White & Wolford, 2011) and on the integrity of ecological systems. Land grabs are a type of foreign investment considered 'arguably is least likely to deliver significant developmental benefits to the host country' (Hallam, 2009, p. 5). This paper highlights factors that exacerbate the challenges associated with monitoring and assessing local rights with respect to land grabs in one country, Ethiopia, using examples from national and local levels.

Ethiopia is a hotspot of land grabbing (Horne, 2011), and agricultural and forest development is a centrepiece of national economic growth and development planning (FDRE, 2011). Some scientists and policy-makers envision increased foreign and domestic investment in Ethiopia's forestlands as a means to alleviate rural poverty and enhance forest ecosystem protection and function (i.e. Bongers and Tennigkeit, 2010). The high demand for wood products in Ethiopia and neighbouring East African countries may justify increased investment in the forestry sector (Bekele-Tesemma, 2007), but a lack of institutional transparency and accountability, in combination with an authoritarian system of government that limits free expression places local forest-based livelihoods in jeopardy. Foreign investors in Ethiopia are not obliged to bring benefits to local communities (Tamrat, 2010), a factor not unique to Ethiopia but of concern given the key role that forests play in bolstering rural livelihoods (Babulo et al., 2009; Yemiru, Roos, Campbell, & Bohlin, 2010). Researchers have described the nature and extent of foreign investment deals in Ethiopia (Lavers, 2012), and analysed the implications for rural livelihoods (Horne, 2011) but have not articulated the specific barriers that affect people's capacity to contest inequitable or unfair forest benefit distributions. This is compounded by the fact that actual and potential forest markets in Ethiopia are difficult to define, may conflict with other uses, are managed by different institutions and are governed by unclear legislation.

Among the proposed responses to the threats to socio-ecological systems posed by land grabs are voluntary guidelines for investment and land management (Table 1), including *principles for responsible agricultural investment* (PRAI) (FAO, IFAD, UNCTAD & World Bank, 2011) and *ten principles for a landscape approach* (Sayer et al., in press). The PRAI, developed by the Food and Agriculture Organisation (FAO), International Fund for Agriculture and Development, United National Commission on Trade and Development and the World Bank, emphasizes livelihoods and aims to 'significantly reduce the chances of generating negative externalities and raise the likelihood of positive impacts [of agricultural investments]' (FAO et al., 2011, p. 4). The ten principles for a landscape approach, developed by a team of ecologists, agronomists, biologists and development experts, 'represent the consensus opinion of a significant number of major actors on how agricultural production and environmental conservation can best be integrated at a landscape scale' (Sayer et al., in press, p. 3) and have been

Table 1.   Principles guiding agricultural investment and land use.

Principles for responsible agricultural investment (FAO et al. 2011)	Ten principles for a landscape approach (Sayer et al., in press)
1. Existing rights to land and associated natural resources are recognized and respected	1. Continual learning and adaptive management
2. Investments do not jeopardize food security but rather strengthen it	2. Common concern entry point
3. Processes relating to investment in agriculture are transparent, monitored and ensure account-ability by all stakeholders, within a proper business, legal and regulatory environment	3. Multiple scales
	4. Multifunctionality
	5. Multiple stakeholders
4. All those materially affected are consulted, and agreements from consultations are recorded and enforced	6. Negotiated and transparent change logic
5. Investors ensure that projects respect the rule of law, reflect industry best practice, are viable economically and result in durable shared value	7. Clarification of rights and respon-sibilities
	8. Participatory and user-friendly monitoring
6. Investments generate desirable social and distributional impacts and do not increase vulnerability	9. Resilience
	10. Strengthened stakeholder capacity
7. Environmental impacts must be quantified, and measures taken to encourage sustainable resource use, while minimizing risk/magnitude of negative impacts and mitigating them	

adopted by the Subsidiary Body on Scientific, Technical and Technological Advice of the Convention on Biological Diversity.

The similarity among the two sets of principles is striking, in particular the emphasis within both on clarification of rights, engagement of stakeholders, and the promotion of transparency and multiple benefits. Evidence from programmes across the forest sector echo a similar need for increased transparency and engagement with local communities. For example, a recent evaluation of *reducing emissions from deforestation and forest degradation and enhancing forest carbon stocks* (REDD +) programme benefit distributions found that unclear or insecure land rights, and under-representation of local people were key weaknesses in project development and implementation (Pham et al., 2013).

So how might advocates, policy-makers and others go about making these needed changes to increase transparency and local engagement in decision-making? Fairly early on in discussions over land grabbing, Zoomers (2010) argued that '"codes of conduct"... are unlikely to work in favour of the poor' (p. 439) because 'processes of land grabbing are broader and deeper than assumed' (p. 430). von Braun and Meinzen-Dick (2009) suggest that a combination of 'international law, government policies, and the involvement of civil society, the media, and local communities is needed to minimize the threats and realize the benefits' (p. 4) of foreign investments in land. These observations are helpful, but still too general to operationalize. This paper strives to address this gap, at least in part, by describing some of these processes in greater detail in Ethiopia, using case-study evidence and document analysis. It engages with the following questions:

What are specific impediments to transparency and engagement with local communities in the context of foreign investments in Ethiopian forests?

What are some initial steps towards addressing them?

To this end, this paper focuses on two impediments, the former at the national level and the latter at the local level:

1. The absence of clear institutional authority and information transparency surrounding land deals affecting forests.
2. Inadequate understanding of and mechanisms to address constraints to local citizen participation.

A background on Ethiopia's forest laws and forest tenure provides context for these impediments. Secondary data and data from a case study of a community in highland Ethiopia provide concrete examples and are the basis of proposed actions to ameliorate the conditions that allow them to persist.

Theoretical grounding

This paper uses the sociological theory of structuration (Giddens, 1986) to understand how societies function and posits a theory of change that involves increased understanding of the channels of contestation available to different actors within a society (Moser & Norton, 2001). Structure in society is both the mechanism through which actors move in the world and the outcome of that movement. Society is composed of a 'multiplicity of structures' that are governed by transposable rules that may 'be applied to an inherently unpredictable range of cases outside the context in which they are initially learned' (Sewell, 1989, p. 20). Reinterpretation of assumed power relations is perhaps most likely during moments when contradictions among rules become increasingly visible. Spaces of incongruity interrupt 'claims of the easy unity of the market and . . . illustrates the creative possibilities of social mobilization' (Tsing, 2005, p. 211).

People with different levels of power and influence have dissimilar access to instruments of economic growth. While neoliberal processes including those associated with land grabs are often thought to accompany increased market openness, Dauvergne and Neville (2010) describe how 'historical legacies of land tenure and control influence the likelihood that rural communities can take advantage of these opportunities' (p. 651). In addition to the practical limitations associated with the capacities of marginalized groups to engage in neoliberal enterprises, neoliberalism can and does thrive in strong authoritarian states. In fact, neoliberalism can actually magnify authoritarian tendencies, particularly 'as those left behind come into conflict with those reaping rewards' (Springer, 2009, pp. 273–274). This extends to debates over whether or not increased formalization of tenure should be a priority in the Global South. Those who argue in favour of enacting policies to ensure more secure and transferable land rights indicate that it will incentivize long-term investments by farmers in their land (Ali, Dercon, & Gautam, 2011) and increase capital availability and livelihood opportunities (Deininger, Ali, & Alemu, 2008; Gebremariam, Bekele & Ridgewell, 2009). Others argue that imported tenure arrangements can have harmful impacts, especially for marginalized groups, when customary and statutory tenure collide (Winter & Quan, 1999). Ethiopia has an ambivalent stance towards capitalism, alternately promoting capitalist and protectionist policies, but critics assert that the poor are likely to be excluded from both:

> The polarity between state and market that was embodied by the first and second republics, and that continues to frame the current land tenure debates, leaves out alternatives based on the self-defined needs of peasant communities, who are conspicuously absent from the cacophony of voices in the public sphere. (Makki, 2012, p. 100)

The channels of contestation matrix provides a concrete mechanism for the analysis of empowerment and transparency through enumeration of the various social, political and policy channels through which citizens can make rights claims (Table 2). It serves to map both the capacity for people to make effective claims as well as institutional, legal and other hindrances that people might face in asserting them (Moser & Norton, 2001).

Paraphrasing Moser and Norton, an enabling environment for rights claims is one in which poor people have the following: access to information; group solidarity; development of skills and capabilities, especially organizational and communication skills; the help of allies capable of providing advocacy at other levels and in distant institutional domains; and access to a 'fair regulator' capable of assessing competing claims according to rights, and provisions without being captured by elite groups (2001, p. x). Enumeration of the channels through which people can assert and question formal and informal rights claims situates rights as a social process embedded in power relations (Diokno, 2011).

This paper uses the channels of contestation matrix to highlight selected institutional channels, types of claims and methods of actions that contemporary Ethiopian can and cannot make with respect to forest-related foreign investment. It argues that a clearer articulation, even of the claims people are unable to make, will support transparency by heightening awareness over incongruities in the structures that govern forest access.

Background: Political context and forest tenure in Ethiopia

The government of Ethiopia has expressed willingness to move towards less authoritarian institutions in its 2010–2015 Growth and Transformation Plan. The Plan

Table 2.   Institutions, types of claims and methods of action in the channels of contestation matrix.

Institutional channels	Types of claims	Method of citizen action
Political	Identification of new rights and freedoms, negotiations over interpretation of rights, demands for transparency and accountability, changing formally recognized rights	Voting, lobbying, open struggle, media reporting, public hearings, advocacy
Legal	Negotiation over interpretation and implementation of laws	Taking legal action, disputing unfair laws, engaging police instead of courts, appealing to third parties and formal monitoring processes
Policy	Negotiation over entitlements such as rights to extension services and credit	Engaging in international, national, and local policy processes, engaging in fiscal reform
Administrative	Negotiation over interpretation and implementation of entitlements, i.e. access to economic and social resources	Making individual claims for resources and services, monitoring public service provision
Social	Negotiation over access to natural and social resources	Negotiating resource claims, debating roles and responsibilities
Private sector	Negotiation over interpretation and implementation of private-sector-related entitlements, i.e. labour rights and access to financial assets	Collectively bargaining for wages and benefits, taking union and civil society action over labour standards

Sources: Adapted from Moser and Norton (2001) and Diokno (2011).

highlights goals of 'establishing a system for citizens' access to information; strengthening the effectiveness of the justice system in terms of its ability to discover the truth through legal procedures; amending laws to ensure that implementation and interpretation of the laws are done in conformity with the constitution; ensuring independence, transparency and accountability of courts and the judicial system; and strengthening law enforcement institutions, among other democratic reforms (FDRE, 2010, p. 11). Still, these changes have yet to materialize, and organizations including Human Rights Watch (HRW) and Amnesty International criticize the current regime for its policies that restrict freedom of expression and association (Amnesty International, 2011; HRW, 2010).

Tenure underpins legal, policy-related, administrative and social aspects of foreign investments. Over half of the factors that plantation investors believe make forest-related investments 'high-risk' are associated with tenure (Bekele, 2011). In Ethiopia, the state owns all forest and agricultural land, granting usufruct rights to citizens in the case of farmland and maintaining all management authority in the case of natural forestlands. The radical land reforms that followed the 1974 Revolution resulted in large-scale land redistributions that shape contemporary landholdings (Rahmato, 2009). The 1975 'Proclamation to Provide for Public Ownership of Rural Lands' established public ownership of forests and agricultural lands, and is consistent with the 1994 Constitution that remains in effect today. It states in Article 40(3) that: 'The right to ownership of rural and urban land, as well as of all natural resources, is exclusively vested in the State and in the peoples of Ethiopia. Land is a common property of the Nations, Nationalities and

Peoples of Ethiopia and shall not be subject to sale or to other means of exchange.' Peters (2009) describes such land relations as 'open to interpretation...[and] careful attention has to be paid to the specific meanings and constructions, including narratives and stories placed by different social actors on the principles justifying access, use, and control' (p. 1322). Indeed, in practice, people routinely access forests for fuelwood, fodder, building materials, medicine and food, among other uses. The 2007 Forest Development, Conservation and Utilization Proclamation No. 542 marked the beginning of a change in direction, and outlined initial provisions for private ownership and private investment in forests, raising concerns over potential inconsistencies with the Constitution (Stebek, 2011).

The federal government devolved land titling to the Regional States in 1997, and regional proclamations allow for the issuance of land certificates that formalize use rights. Ethiopia does not have a federal institution responsible for land administration (ARD, 2004). Most regional provisions permit temporary land leasing and inheritance-based transfers, but prohibit land sale or mortgage. Changes to the Family Code made in 2000 gave women equal rights to household assets including land upon the death of their spouses or divorce, marking a radical shift towards increased gender equity (Kumar & Quisumbing, 2012), but implementation is devolved to the state level, and varies significantly in terms of progress made. As of 2010, over half of Ethiopia's regional states (including Benishangul-Gumuz, Afar, Gambella, Somali and Harari regional states) had not devised a land administration system (Tamrat, 2010). Grey areas within regional proclamations 'lead to confusion and provide[s] scope for bureaucratic discretion' (Deininger, Ali, Holden, & Zevenbergen, 2007, p. 5).

The 2007 Oromia Rural Land Use and Administration Proclamation outlined a number of general articles relevant to forest investments. Investors are obliged to 'plant indigenous trees at least on 2% of the given land' and investments 'shall be determined in the way that it shall protect the natural resources'. Remaining natural forest patches 'shall be identified, demarcated, protected, conserved, and sustainably used by the local community' and '[l]and users are obliged to conserve and protect mother trees found on their holdings.' These provisions may provide a means to increase the accountability of different forest-based investments, although a number of documented land deals have taken place without due consultation with communities (Horne, 2011).

Methods

This paper uses document analysis and case-study evidence to identify and describe impediments to transparency and engagement with local communities in the context of foreign investments in Ethiopian forests.

Case-study evidence is based on 10 months of field research conducted in highland Ethiopia in 2009 and 2010. During this period, the author resided in a highland Oromo community of about 7000 residents adjacent to a forest plantation and natural forest area of approximately 149 and 1209 hectares, respectively. Located some 180 km south of Addis Ababa, the forests were managed by a government-operated Forest Enterprise (referred to subsequently as the Enterprise). Data were collected from open-ended interviews with 38 purposively selected community members and resource managers, a household livelihoods survey, forest inventory, ethnographic field notes and analysis of secondary sources. Interviews were conducted in English and Oromiffa, with translation assistance provided by a community member (author speaks English and some Amharic and

Oromiffa). Reports and historical records were obtained through archival research in Ethiopia and the United States.

Case-study evidence describes community access to a state-managed plantation and natural forest area and the channels of contestation available to local people. It is an 'exemplary case' in that it addresses 'those alternatives that most seriously challenge the assumptions of the case' (Yin, 2003, p. 187). In other words, the community described in the case possesses a number of attributes that make it likely for people to have comparatively robust channels of contestation. These include:

- location in the Oromia Regional State, a region with strong forest legislation that has made progress towards implementing land titling reforms;
- clear demarcation of the natural forest area with permanent boundary markers in place for multiple decades;
- presence of a government-run forest enterprise, referred to as a 'radically new forestry institution' (Bongers & Tennigkeit, 2010, p. 51) that is staffed by well-educated forestry experts who are sensitive to local livelihood needs and willing to experiment with new approaches;
- existence of a permanent staff of forest guards and
- proximity to external judicial enforcement institutions and existence of local institutions for conflict resolution.

Institutional transparency

Early evidence on foreign investments in Ethiopia's forests and agricultural lands indicates that the processes governing forest leases are nebulous and challenging to track. The absence of clear institutional authority among federal agencies hampers planning, coordination and overall transparency in forest management and makes it difficult for citizens and others to obtain information and ensure that proper administrative procedures are followed. Conflicting definitions of forest and the absence of a definitive map of existing forests make it difficult to assess whether emerging agricultural investments affect forests, or which forests are available for private investment. As many as four separate federal ministries are involved in administering land-related investments, and the complicated nature of their authority to approve and oversee investments makes it difficult for citizens and advocates to ensure due process is followed and assert competing claims in a timely manner.

Forest investors are required to submit a Forest Management Plan to the Ministry of Agriculture (MoA), although only projects that fall within the forestry sector are required to develop these plans (i.e. projects involving forest clearing for agriculture are not necessarily subject to review by forestry experts). Land allocations above 5000 hectares are managed through the Agricultural Investment Support Directorate under the MoA, while others are managed through the Ministry of Trade and Industry's Investment Agency. To add further complexity, investments involving irrigation are administered by the Ministry of Water Resources' River Basin Authorities. There are no known formal channels through which Ministries and the various agencies within them communicate with each other about forest-related investments.

Figure 1 describes federal-level institutions involved in forest-based investments, but regional actors also play a role in lease approval and administration. While procedures vary among states, thresholds based on lease size often determine who has jurisdictional authority over investments. For example, in the Regional State Beninshangul Gumuz,

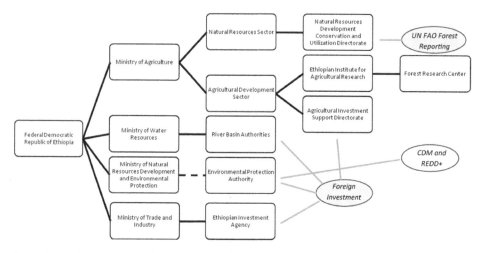

Figure 1.   Federal entities and authority over forest-related reporting and management.

investment leases for fewer than 1000 hectares are administered by the regional Land Protection office while those for more than 1000 hectares are administered by the MoA (Zebene, 2012).

Although highlighted by the Ethiopian government as one of eight sectors expected to play a central role in sustainable economic development in the coming decades (FDRE, 2011), forestry lacks a strong institutional presence at the federal level (World Bank, 2012). Ethiopia's head of forestry works in the Forestry Research Centre, three levels subordinate to the Minister of Agriculture (Figure 1). In part, forestry may receive short shrift as agriculture historically served as a primary means through which leaders demonstrated political legitimacy. Annual crop production figures are closely monitored in election years, and high production is associated with political success, compelling officials to use the means at their disposal to favour agricultural output, even at the expense of other land uses such as forestry (personal communication, community member, 4 April 2010).

While not linked directly to forest investments, the FAO Global Forest Resources Assessment (GFRA) 'provides the data and information needed to support policies, decisions and negotiations in all matters where forests and forestry play a part' (FAO, 2010, p. xi). The forestry specialists who prepare GFRA reports are housed in the Forestry Research Centre, a subdivision of the MoA. Preparation and planning for the bilateral forest carbon payment mechanisms known as CDM and REDD + are managed through the Environmental Protection Agency (EPA). Initially established as part of the Ministry of Natural Resources Development and Environmental Protection, the EPA is now an autonomous entity (indicated by dashed line in Figure 1) that also oversees permits for licensing and land allocation phases of land investments. The sometimes conflicting and usually nebulous nature of permit requirements leads to confusion (Gebremariam et al., 2009) and lack of enforcement (Tamrat, 2010).

Conflicting forest definitions and designations

Federal and regional land administration laws lack clarity and seem to exclude community holdings from eligibility for compensation that would otherwise be granted through the Constitution and Regional Proclamations. Ethiopia's country report submitted to the FAO as part of the Global Forest Resource Assessment indicated that as of 2010, no forestland

Table 3.   Ethiopian forest cover and ownership class designation.

Variable	Area (ha)
Forest area	12,296,000
Private forest	0
Public ownership	13,000,000
Regenerated forest	11,785,000
Forest designation production (plantations)	511,000

Source: FAO (2010).

in Ethiopia was managed under private ownership (Table 3), information that conflicts with reporting on Participatory Forest Management, which technically constitute private holdings and in 2010 extended well over 210,000 hectares (Winberg, 2010). Disparate reporting requirements and lack of information sharing among ministries make it difficult for citizens to a complete picture of the extent and nature of forest cover and location and investments that affect them.

Integration across agencies is further hampered by financial benefits that are granted to those who succeed in attracting foreign investors. Regional actors have incentive to attract and retain foreign investors to their districts because it allows them to compete more effectively for scarce regional development funds for infrastructure improvements that bring status and additional economic development opportunities (personal communication, government worker, Addis Ababa 18 May 2010). There exist a number of financially unattractive aspects of forest sector investment in Ethiopia, but foreign investors are perceived as having securer rights in comparison to domestic investors, giving them a comparative advantage. As one scientist explained:

> There is unwillingness on the behalf of domestic investors to invest in forest resources for a number of reasons: length of time for return on investment, insecure land tenure, disputes with local people, problems in the courts because judges and police are subject to bribes. [Foreign investors are less vulnerable to these problems because] their interests are more visible. (personal communication, scientist, Addis Ababa 20 May 2010)

Formally recognized private foreign investment in Ethiopia's forestry sector, defined here as activities involving afforestation, reforestation, conservation and non-timber forest product market development, is currently limited. Of the handful of foreigners who made inquiries about investment opportunities to a government forestry official over the past few years, only one was moving forward with developing a business plan and securing appropriate permissions (personal communication, government worker, Addis Ababa 18 May 2010). The Ethiopian Investment Authority and MoA each list only one forestry-related project on public websites, a 5000-hectare match stick plantation in the Southern Nations and Nationalities Peoples Republic Regional State and a 50,000-hectare *Pongamia pinnata* plantation in Beninshangul Gumuz, respectively.

There is broad recognition that definitions of what constitutes 'forest' vary greatly, reducing the temporal and intra-country comparability of forest data (FAO, 2002). Definitions of forests affect assessment results, confer eligibility for different funding mechanisms, and trigger enforcement of laws, regulations and acceptable land uses. Natural forests in Ethiopia are believed to have once covered 40% of the country's land area (FDRE, 2001) but data on contemporary forest cover vary widely by reporting entity. This is due in part to variation among definitions of forests and forest types. The 2007 Forest Development, Conservation and Utilization Proclamation No. 542 defines forest as 'a community of plants, either naturally grown or developed by planting and mainly consisting of trees and other plants having woody character', a designation that is not particularly helpful from a jurisdictional standpoint. Ethiopia's Country Report for the 2010 GFRA recorded total forest cover at over 13 million hectares, or 10.5% of the land area, while a separate report written on the same year and with the same underlying data-set (see WBISPP, 2005), recorded forest cover at over 34 million hectares, or 27.5% of the country's land area (Table 4). Including shrublands, permissible under the IPCC definition, some 49% of Ethiopia's land area could be classified as forest.

Conflicting forest designations make it difficult for citizens to monitor change over time, to ensure that agreements are vetted through appropriate institutional channels and to confirm that rights regimes are enforced. Sasaki and Putz (2009) highlight concerns that UNFCCC forest area definitions do not adequately disincentivize forest degradation as all forests that meet minimum thresholds are considered equal (i.e. making it permissible to degrade forest while maintaining status). This paper advances these arguments further, highlighting challenges associated with the needs of citizens to access information to assert legal claims and ensure due diligence of relevant laws and procedures under inconsistent definitions.

Local social channels of contestation: Case-study evidence

Contemporary and historic political repression and a lack of accountability of government institutions to local people are thoroughly documented in the case of Ethiopia (see, e.g. de Waal, 1991; HRW, 2010, 2012; Rahmato, 2009). These political realties cannot be effectively countered through the rapid consultations with local communities that are often used to confer consent. This section uses case-study evidence to describe on the ground realities that affect community participation in decision-making over forests.

Site history

According to community elders, as recently at 70 years ago, forests in the area extended 17 km west to the town of Arsi Negele and about 20 km south to the town of Kofele. Forests were punctuated by highland bamboo thickets, pastures and *chafas* (wetlands) which were used as seasonal grazing areas. Areas that have remained too wet for cropping comprise what is left of community grazing lands. Discrepancies among resource ownership claims on paper and in practice can be traced from the present back to the early days of Amhara rule in the region. Following conquest of the Arsi area at the end of the nineteenth century, forests became the property of the state. Concessions of land, with accompanying rights to local labour, were granted by the Emperor primarily to Amhara military officials, widows and other outside elites (Poulsen, 1973). Resistance to new management regimes has manifested over time through various channels including open hostility and refusal to supply information (Poulsen, 1973), trampling and grazing of newly planted seedlings, and household encroachment into forested areas. While regulations governing forest access have remained relatively uniform over the past four decades, enforcement has varied dramatically over time.

Forests were heavily exploited by Italian and Ethiopian sawmill operators during the reign of Haile Selassie (1930–1974). Forest concessions were granted by Emperor Haile Selassie to military officials, religious institutions and patrons. Concessions contracted to sawmillers included mandatory replanting obligations, but regulations were not enforced and companies neglected to follow them (Poulsen, 1973). A dramatic conversion of natural forests to farmland occurred in the study area between 1976 and 1988 under the

Table 4. Forest cover estimates from (a) Ethiopia ECRN-UNDP Report (2010) and (b) Ethiopia GFRA Country Report (2010).

(a) Forest area

Land cover type	Area in hectares	Land area (%)
Forest Area*	34,154,754	27.5
Forest Area, with Shrubland*	60,557,802	49.0
High forest	4,073,213	3.3
Plantation	501,522	0.4
Woodland	29,549,016	23.7
Highland bamboo	31,003	0.0
Shrubland	26,403,048	21.2
Lowland bamboo	10,701,981	8.6
Afro-alpine	245,326	0.2
Grassland	14,620,707	11.8
Swamp	810,213	0.7
Cultivated land	21,298,529	17.1
Bare rock and soil	15,359,409	12.3
Water	828,277	0.5
Total land area**	124,422,244	99.3

(b) Forest cover

Land cover type	Area in hectares	Land area (%)
Total forest area*	13,000,261	11.9
Forest	3,219,186	2.9
Plantation	491,291	0.4
High woodland	9,289,784	8.5
Low woodlands and shrubs	44,649,764	40.7
Other land	51,981,177	47.4
Water	798,798	0.6
Total land area**	109,631,202	100.0

Sources: FAO (2010) and Moges, Eshetu, and Nune (2010).
*Totals may appear different due to rounding.
**Excludes land cover classified as water.

Derg regime. During this period, every household was granted a small farm, usually around two hectares, based in part on household size. At the same time, additional organized timber harvesting was undertaken by the state-run Forest Enterprise with technical assistance from the Swedish government.

Today, plantations are considered well-guarded in comparison to natural forests. With the exceptions of limited grazing and periodic access to slash from plantation thinnings, plantation production feeds urban rather than local markets. Community forest product consumption goes largely unregulated in natural forests. Higher-order offenses such as timber harvest are sometimes brought to the attention of local police, but rarely result in legal convictions. Enforcement of forest regulations involves a range of actors with different levels of authority (Figure 2). Local forest experts identified what they saw as challenges to effective enforcement at different levels of government, and their responses are shown under the heading 'Challenges' in Figure 2. Inattention to forest regulatory enforcement is emphasized throughout. Forest protection is a common rallying point in political speeches and community events, but it rarely leads to substantive action. Forest guards expressed frustration at the weak enforcement by government officials: 'Officials are afraid to enforce regulations because they don't want to harm their standing in the community or their chances of re-election' (118, Forest Guard). This quote exposes the political nature of enforcement and reveals the tension between rhetoric and action. Leaders routinely advocate for forest conservation while simultaneously working to maintain their identity as egalitarian men of the people.

Foreign actors often engage with *Kebele* leaders to make decisions on behalf of a community or to identify households or individuals for consultation, despite the fact that Kebele leaders are nearly always supporters of the ruling national party, and are not generally accountable to local democratic processes of decision-making (Pausewang, 2009).

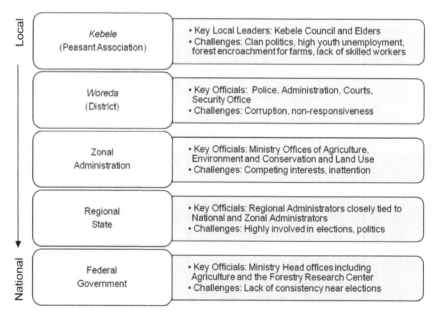

Figure 2.   Government entities involved in forest regulation enforcement, Arsi Forest. *Source*: Interview with local forest experts, 17 May 2010, Arsi Forest.

Enforcement and conflict over forest access

Processes used to enforce forest boundaries reveal inequities in power relations and the absence of local channels of contestation among local people. In 2009, a forest boundary assessment conducted during the winter of 2009 and spring of 2010 revealed that 54 households (8% of all households in the community) had expanded their farms or established new homesteads (ranging in size from 0.25 to 11.25 hectares) within the boundaries of the natural forest area. These homes were demolished (Photo 1) and households were relocated to community grazing lands, despite the fact that these lands that consisted of seasonal wetlands are considered unsuitable for farming due to soil characteristics and seasonal inundation.

Households located on its periphery relied on the land to graze livestock and were not pleased with the decision to relocate households there. When asked about the decision, one man responded: 'Why do you ask this question? We do not agree. The government is powerful. We are afraid. We have attended many meetings and separated without resolution' (Personal communication, community member, Arsi Forest 5 May 2010). This remark highlights the perception among locals that they are playing a 'losing game' in fighting government decisions.

Discussion

In investigating the channels of contestation that affect people's control over forests in Ethiopia, a complicated system lacking in consistency and transparency emerges. Incongruent definitions of forest become not only a scientific hurdle, but a political hurdle, as the absence of coherent data on forest cover prohibits people from rectifying on the ground land investments with land cover classifications. This impedes the search for coherency, a central focus of the 'collective practice of social actors and the restructuring of existing political economies of truth' (Pollock, Babha, Breckenridge, & Chakrabarty, 2000,

Photo 1. Homestead within forest boundaries after demolition. Bundled household items (foreground) and housing materials border forest edge (rear).

p. 216). As emerging investments play out, non-standard definitions of forests undermine determinations of jurisdictional authority, permitting, review, approval of investments, tracking of progress, outcome monitoring, tax assessment and human rights claims.

Transparency and uniformity in documentation also allows ministries and other agencies to maintain some level of accountability with one another. While there have been recent discussions in Ethiopia concerning the potential of establishing a single agency to manage all investments, this could augment rather than reduce the climate of impunity that characterizes many contemporary investments. As forest and agricultural resources grow increasingly scarce, uniform standards and clear communications pathways will be essential to discourage conversion of forests to agricultural lands, or the granting of forest concessions to investors that should be conserved or managed by communities.

Emerging forest-related investments tighten the linkages between the central state and local spaces. Community-state relations are characterized by 'political marginalization, heavy state intervention and highly extractive relations between state and peasants' (Milas & Latif, 2000, p. 363). Limits to protest may be even greater as neoliberal processes are brought in to contested spaces. Given the preferential protections afforded investors, local claims to forest resources may be further marginalized as economic interests come to supersede historically negotiated value-based claims.

Conclusion

Forest-based land investments affect rural livelihoods due to the interconnected nature of forest and agricultural incomes at forest margins. In Ethiopia, foreign investments in forests take many forms, including direct harvest of forest products, plantation establishment, forest conversion for agriculture and payment incentives for ecosystem services such as carbon.

Citizen channels of contestation, which comprise the legal, policy-level and administrative avenues through which people can make their voices heard, are currently limited, at the best. Secondary and case-study evidence highlights the lack of free expression and accountability of political leaders to local people. How can we help promote institutions that are more accountable to citizenry? Citizens are by no means the only actors who can promote equity and justice in forest-related investments, and in the context of an authoritarian state such as Ethiopia, outsiders may take proactive steps towards increasing transparency in forest management and foreign investments affecting forests. International and domestic corporations, advocacy groups, lenders, donors and others can and should leverage their influence to develop progressive policies and ensure their implementation. For example, the Land Matrix[1] produces a global map of land-related investments which allows anyone with access to the Internet to review documented investment deals by country and region. However, in the case of Ethiopia, these deals are rarely tied to specific spatial coordinates, making it impossible to determine whether leased land consists of forest or pasture, is occupied by people or high-value wildlife, and so on.

Household-level forest benefit claims are rooted in customary and historical access to forest resources, and local rights are woven into understandings of what constitutes legitimate use. These are increasingly threatened with the emergence of new foreign investment opportunities in forested areas. Informal forest benefit distributions are not guaranteed because rights were never formally devolved, disadvantaging local people in person or on paper attempts to assert access claims in the face of 'new' tenures. Rather than focusing on vague calls for empowerment, this paper tries to describe the specific obstacles and institutional arrangements that make it difficult for citizens to participate effectively in discussions over land rights. Recommendations for enhancing channels of citizen contestation within these areas include the following:

- Determination of uniform definitions and designations of 'forestlands'.
- Articulation of the roles, duties and responsibilities of all ministries and agencies having authority over land-related investments.
- Articulation of a process through which ministries and agencies provide information to one another concerning current and prospective investments.
- Creation of a forum for sharing all agreements, applications and other documents associated with forest-related investments, with documents translated into major regional languages.
- Description of precise coordinates associated with foreign land leases, so that citizens and outsiders may track the locations of foreign investments in forestlands.

If implemented, these recommendations would make incremental progress towards enabling citizens and advocates to more effectively understand the implications of forest-related investments and voice resource claims that promote just resource allocation.

Note

1. See http://landmatrix.org/get-the-idea/global-map-investments/, retrieved 3 March 2013.

Notes on contributor

Dr. Kathleen Guillozet is currently a Postdoctoral Scholar with Virginia Tech. She is interested in forest-based livelihoods, riparian forest management, ecosystem services, and associated markets. She gratefully acknowledges the two anonymous reviewers, guest Editor Dr. Fassil Demissie, Journal Editors and Dr. John C. Bliss for their comments and edits which greatly improved the content of this article. She is especially thankful to the dedicated forestry experts and community members in Ethiopia whose concern for and knowledge of their country's forests is a source of inspiration.

References

Ali, D. A., Dercon, S., & Gautam, M. (2011). Property rights in a very poor country: Tenure insecurity and investment in ethiopia. *Agricultural Economics, 42*, 75–86. doi:10.1111/j.1574-0862.2010.00482.x.

Amnesty International. (2011). *Ethiopia submission to the United Nations Human Rights Committee*. London: Author.

ARD. (2004). *Ethiopia land policy and administration assessment*. Burlington, VT: Author.

Babulo, B., Muys, B., Nega, F., Tollens, E., Nyssen, J., Deckers, J., & Mathijs, E. (2009). The economic contribution of forest resource use to rural livelihoods in Tigray, northern Ethiopia. *Forest Policy and Economics, 11*, 109–117. Retrieved October 01, 2010, from http://www.sciencedirect.com/science/article/pii/S1389934108000889

Bekele-Tesemma, A. (2007). *Economic significance of industrial-forest cum forest-industry development focus: Important poverty alleviation opportunity being squandered in Ethiopia.* Shashemene: Economic and Institutional Aspect of Forestry in Ethiopia – Debub University, Wondo Genet College of Forestry.

Bekele, M. (2011). *Forest plantations and woodlots in Ethiopia*. Nairobi: African Forests Forum Working Paper Series.

Bongers, F., & Tennigkeit, T. (Eds.). (2010). *Degraded forests in eastern Africa: Management and restoration*. Washington, DC: Earthscan.

Borras, S. M., Hall, R., Scoones, I., White, B., & Wolford, W. (2011). Towards a better understanding of global land grabbing: an editorial introduction. *Journal of Peasant Studies, 38,* 209–216.

Dauvergne, P., & Neville, K. J. (2010). Forests, food, and fuel in the tropics: The uneven social and ecological consequences of the emerging political economy of biofuels. *Journal of Peasant Studies, 37,* 631–660. Retrieved September 24, 2010, from http://www.informaworld.com/10. 1080/03066150.2010.512451

de Waal, A. (1991). *Evil days: 30 years of war and famine in Ethiopia.* Watch, NY: Human Rights Watch.

Deininger, K., Ali, D. A., & Alemu, T. (2008). Assessing the functioning of land rental markets in Ethiopia. *Economic Development and Cultural Change, 57,* 67–100.

Deininger, K., Ali, D. A., Holden, S., & Zevenbergen, J. (2007). *Rural land certification in ethiopia: Process, initial impact, and implications for other african countries.* Washington, DC: World Bank.

Deininger, K., Byerlee, D., Lindsay, J., Norton, A., Selod, H., & Stickler, M. (2011). Rising global interest in farmland: Can it yield sustainable and equitable benefits? Agriculture and Rural Development (pp. 1–264). Washington, DC: The World Bank.

Diokno, M. S. I. (2011). Chapter 5: Human rights based approach to assessment. *Human rights based approach to development planning toolkit,* 1–42. Retrieved December 7, 2013, from http:// www.hrbatoolkit.org/?page_id=130

FAO. (2002). Expert meeting harmonizing forest-related definitions for use by various stakeholdersed. *Harmonizing forest-related definitions for use by various stakeholders.* Rome.

FAO. (2010). *Global forest resources assessment, main report.* Rome: Author.

FAO, IFAD, UNCTAD, World Bank. (2011). *Options for promoting responsible investment in agriculture.* Rome: Inter-Agency Working Group on the Food Security Pillar of the G-20 Multi-Year Action Plan on Development.

FDRE. (2001). Initial national communication of ethiopia to the United Nations Framework Convention on Climate Change (UNFCCC). In NMS Agency (Ed.), *MOW Resources.* Addis Ababa: Author.

FDRE. (2010). *Growth and transformation plan (gtp) 2010/11-2014/15* (p. 85). Addis Ababa: Author.

FDRE. (2011). *FDRE Ethiopia's climate-resilient green economy: Green economy strategy.* Addis Ababa: Author.

Gebremariam, A. H., Bekele, M., & Ridgewell, A. (2009). *Small and medium forest enterprises in Ethiopia.* London: IIED.

Giddens, A. (1986). *The constitution of society: Outline of the theory of structuration.* Berkeley: University of California Press.

Hallam, D. (2009). *Foreign investment in developing country agriculture – issues, policy implications and international response.* Paris: OECD Global Forum on International Investment.

Horne, F. (2011). *Understanding land investment deals in Africa country report: Ethiopia.* Oakland: Oakland Institute.

HRW. (2010). *Ethiopia, development without freedom: How aid underwrites repression in Ethiopia.* New York, NY: Author.

HRW. (2012). *"Waiting here for death" forced displacement and "villagization" in Ethiopia's gambella region* (p. 119). New York, NY: Author.

Kumar, N., & Quisumbing, A. (2012). Inheritance practices and gender differences in poverty and well-being in rural ethiopia. *Development Policy Review, 30,* 573–595. doi:10.1111/j.1467-7679.2012.00589.x.

Lavers, T. (2012). Patterns of agrarian transformation in ethiopia: State-mediated commercialisation and the 'land grab'. *The Journal of Peasant Studies, 39,* 795–822. doi:10.1080/03066150.2012. 660147.

Makki, F. (2012). Power and property: Commercialization, enclosures, and the transformation of agrarian relations in ethiopia. *The Journal of Peasant Studies, 39,* 81–104. doi:10.1080/ 03066150.2011.652620.

Milas, S., & Latif, J. A. (2000). The political economy of complex emergency and recovery in northern Ethiopia. *Disasters, 24,* 363.

Moges, Y., Eshetu, Z., & Nune, S. (2010). *Ethiopian forest resources: Current status and future management options in view of access to carbon finances*. Addis Ababa: Literature Review Prepared for the Ethiopian Climate Research and Networking Groups and United Nations Development Program.

Moser, C., & Norton, A. (2001). *To claim our rights: Livelihood security, human rights and sustainable development*. London: Overseas Development Institute.

Pausewang, S. (2009). *Exploring new political alternatives for the Oromo in Ethiopia: Report from Oromo workshop and its after-effects* (pp. 1–98). Bergen: Chr. Michelsen Institute.

Peters, P. (2009). Challenges in land tenure and land reform in africa: Anthropological contributions. *World Development, 37*, 1317–1325.

Pham, T. T., Brockhaus, M., Wong, G., Dung, L. N., Tjajadi, J. S., Loft, L., ... Luttrell, C. (2013). *Approaches to benefit sharing: A preliminary comparative analysis of 13 REDD+ countries*. Working Paper 108. Bogor: CIFOR.

Pollock, S., Bhabha, H. K., Breckenridge, C. A., & Chakrabarty, D. (2000). *Cosmopolitanisms. Public Culture, 12*, 577–589.

Poulsen, G. (1973). *CADU forestry activities*. Asela: Chilalo Agricultural Development Unit.

Rahmato, D. (2009). *The peasant and the state: Studies in agrarian change in Ethiopia 1960–2000s*. Addis Ababa: Addis Ababa University Press.

Rice, A. (2009, November 20). Is there such a thing as agro-imperialism? *New York Times Magazine*.

Sasaki, N., & Putz, F. E. (2009). Critical need for new definitions of "forest" and "forest degradation" in global climate change agreements. *Conservation Letters, 2*, 226–232. doi:10.1111/j.1755-263X.2009.00067.x.

Sayer, J., Sunderland, T., Ghazoul, J., Pfund, J. -L., Sheil, D., Meijaard, E., ... Venter, M. (2013). Ten principles for a landscape approach to reconciling agriculture, conservation, and other competing land uses. *Proceedings of the National Academy of Sciences, 110*, 8349–8356.

Sewell, W. H. (1989). *Toward a theory of structure: Duality, agency and transformation*. Ann Arbor, MI: Center for Research on Social Organization.

Springer, S. (2009). Renewed authoritarianism in southeast asia: Undermining democracy through neoliberal reform. *Asia Pacific Viewpoint, 50*, 271–276. doi:10.1111/j.1467-8373.2009.01400.x.

Stebek, E. N. (2011). Between land grabs and agricultlural investment: Land rent contracts with foreign investors and ethiopia's normative setting in focus. *Mizan Law Review, 5*, 175–214.

Tamrat, I. (2010). Governance of large scale agricultural investments in africa: The case of Ethiopia. *World Bank Conference on Land Policy and Administration*. Washington, DC.

Tsing, A. (2005). *Friction: An ethnography of global connection*. Princeton, NJ: Princeton University Press.

IPB, von Braun, J., & Meinzen-Dick, R. (2009). Ed. (). *'Land grabbing' by foreign investors in developing countries: Risks and opportunities*, Paper Number 13 (pp. 1–9). Washington, DC: International Food Policy Research Institute (IFPRI).

WBISPP. (2005). *Woody biomass inventory and strategic planning project: A national strategy plan for the biomass sector*. Addis Ababa: Author.

Winberg, E. (2010). *Participatory forest management in Ethiopia, practices and experiences*. Addis Ababa: FAO.

Winter, M., & Quan, J. (1999). *Land tenure and resource access in West Africa: Issues and opportunities for the next twenty-five years*. London: IIED.

World Bank. (2012). *Ethiopia readiness preparation proposal (r-pp) assessment note*. Washington, DC: World Bank.

Yemiru, T., Roos, A., Campbell, B. M., & Bohlin, F. (2010). Forest incomes and poverty alleviation under participatory forest management in the Bale highlands, Southern Ethiopia. *International Forestry Review, 12*, 66–77.

Yin, R. K. (2003). *Case study research: Design and methods*. Thousand Oaks, CA: Sage.

Zebene, W. (2012). *Benishangul Gumuz unhappy over investment implementation*. Addis Ababa: The Reporter.

Zoomers, A. (2010). Globalisation and the foreignisation of space: Seven processes driving the current global land grab. *Journal of Peasant Studies, 37*, 429–447.

Scrambling for the promised land: land acquisitions and the politics of representation in post-war Acholi, northern Uganda

Anders Sjögren

Department of Political Science, Stockholm University, Stockholm, Sweden; The Nordic Africa Institute, Uppsala, Sweden

In the wake of return to relative peace in Acholi region, northern Uganda, from 2006, land matters have taken centre stage. After having been displaced into camps for many years, people have started to go back home. Their return is complicated by many factors, including above all, land disputes. While the Ugandan constitution and land legislation protects customary tenure, the social and economic institutions that uphold this tenure regime have been severely weakened as a result of war and displacement. The combination of demographic changes following large-scale displacement and gradual return; social and economic conflicts emanating from biting poverty for most and accumulation by a few; uncertain territorial demarcations by way of changing and contested statutory and communal boundaries in the context of weak and subverted regulatory institutions, together deepen conflicts over resources. This article analyses these issues by examining a case of land acquisition in Amuru: a bid by the Madhvani business group to access huge tracts of land in western Acholi for purposes of growing sugar cane, and the heated debates and protests this case has generated, as played out by political representation in different arenas such as the media, courts and representative assemblies.

Introduction: struggles over land in the wake of war

Over the last few years, one of the most frequently and hotly debated issues concerning the political economy of sub-Saharan Africa has been the rise of large-scale land acquisitions (among an already vast literature, see Cotula [2012] and Zoomers [2010]). This continent-wide tendency is also visible in Uganda, where, as elsewhere, it takes on different regional expressions. In Acholi sub-region, northern Uganda, land acquisitions are particularly sensitive, occurring as they do in the wake of long-standing displacement of the majority of population and their recent uncertain return. For two decades, the region suffered from rebellions and civil war. Armed conflict subsided in 2006, but the majority of the displaced population only began to return home a few years later after having been forced to spend many years in refugee camps. Their resettlement has been complicated by many factors. The vast, fertile and oil-rich land in Acholi has attracted the attention of prospective investors, willing and able to take advantage of an impoverished population. In addition to the many local land disputes at household and village levels, the region has recently witnessed a growing number of cases of controversial purchases, leases and allocations; all of this is fuelling anxiety and tension among local communities.

As the internally displaced population returns home and as attempts at large-scale acquisition of land intensify, the regulatory framework is being put to test. Through the 1995 constitution and the 1998 Land Act, customary tenure – the dominant tenure form in the region – is constitutionally and legally anchored and, in an African comparative perspective, strongly supported, at least on paper (Alden Wily, 2011, p. 745). Security of tenure for ordinary Acholi evidently depends on much more than the letter of the law. The interpretation and application of law in practice may be an entirely different matter, linked as it normally is to processes of individuals, groups and institutions claiming and exercising authority in other spheres of society (Alden Wily, 2012). Furthermore, 'customary land tenure' is merely an umbrella term for a wide set of relations, and any particular context is regulated in the interface between law and practice, and in some cases by practice alone (Cotula, 2007; Pottier, 2005). The coexistence in Acholi of relatively strong legislation with regard to land, and the extreme social, economic and political vulnerability that characterises the region makes it particularly relevant to interrogate how, in the interplay between law and practice, different social forces seek to access land with particular emphasis on the implications for security of tenure in terms of effective control (Borras & Franco, 2012, p. 55). The present article argues the necessity of analysing the politics of land acquisitions in a manner that carefully examines the nuances of the local context, including competing local interests. Many actors aspire for political involvement around land issues through demand-making and interest representation, and do so in many overlapping statutory and customary arenas, such as clans, councils and courts. How does the politics of demand-making and interest representation in this multiplicity of arenas shape the modes of regulating access to land in Acholi, or, in the terminology used here, the form and content of the land tenure regime?

This article explores the issue of social and political struggles around large-scale land acquisitions by examining a controversial case in Acholi sub-region. It draws on secondary literature for the wider context and on a combination of media reports, official documentation and interviews and observations conducted during fieldwork in 2009 and 2010 for empirical details. The case made national headlines in 2007. When it became known that the Madhvani Group, a local business conglomerate, had the intention of getting access to 40,000 hectares in Amuru in the western part of Acholi for the purpose of growing sugar cane, the response was fierce and immediate. Sections of local communities and opposition politicians were adamant in demanding that any investor may operate only with the consent of the local population, and the matter has continued to evoke strong reactions. The case went to court, but struggles over regulating access have been fought in a number of other arenas at local and national levels.

The first section of the article presents an overview of the literature on land conflicts in sub-Saharan Africa, and then engages with theoretical perspectives on the political struggles over land. The second section discusses recent land issues in Uganda and outlines the main features of the land tenure regime in Acholi sub-region. Section three then moves on to examine the empirical case, following which the concluding section offers an analytical summary of the findings by relating them to the theoretical arguments.

Land struggles and land tenure regimes

The first part of this section situates and theorises competition over resources and the forms of stratification that follow. In the second part, I link the socio-economic processes identified in the literature to their political regulation by developing theoretical arguments about mechanisms of access, institutional mediation and interest representation. These arguments are anchored in an analytical framework drawing on the concept of land tenure regimes, denoting the rules and practices that regulate access to land.

Land acquisitions, competition and social stratification

Recent overview articles (Bernstein, 2004; Berry, 2002, 2009; Peters, 2004, 2009) point to the multidimensional nature of the land question in Africa and summarise rich and growing evidence from across the continent of increasing competition and conflict over land over the last two decades. Land is not only an economic resource for agricultural production and accumulation for individuals, agribusiness and the state, but it is also a source of social status, political power and cultural heritage and belonging, something accentuated by its territorial dimension. Combinations of demographic, economic, ecological and political factors generate a galaxy of forms of competition and conflict, ranging from intra- and inter-family feuds to acquisition processes shaped by governmental and business actors at the international level (Berry, 2002, pp. 638–639; Peters, 2004, pp. 301–305); all competition crucially involves struggles over political connections. Creating access to land is linked to defining, recognising and exercising private and public authority in a broad sense (Berry, 2009, p. 24; Lentz, 2006; Peters, 2009, p. 1321; Sikor & Lund, 2009).

The observation about the interplay between access to resources and the exercise of authority is approached from a particular angle in Peters' key argument: that struggles over land are premised on social relations of domination and develop in ways that more often than not reinforce social differentiation, revolving around accumulation among the better off and survival for the majority (Peters, 2004, p. 305; 2009, p. 1319). Peters' emphasis on stratification of opportunities and constraints, systematically benefiting the wealthy and powerful, is in explicit contrast to what she calls 'a currently influential approach [...] which privileges flexibility and indeterminacy in analyses of social relationships over land' (2004, p. 269). This article broadly shares Peters' concern with the importance of analysing not only the nuances of local settings, but also more general patterns of domination.

Whereas relationships over land are not, then, characterised by flexibility for all and open-ended negotiability, conflict dynamics are nevertheless contradictory. Bernstein (2005, pp. 87–89) and Peters (2004, pp. 301–302, 305) argue that in most of contemporary sub-Saharan Africa, competition over land 'in the context of a generalized crisis of reproduction' (Bernstein, 2005, p. 92) is linked to social differentiation, which may be described as a class dynamics of sorts. However, both Bernstein and Peters stress that it is a class formation dynamic that is typically played out in fragmented and overlapping ways along lines of gender, ethnicity, clan and generation. This is said to be the case both for the forms of social stratification and for the political struggles around them. Such complexity is well articulated by Bernstein (2004, p. 218):

> The translation of such 'social facts' into 'political facts' [...] includes how the kinds of processes sketched are mediated through the often fragile political alliances and erratic practices of local accumulators and the similarly erratic, and contested, interventions of the local state, in which 'native'/'stranger' distinctions, 'squatting' and eviction also feature.

Elsewhere, Bernstein (2005, pp. 87–88) suggests three reasons why fragmentation of conflict types and identities should be the typical pattern: the absence in much of Africa of both large-scale landed property and generalised land alienation of a Latin American variant; the fractured nature of local state and society along lines of ethnicity promoted by colonialism and rarely discontinued after it; and the limited historical experience of popular rural political organisation. Similarly, Boone (2013) argues that the level of authoritative jurisdiction of land can be predicted to correspond to the scope of conflicts around the same, to the effect that land tenure regimes under customary authority, be they centred on household or chieftaincy, tend to localise conflicts and deflect them away from public political decision-making so as to undercut the prospects for broad-based mobilisation. Structural and subjective factors thus combine in generating multiple forms of political identities and organisation, often structured by local dynamics, hence making the politics of claiming access highly variable.

Access to land: mechanisms, regulation and representation

One theoretical perspective for approaching the multiplicity of actors, arenas and strategies in relation to resources has been proposed by Ribot and Peluso (2003), who argue that analysts would do well to broaden their scope of inquiry from concerns with legal and legitimate claims to property to the study of mechanisms for gaining, controlling and maintaining access in a broader sense. They define access as 'the ability to benefit from things – including material objects, persons, institutions and symbols'. (2003, p. 153). Rather than concentrating on 'bundles of rights', including the rights to use, manage and transfer land, Ribot and Peluso suggest that 'bundles of powers' (2003, p. 154) are necessary for understanding the 'array of institutions, social and political-economic relations and discursive strategies that shape benefit flows' (2003, p. 157) – or in other words: the capacity to control the use, management, transfer and so on, based on rights or not.

These arguments, which are drawn on in the analysis in this article for purposes of capturing the significant interplay between law and practice, suggest that strategies for accessing land, including claims for land rights, are made from a range of interrelated perspectives for overlapping purposes. It further means that the politicisation of such social struggles is likely to attract a great number of actors, all of whom claim to be legitimate and authoritative representatives or adjudicators in matters of land, and who bring concerns and disputes to various arenas, including courts, political assemblies, the media or the popular politics of the streets. As emphasised by Sikor and Lund (2009), contestation over material resources at the same time constitute struggles over the making and authorisation of the more or less formal institutions that regulate access.

Such institutional crystallisation by way of mediation of structural processes and agency may be captured analytically by the concept of land tenure regimes, denoting the laws, rules, norms and practices that regulate access to land for use, control, ownership, transfer and so on. The capacity of various actors to make use of institutions will differ significantly, as will the autonomy and capacity of institutions in relation to different social forces. Actors' choices of modes of engagement and arenas for pursuing their interests will depend on the manner in which regimes are organised in terms of rules, channels and arenas, as well as on the competing acquisition strategies of other actors. They may use, override or bypass laws and formal arenas, drawing on different instruments of domination and resistance for getting access, such as law, administration, policy, money and violence (Ribot & Peluso, 2003). Within parameters of relations of domination, laws and rules are constantly contested by political practices and locally specific and often informal social institutions; this is particularly salient in the context of customary tenure.

While customary tenure has an acknowledged openness expressed in shifting local practices, this does not preclude competition and commodification. As has been repeatedly emphasised, customary land tenure regimes are neither inherently weak in preserving security of tenure due to the absence of formalised ownership nor intrinsically protective or egalitarian. There are many examples of how customary practices might encompass a layering of protected access, from the individual to the communal (Peters, 2009, p. 1318), as well as of how they under other circumstances may uphold forms of inequality (Alden Wily, 2011, p. 737; Peters, 2009, p. 1319). It is posited here that variations in security of tenure is not so much determined by the tenure form per se as by the social, economic and political relations that shape its content. In the context of intensified competition, it is not surprising that most particular instances of customary tenure are arenas for contestation, and that the flexibility of the tenure form opens up for many mechanisms of seeking access as well as for many actors and institutions aspiring to regulate these processes. One example of competition over access to customary land is de facto commodification through the so-called vernacular land markets (Chimhovu & Woodhouse, 2006) or informal formalisation – a wide array of transfer techniques beyond the legal title (Peters, 2009, p. 1320). Discussing the prospects for customary tenure in the context of the recent wave of large-scale land acquisitions, Alden Wily (2011, pp. 733, 736) shows that forests, grazing land and other unfarmed lands appear to be particularly targeted.

In view of the unwritten character of customary law and the current weakness of many of the formal institutions that relate to it, one may expect a fairly wide scope for, and significance of, the practices of access, including demand-making and interest representation. The most obvious expression of interest representation is party politics; this article discusses the role played by representatives of political parties locally and nationally. The politics of interest representation in a broader sense is often discussed in terms of state–civil society relations (for the theoretical debate, see Gibbon [1996] and White [1994]; for the debate on civil society in Africa, see the volumes edited by Harbeson, Rothchild, & Chazan [1994] and Kasfir [1998]). Against perspectives that tend to view civil society as a pluralising social phenomenon with relatively homogeneous core properties and liberal-democratic political implications (Diamond, 1994), it is argued here that civil society is better understood as an analytical as opposed to a prescriptive term for a wide range of more or less formal social groups without specific predetermined political properties.

The composition of civil society emerges from the organisation around social relations, and state institutions and policies are shaped by demands from domestic and external political forces, including those in civil society. The state intervenes in different ways on behalf of certain groups in civil society and subordinates others (for extended versions of this argument, see Gibbon [2001] and Sjögren [2001]). This perspective is better equipped to capture the theoretical interplay, the empirical diversity and the contradictory political orientations of state–civil society relations, and will be used in this article to analyse how various civil society groups engage with the conflict in rather different ways. The complexity of representation is visible not only through the many actors that engage in it, but also with regard to the many arenas that they target. One consequence of customary tenure being generally anchored in statutory law, but vaguely operationalised and weakly implemented, is legal pluralism and institutional confusion. Actors bring their claims to different arenas for authoritative interpretation and decision-making, further complicating interest representation.

The politics of land in Uganda and Acholi

In order to discuss the land tenure regime in Acholi, it is necessary to first summarise recent developments of land matters at the national level. The modern history of Uganda has to a large extent revolved around land. After independence in 1962, relations between successive central governments and regions and localities have been consistently unstable, and land has been a key political resource for stirring up or calming tensions. After taking over state power in 1986, the National Resistance Movement (NRM) found itself facing the land question with dual loyalties to consider between landed interests and radicals who pushed for land reform. The principles for a new legal and institutional framework for governing land were incorporated into the 1995 constitution, following which their operationalisation was pushed forward a few years (Green, 2006, pp. 376–377).

By the time the Land Act was passed by the parliament in June 1998, the above-mentioned divide in the NRM was reproduced in the legislation. The Act states that land is vested with the people of Uganda and recognises four systems of land tenure: freehold, leasehold, *mailo* and customary tenure. At the policy level, however, the Act pulled in different directions: it claimed to create security of tenure for different categories of occupants, including those covered by customary tenure, but at the same time sought to promote a land market for liberalised production, thereby essentially privileging private tenure and undermining customary tenure. Its instruments for implementation were vague and contradictory, and funding proved to be inadequate. The general assessment is that rather than having enabled a productive compromise, the Act produced a stalemate (Green, 2006, p. 377; Hunt, 2004). It should also be noted that while legislation and systems for land administration have been in place since the late 1990s, albeit imperfectly implemented, developments in the policy area have been lagging. After many years, a final draft of the National Land Policy was presented to the Cabinet in March 2011, but has as yet not been adopted by the parliament. Indistinct policy directions and weak implementation is one reason land issues have refused to go away. Another is the – partly related – spread of land conflicts across the country; for a recent national overview of its different forms and regional spread, see Rugadya (2009). Some of the conflicts are local, often ethno-regional, in nature. Others are cases of alleged land grabbing – rampant over the last decade – in which the government has frequently been accused of being negligent or complicit (*The Independent*, January 3, 2012; National Association of Professional Environmentalists 2012; Oxfam, 2011). These trends have triggered widespread protests with critics accusing the government of acting in bad faith, and have further polarised the debate on land, one instance of which being a strand of popular and elite discourse centred on perceived land grabbing by ethnic outsiders.

The emerging Acholi land tenure regime

The structural features that condition contemporary Acholi society and politics are historically rooted in the uneven regional development of Uganda. Lopsided economic expansion strategies and state structures of indirect rule under colonialism resulted in deep regional disparities. The northern parts of Uganda, including Acholi, essentially served as a 'labour reservoir for the cash crop economy of the south' (Mamdani, 1976, p. 52) as well as for the police, the armed forces and the civil service (Branch, 2011, p. 50). However, from 1962 to 1986, national political and military power was vested in groupings from different parts of the north. With the takeover of state power by the NRM in 1986, power suddenly shifted to the south. This intensified the leadership crisis in Acholi that had begun during the 1970s and 1980s, and would, during the years of war and displacement, develop into a profound social crisis (Branch, 2011, pp. 56–62). For 20 years, between 1986 and 2006, the Acholi region suffered from war, with subsequent rebel groups, most notoriously the Lord's Resistance Army (LRA) fighting the government and attacking the civilian population. At the same time, government troops committed gross human rights violations. It is estimated that more than one million Acholi lived in camps for internally displaced, where, by government policy, they had been forced to reside during the last few years of the conflict; for elaborate analyses, see Branch (2011) and Finnström (2008). Since 2006, the sub-region has seen relative peace. While the vast majority of the population has now left the camps, many were hesitant to do so for several years, due to uncertainty over where and what to return to. Another aspect, crucial for understanding interest representation in Acholi, is that the government's long-standing heavy-handed military presence and simultaneous political marginalisation of the sub-region made it a solid opposition stronghold; it was not until the 2011 elections that the NRM succeeded in making inroads there.

In Acholi, land as a political issue is fairly recent. Because of the war, the 1998 Land Act did not begin to have an impact until lately. Legislation as such was at first not controversial. This is perhaps unsurprising; as stated above, customary tenure is protected by Ugandan law – the Land Act recognises 'local customary regulation' (Government of Uganda, 1998, section 3(1)(d)). Polarisation, however, became evident when, in 2007, the government tabled a motion with the aim of revising the Land Act. Among other controversial matters, the proposals included a widened scope for the government in expropriating land for development. The Land (Amendment) Bill also included a proposal about protecting occupants 'claiming interest in land under customary tenure' against evictions, as stated in Clause 32B. This attracted fierce criticism from Members of Parliament from the greater north, including Acholi, Lango, Teso and Karamoja, who voiced the fear that this would be open to abuse and serve as an opening for grabbing of land. This concern was particularly strongly felt in Acholi, as resettlement had only just begun. After two years of intense debate, the Bill was passed by the parliament in November 2009. By that time, Clause 32B had been dropped, to the effect that the opposition to the Bill by the Members of Parliament from northern Uganda softened.

While at a general level legal issues are relatively straightforward, their application in practice has turned out to be much more complicated. Clan leaders are to be in charge of land allocation and dispute resolution, although land disputes can be (and often are) taken to the statutory legal system through Local Council and Magistrate courts as well. Customary land is typically unregistered and under the ownership (in a loose sense) and custody of one of several social units, in Acholi ranging from the individual to the clan, but cannot be sold without the consent of all parties involved. Under the current law there is no titling in areas covered by customary law, but an approximate, Certificates of Customary Ownership (CCOs), was introduced by the 1998 Land Act; it was however not available until 2012. The introduction of CCOs has been viewed with suspicion by proponents of customary tenure who regard it as a way of introducing freehold through the back door. Meanwhile, land continues to be sold in vernacular markets.

Land administration has proven to be deficient. In line with general political directions, administration was decentralised by the Land Act, which also created a number of institutions with respective mandates to regulate demarcation, registration, dispute resolution and so on. The subdivision of districts, such as the 2010 carving out of Nwoya district from Amuru, has created still more fiscally and administratively weak entities. Implementation has been predictably weak. As the proposed National Land Policy acknowledges, 'The land administration system is inadequately resourced and performing poorly below expected standards with tendencies of fraud and corruption. The dual system of land administration (the formal/statutory and informal/customary) breeds conflict, confusion and overlaps in institutional mandates' (Government of Uganda, 2011, p. 7).

One example of this would be that after a long period of erratic existence, District Land Tribunals were discontinued in 2006. Another statutory institution, District Land Boards, was tasked with, among other things, holding and allocating land deemed not to belong to any individual or institution; this has played an important role in the empirical case examined in this article.

Turning to the more informal aspects of the land tenure regime in Acholi, Sebina-Zziwa, Nabacwa, Mwebaza, Bogere, and Achiro (2008) identify four recent major shifts that seriously impede the effective functionality of customary tenure; for similar observations and arguments, see Adoko and Levine (2004). The first shift is demographic, which, just like anywhere, means that more people share the same (or possibly less – ecological factors are not taken into account by the authors) amount of resources. The second one is political. The policy of decentralisation and the introduction of ever more districts and associated sub-units bring about new boundaries and political structures, new political constellations and power struggles, and new institutional channels for accessing land. The third shift is social. Life in the camps has torn the social fabric apart. Clan leaders have often lost their specific knowledge, and their authority has been weakened.

The fourth shift is economic. At the macro-level, the national policy orientation promotes privatisation; at the micro-level, this creates incentives to treat land as not merely a cultural asset. Under current conditions, land is turning into a commodity. The soil is extremely fertile after largely having lain fallow for a decade and attracts a lot of attention. Suspicion has been rife among the local population for years that outsiders or local elites are either planning to grab the land or buy it at a throwaway price (Adoko & Levine, 2004, p. 15; Atkinson, 2008; Finnström, 2008, pp. 174–180), and tension has been heightened by rumours of oil deposits. All of this has triggered what was frequently referred to in conversations during fieldwork as 'a mad scramble for land' in Acholi region in general, and in Amuru and Nwoya districts in the south-western part of the sub-region in particular. This scramble encompasses different types of potential and existing conflicts, such as boundary disputes that occur at many levels: within and between families and households; clans and communities; parishes, sub-counties and districts; and large-scale land acquisitions which come by way of well-connected individuals who, often situated in the nexus of political, business and military activity, have been able to make use of the fluid and uncertain situation for personal gain (Adoko & Levine, 2004, pp. 49–55; Refugee Law Project, 2012; Sebina-Zziwa et al., 2008, pp. 14–15).

The Madhvani case: sugar cane for development or government grab?

During the then ongoing peace talks between the government of Uganda and the LRA, animated debates arose in the latter months of 2006 about the return of displaced persons and the future of land in Acholi. Against the backdrop of long-standing rumours of investors targeting land, Acholi Members of Parliament and local government leaders repeatedly cautioned against any such attempts (Atkinson, 2008, pp. 6–7). That was the context in which the Madhvani Group in January 2007 made public its intention to acquire land in Acholi to cover an outgrower plantation for sugar cane and a factory to process it; in July that same year this was specified to 40,000 hectares in the western parts of Amuru district. The proposal triggered strong protests. The Acholi Parliamentary Group gave a public warning that any investor who tried to grab land in Acholi would fail – one Member of Parliament (MP) allegedly threatened that they would be speared. The main demands made by the critics of the project were threefold: that no land in Acholi should be allocated until everybody was resettled on their land; that while investments may be welcome, any negotiation needed to be made directly with the community in question; and in the event land was allocated, it needed to be on the basis of lease – selling land would not be an option.

The project had the strong backing of the government, which, according to media reports in November 2008, in early 2008 had directed that half of the requested land, 20,000 hectares, should be leased to the Madhvani Group, and that the Government should hold 40% of the shares in the venture (Atkinson, 2008, p. 7). This reinforced local disapproval; President Museveni and the NRM were deeply unpopular in the region. Around the same time, in November 2008, it, however, transpired that Amuru District Land Board had already done what the government proposed, namely allocated 20,000 hectares to the Madhvani Group for a long-term lease on the pretext that the land in question was unoccupied. This prompted some Members of Parliament and private citizens to take members of the Board, representatives of the Madhvani Group and local politicians to court on the basis of illegal procedures for allocation of customary land. They succeeded in securing a court injunction from the High Court in Gulu, barring any activities in relation to the land in question (Atkinson, 2008, p. 8). The defendants coalesced around Amuru Sugar Works Limited, a company that as its owners has the Madhvani Group, Major General and MP Julius Oketa, holding 1 of the 10 parliamentary seats allocated to the military, and the former acting secretary of Amuru District Land Board. In February 2012, after many years of hearings, Gulu High Court finally ruled in favour of the defendants, thus opening up for the project to go ahead; the complainants stated that they were determined to appeal (*Sunday Monitor*, February 5, 2012).

Turning to the politics of representation, the Madhvani proposal has drawn many actors into the fray, all claiming an authoritative role in land matters. Starting with political party representatives, Acholi MPs – all of whom but one belonged to the opposition in the 2006–2011 parliament – predictably made much political mileage out of this; some solidified their already strong positions, for others it served as a temporary lifeline, as shown by their electoral defeat in 2011. Furthermore, some opposition MPs and local leaders have also been rumoured to have engaged in dubious land acquisition. On the side of civil society, a controversial role is played by Acholi cultural/traditional leaders under the umbrella of *Ker Kwaro Acholi*. This institution, headed by the paramount chief, *rwot Achana*, is a recent creation, formally instated in 2000, that mirrors similar ones in other regions of the country. It seems, however, to enjoy only limited public confidence (Allen, 2006, pp. 147–148). There is a widespread feeling that its top leaders have been compromised; some of them have openly been siding with the Madhvani Group. In 2009, one clan leader was attacked by an agitated crowd following such allegations, and continuously, accusations are being made by the Acholi Parliamentary Group against *Ker Kwaro Acholi* for clandestine collaboration with the government (*Acholi Times*, March 26, 2012). On a more theoretical note, it may be suggested that *Ker Kwaro Acholi* straddles between civil society- and state-like roles, both aspiring to represent the Acholi community in relation to the Madhvani Group and the central government, and claiming regulatory authority with regard to access to land.

During the final years of the war, external civil society organisations came to Acholi sub-region. Many of those who have remained now address various aspects of the land in question, though the foreign ones among them are very restricted in offering avenues for interest representation. One locally anchored umbrella organisation with a relatively high degree of credibility, much due to the role of some of its members during the conflict, is Acholi Religious Leaders Peace Initiative (ARLPI). Already during the war, ARLPI confronted the government over alleged plans to acquire land in Acholi. ARLPI's relative moral authority has made it possible for the organisation to create arenas for negotiation, though mainly over local conflicts. The Madhvani saga further witnessed the emergence of Amuru Anti-Land Grabbers Association, a local pressure group which managed to disrupt a high-profile visit to the area, and which transported people to a protest meeting. On closer examination, it appears that this group is a small ad hoc entity run by a local associate of a prominent regional MP.

The Madhvani conflict goes beyond Acholi sub-region and enters the wider scheme of things. A conspicuous feature in the eyes of many critics has been the pronounced role played by the government in pushing for the project, in marked contrast to the rather low-key profile of the Madhvani Group itself. President Museveni himself visited Amuru a number of times in late 2007, only to be told repeatedly that the targeted land was and would remain under customary tenure. Government activity has led to widespread speculation on the topic – brought up by almost every respondent during fieldwork interviews – that the Madhvani Group's sugar cane factory may be just a front activity for the real venture: oil exploration within the designated area; Amuru is within the oil belt. Government intervention in the matter has ebbed and flowed. After an initial period of active engagement, the Government kept a lower profile for some time. However, in the context of a sugar production crisis (and in the comfort of having just won an election), President Museveni in August 2011 reactivated some controversial ideas from the past, namely to allocate large tracts of land to sugar-producing companies. The most contentious of these was the proposal to assign a part of Mabira forest in central Uganda to the Mehta group. The latter suggestion resulted in riots all across the country in 2007 and would be certain to cause conflicts, should the President decide to push it further. But Museveni also referred to the Madhvani project in Amuru, allegedly saying he expected that matter to be concluded within three months, branding the opponents of the project 'enemies of development' (*New Vision*, August 15, 2011).

The challenged credibility of most actors and arenas for representation renders demand-making fluid and representation unpredictable from the perspective of local communities. These are, to start with, not necessarily united in their views. Even though opposition to the project appears to be fairly widespread, opinions range from hostility to support – the latter mainly being tagged to hopes for employment opportunities. Alliances are tenuous. The resistance to the Madhvani project largely depended upon the foothold created by the court injunction in combination with outspoken political representatives. For some time, it was possible for opposition politicians to create a relatively broad common front, but the 2011 elections, following which a number of NRM parliamentary candidates captured what used to be opposition seats, changed the political dynamic in Acholi. Some of the losing opposition MPs and local councillors formed the Acholi Land Forum after the elections (*New Vision*, March 22, 2011), but such a pressure group is unlikely to have as much bargaining power as the Acholi Parliamentary Group did, particularly in view of the High Court verdict.

Conclusion

It is entirely predictable that Acholi sub-region should be the target of attention from wealthy groups and individuals. The combination of fertile and supposedly oil-rich lands, a recently displaced and vulnerable population and land tenure regulated by weak political and cultural institutions has opened up for informal manoeuvring. Many modes of accumulation by land acquisition – some of them by dispossession, justificatory narratives about 'unoccupied land' notwithstanding – are visible in post-war Acholi, generating stratification and exclusion (Adoko & Levine, 2004; Sebina-Zziwa *et al.*, 2008). These accumulation projects occur through a wide array of mechanisms of access, with actors combining resources rooted in property, power, status and violence. Coming as it does against the background of recent displacement and long-standing rumours of planned land grabbing, the fierce scramble for land has triggered fear and further conflicts among the local population.

The scramble also generates competition for authority over customary tenure. This of course is nothing new. While it may be true that prior to the war, the social, economic and political underpinnings of the land tenure regime were probably more closely connected and internally coherent than are the current ones, this should not be taken to suggest a land tenure regime of the past characterised by communal harmony; it needs to be recalled that the content of customary tenure has been historically shifting and culturally contested and remains so today. Branch (2011, pp. 52–53, 61–62) argues that in the context of Uganda's ethno-regionally fractured polity before and after independence, the construction of a Acholi political identity with internal and national dimensions unfolded through fluid political alliances between a stated-based middle class, another group relying on lineage and generation based authority, and state-appointed chiefs, each with their own interpretation of customary law.

Similar processes are at work in contemporary Acholi, where the responses to land acquisitions are setting off a complex field of interest representation at the level of party politics and civil society. Political representatives, religious institutions, traditional leaders and others claim legitimate authority to define and speak on behalf of the Acholi community. The ways in which such actors intervene in processes of large-scale acquisitions by making claims to authority based on particular notions of community have ramifications for more local and intra-communal land struggles too, at both discursive and practical levels, especially when, as is often the case, different kinds of conflicts interlock. The latter observation points towards a general ambiguity regarding security of tenure under customary law. If respected and effectively upheld, customary tenure may serve as protection of access to land against market-based appropriation. At the same time, and especially if community is defined in terms of ancestry, it may reproduce nativist forms of exclusion internal to the tenure form and set off a logic of fragmentation and localisation (Boone, 2007, pp. 576–580).

A key feature of the Acholi land tenure regime, which in broad terms structures strategic considerations and behaviour, is the disjuncture between legislation on the one hand and institutional and social practices on the other. The post-1998 regime has introduced administrative and legal ambiguity, where relations between the formal and informal elements tend to be contradictory rather than complementary. In contemporary Acholi, legal and institutional multiplicity and weaknesses open up for actors to bring conflicts to arenas at different levels – which they do, from the household to the district. The incorporation of customary tenure into statutory law without clear divisions of labour between entities furthers institutional confusion. In this context, people are likely to take their grievances from one institutional arena to the other without necessarily having much faith in any. The issue of who should exercise authority with regard to land is fundamentally uncertain, and the competition around the rights to define, interpret and execute rules, laws and procedures – the internal 'constitutional' aspects of customary law – easily lends itself to manipulation. While there is a multitude of actors and institutions aspiring to regulate access to land, the majority of the population has limited influence over effective decision-making in any of these institutions. Indeed, landscapes of multiple and competing institutions often tend to create scope for grey-area manoeuvring, and, in the context of poverty and inequality, frequently to the detriment of vulnerable categories.

The uncertainty surrounding administrative and judicial authority makes the territorial and communal scale dynamics of the conflicts rather fluid. There are signs of a localising effect taking place in Acholi, expressed in the growing number of conflicts revolving around clan, and the multiplication of self-proclaimed chieftaincies, to the extent that the prime minister of *Ker Kwaro Acholi* has banned the creation of new chiefdoms (*New Vision*, March 16, 2012). Another factor that may deepen localisation is the changing structure of the state in terms of administrative subdivision; however, border disputes may also move the level for fighting out conflict upwards. Obviously, such tendencies complicate the conditions for broad-based politicisation of land issues in general. But there are also examples, including the case analysed here, of conflicts being politicised and elevated to grander scales.

The long-term prospects for resistance to the acquisition project studied here appear uncertain. Local communities are exposed in the wake of war and displacement, and vulnerable to persuasion. Effective demand-making requires continuous presence not only in the courts of law, but also in other arenas of decision-making, including political assemblies and the backrooms of informal deal-making. Disputes of a more distinct local nature are evidently easier to resolve by the use of local mechanisms. The Madhvani case, with its high-stake, high-profile involvement from the President, is different in a double-edged way, in that its particular features have increased the importance of both the exercise of power and resistance to it. In the long run, successful engagement depends on forceful commitment in many arenas not only locally, but also at the level of national politics. It remains to be seen whether the groups claiming to speak on behalf of those resisting the project will have the necessary tenacity, strategic skills and resources for sustained representation.

Acknowledgements

Many thanks to Jimmy Otim for research assistance, and to Ronald Atkinson for comments on an earlier draft.

Funding

This research was funded by Riksbankens Jubileumsfond.

Notes on contributor

Anders Sjögren is lecturer and researcher in the Department of Political Science, Stockholm University, Sweden, and researcher at the Nordic Africa Institute, Uppsala, Sweden. This article is part of his ongoing research on land tenure regimes, citizenship and state formation in Kenya and Uganda.

References

Adoko, J., & Levine, S. (2004). *Land matters in displacement: The importance of land rights in Acholiland and what threatens them.* Kampala: CSOPNU.

Alden Wily, L. (2011). 'The law is to blame': The vulnerable status of common property rights in sub-Saharan Africa. *Development and Change, 42,* 733–757.

Alden Wily, L. (2012). Looking back to see forward: The legal niceties of land theft in land rushes. *Journal of Peasant Studies, 39,* 751–775.

Allen, T. (2006). *Trial justice: The International Criminal Court and the Lord's Resistance Army*. London: Zed Books.

Atkinson, R. R. (2008, December). Land issues in Acholi in the transition from war to peace. *The Examiner*, Issue 4, 3–9, 17–25.

Bernstein, H. (2004). 'Changing before our very eyes': Agrarian questions and the politics of land in capitalism today. *Journal of Agrarian Change, 4*, 190–225.

Bernstein, H. (2005). Rural land and land conflicts in sub-Saharan Africa. In S. Moyo & P. Yeros (Eds.), *Reclaiming the land: The resurgence of rural movements in Africa, Asia and Latin America* (pp. 67–101). London: Zed Books.

Berry, S. (2002). Debating the land question in Africa. *Comparative Studies in Society and History, 44*, 638–668.

Berry, S. (2009). Property, authority and citizenship: Land claims, politics and the dynamics of social division in West Africa. In T. Sikor & C. Lund (Eds.), *The politics of possession: Property, authority and access to natural resources* (pp. 23–45). London: Wiley-Blackwell.

Boone, C. (2007, October). Property and constitutional order: Land tenure reform and the future of the African state. *African Affairs, 106*, 557–586.

Boone, C. (2013). *Property and political order in Africa: Land rights and the structure of politics*. Cambridge: Cambridge University Press.

Borras, S. M. Jr, & Franco, J. C. (2012). Global land grabbing and trajectories of agrarian change: A preliminary analysis. *Journal of Agrarian Change, 12*, 34–59.

Branch, A. (2011). *Displacing human rights: War and intervention in northern Uganda*. Oxford: Oxford University Press.

Chimhovu, A., & Woodhouse, P. (2006). Customary vs private property rights? Dynamics and trajectories of vernacular land markets in sub-Saharan Africa. *Journal of Agrarian Change, 6*, 346–371.

Cotula, L. (Ed.). (2007). *Changes in 'customary' land tenure in Africa*. London: IIED.

Cotula, L. (2012). The international political economy of the global land rush: A critical appraisal of trends, scale, geography and drivers. *Journal of Peasant Studies, 39*, 649–680.

Diamond, L. (1994). Rethinking civil society: Toward democratic consolidation. *Journal of Democracy, 5*, 4–17.

Finnström, S. (2008). *Living with bad surroundings: War, history and everyday moments in northern Uganda*. Durham, NC/London: Duke University Press.

Gibbon, P. (1996). Some reflections on 'civil society' and political change. In L. Rudebeck & O. Törnquist (Eds.), *Democratisation in the third world: Concrete cases in comparative and theoretical perspective* (pp. 21–50). Uppsala: Seminar for Development Studies.

Gibbon, P. (2001). Civil society, locality and globalization in rural Tanzania: A forty-year perspective. *Development and Change, 32*, 819–844.

Government of Uganda. (1998). *The Land Act (Cap. 227)*. Kampala: Government Printer.

Government of Uganda. (2011). *The Uganda national land policy final draft*. Kampala: Ministry of Lands, Housing and Urban Development.

Green, E. D. (2006). Ethnicity and the politics of land tenure reform in central Uganda. *Commonwealth and Comparative Politics, 44*, 370–388.

Harbeson, J., Rothchild, D., & Chazan, N. (Eds.). (1994). *Civil society and the state in Africa*. Boulder, CO: Lynne Rienner.

Hunt, D. (2004). Unintended consequences of land rights reform: The case of the 1998 Uganda Land Act. *Development Policy Review, 22*, 173–191.

Kasfir, N. (Ed.). (1998). *Civil society and democracy in Africa: Critical perspectives*. London: Frank Cass.

Lentz, C. (2006). Land rights and the politics of belonging in Africa: An introduction. In R. Kuba & C. Lentz (Eds.), *Land and the politics of belonging in West Africa* (pp. 1–34). Leiden: Brill.

Mamdani, M. (1976). *Politics and class formation in Uganda*. Kampala: Fountain Publishers.

National Association of Professional Environmentalists. (2012). *Land, life and justice: How land grabbing in Uganda is affecting the environment, livelihoods and food sovereignty of communities*. Kampala: Author.

Oxfam. (2011). *The new forest company and its Uganda plantations*. London: Author.

Peters, P. E. (2004). Inequality and social conflicts over land in Africa. *Journal of Agrarian Change, 4*, 269–314.

Peters, P. E. (2009). Challenges in land tenure and land reform in Africa: Anthropological contributions. *World Development*, *37*, 1317–1325.

Pottier, J. (2005). 'Customary land tenure' in sub-Saharan Africa today: Meanings and contexts. In C. Huggins & J. Clover (Eds.), *From the ground up: Land rights, conflict and peace in sub-Saharan Africa* (pp. 55–75). Pretoria: Institute for Security Studies.

Refugee Law Project. (2012, August). Land and investment: Balancing local and investor interest. *Conflict Watch*, *5*. Retrieved September 10, 2012, from www.refugeelawproject.org/accs/activity_briefs/Land_and_Investment;_Balancing_Local_and_Investor_Interests.pdf

Ribot, J. C., & Peluso, N. L. (2003). A theory of access. *Rural Sociology*, *68*, 153–181.

Rugadya, M. A. (2009). Escalating land conflicts in Uganda: A review of evidence from recent studies and surveys. Mimeo.

Sebina-Zziwa, A., Nabacwa, M., Mwebaza, R., Bogere, G., & Achiro, R. (2008). *Emerging land related issues in the Acholi sub-region: Northern Uganda*. Kampala: Makerere Institute of Social Research.

Sikor, T., & Lund, C. (Eds.). (2009). Access and property: A question of power and authority.. *The politics of possession: Property, authority and access to natural resources* (pp. 1–22). London: Wiley-Blackwell.

Sjögren, A. (2001). State, civil society and democratisation: Theoretical debates past and present. In B. Beckman, E. Hansson, & A. Sjögren (Eds.), *Civil society and authoritarianism in the third world* (pp. 21–48). Stockholm: PODSU.

White, G. (1994). Civil society, democratization and development (I): Clearing the analytical ground. *Democratization*, *1*, 375–390.

Zoomers, A. (2010). Globalization and the foreignisation of space: Seven processes driving the current global land grab. *Journal of Peasant Studies*, *37*, 429–447.

Asian capitalism, primitive accumulation, and the new enclosures in Uganda

David Ross Olanya

Department of Public Administration and Management, Gulu University, Gulu, Uganda

The new scramble for farmlands, similar to the colonial practice of allocating productive land for plantation agriculture, needs analysis. The failure of a dual economy resulted in the emergence of Asian capitalism, progressively changed from a colonial cotton frontier to a more lucrative sugar industry. The existence of relatively balance domestic power relations during British colonialism protected the local indigenous population from land alienation. A maximum cap of 10,000 acres was institutionalized to limit the amount of land owned by non-Africans. However, both Metha and Madhvani companies circumvented the cap to acquire more land, an insight not really being appreciated in the current land grab discourse. Using economic historical analysis, this article reviews how Metha and Madhvani accumulated more land, and compares with their current quest for primitive accumulation of 7100 hectares in Mabira Forest Reserve and 40,000 hectares of communal land in Amuru district.

1. Introduction

In order to understand the new enclosure policies, let us first explore the historical enclosure policies employed during the colonial government and postindependent governments. Asian capitalism in Uganda arose from the failure of settler class and peasantry classes. The Indian-based companies, the *Metha* and *Madhvani*, embarked on acquisitions of more land although the policy environment was not favorable to foreigners of non-colonial government root in Uganda. The beginning of primitive accumulation in Uganda was when British colonialism, through 1900 Buganda Agreement, introduced *mailo, native freehold*, and *leasehold* and *Crown* land ownerships. Subsequently, the 1900 Buganda Agreement created a landlord class in Buganda, Toro, and Ankole. The ruling elites excluded their subjects from the accumulation process, and those on *mailo* land became tenants and private freeholds were given to kings and notables individuals in Toro and Ankole. The *mailo* system is an equivalent to *freehold* with individual rights. However, this was not applicable in Northern and Eastern Uganda since they lacked strong administrative systems that could threaten the possibility of resistance to the colonial authorities. The landlord class in Buganda was a private estate '*mailo*', while '*native freehold*' was granted in Toro and Ankole. The *mailo* and *freehold* ownerships were created to accommodate the interests of the ruling oligarchies and loyalty to the British colonial authorities. The rest of Uganda was declared 'Crown land' under the control of British authority with control rights, and a limited number of freehold estates were given to individuals and corporations (Ahluwalia, 1995; Ministry of Lands, Housing and Urban

Development [MLHUD], 2007a; Nkioki, 2006). To illustrate the process of primitive accumulation, article 15 of the 1900 *Buganda* Agreement specified that out of the total 19,700 square miles (Juma, 2006), the Kabaka and 4000 of his chiefs received freehold rights to 9003 lots of 1 square mile each, known as *mailo*, and passed them to their heirs (Ofcansky, 1996, p. 24). In Ankole, the 1901 agreement demarcated 50 square miles for private freeholds and 26 square miles for the official estates. In addition, in Toro, 255 square miles were given as private freeholds and 122 square miles as official estates to Omukama and his chiefs (Mugambwa, 2002, p. 5). During this period, land alienation was in *mailo* and Crown land. Under *mailo* system, Kabaka, his chiefs and some notables benefited from the alienation. Under Crown land, alienation was for government purposes and this land was vested in the custody of the Queen of England.

The increased demand for cotton in Britain was related to the expansion of domestic clothing industry as well as the expansion of international markets, and this led to the emergence of landed class in Buganda. The Buganda parliament, *Lukiiko*, passed Land Law in 1908, defining the system of tenure introduced by the 1900 Buganda Agreement, requiring tenants and peasants to pay rent. The tenants and peasants were to pay dues every year, *busulu* for the tenants and *envujjo* for each acre. Baganda peasants and immigrants on large tracts of undeveloped land were legally rendered landless and actually had to pay to pay 'Busuulu' or 'Enjunjo' rent to *mailo* holders. As noted by Ahluwalia (1995), the 'Busulu' and 'Nvujju' laws legalized as a way of dominating the peasants in order to control their economic surplus since Buganda *Lukiiko* (parliament) was mainly dominated by landlords. This later led to the *Bataka Movement*. The colonial authorities in 1928, however, responded by enacting the *Busulu* and *Envujji* to limit the amount of rent the landlord could levy and guaranteed tenants complete and hereditary security of tenure provided they used the land productively (Juma, 2006). The rights of the tenant in Clause 11 provided that no peasant could be evicted by the *mailo* owner from the *kibanja* unless the order was made by court having the jurisdiction (Mugambwa, 2002, p. 5). Therefore, it became very difficult for the *mailo* landowners to remove sitting tenants in order to turn their land into a single large estate since they had certificates of occupancy (Ahluwalia, 1995).

The peasants depended on the chiefs who were turned into landlords. This was the harbinger of individual land registration in Buganda, Ankole, and Toro. The Buganda Agreement of 1900 provided a detailed land settlement whereby the waste and uncultivated land was vested in the Crown and the remainder divided into private and official estates. The Crown Lands Ordinance allowed the governor to allocate crown. However, the Crown Land Ordinance 1922 stated that other than the unoccupied land, land acquired for public purposes and covered by the agreements must be clarified. In *Kigezi* region, the 1902 Uganda Order in Council and the 1903 Crown Land Ordinance declared all land in Uganda to be 'Crown land', legally vesting ownership in the Crown while the rights of African were protected. Crown land, however, excluded land allocated to chiefs under the agreements signed with leaders in the kingdoms of Buganda, Ankole, Toro, and Bunyoro. It was only meant for land outside these Kingdoms. Even the 1950 pronouncement on the colonial policy on land outside Buganda stated that Crown land was held 'in trust for the use and benefit of Africans'. However, while the official policy of protecting African interests was non-alienation in the freehold, in few cases land under the freehold was granted to missions through leasing to the Native Anglican Church and White Father Mission. Also, leaseholds were given for pyrethrum plantations as well as certificates of occupancy were granted to a number of Buganda Agents for the land they held in Kigezi (Carswell, 2007, p. 86–87).

Since the global financial and food crises of 2007 and 2008, respectively, the motivation to acquire land in the global south has increased in both public and communal lands as state geared to sustain their economic viability. As such the new enclosure polices in Uganda are driven by powerful corporate interests in the name of transforming the agricultural-based economy, mainly for food, energy, biofuels, reducing emissions from deforestation and degradation opportunities, and conservation purposes, generally supported by the state. For example, Norwegian Forest Company, through Busoga Cooperative Co. Ltd., acquired 100,000 ha of Bukaleeba Central Forest Reserve and replaced with pine and eucalyptus, displacing more than 8000 people from 13 villages in Mayuge district who encroached on the land during the political turmoil of 1975–1985. They were neither consulted nor compensated. In addition, 20,000 ha of Luwunga Forest Reserves have been allocated for tree project, evicting more than 200,000 peasants (Friend of the Earth Uganda/NAPE (National Association of Professional Environmentalists), 2012). Lie Jianjun has acquired 4000 ha of land for 99-year leases at US$1 or less than for faring in 2008. Similar, Uganda government has agreed to allocate 800,000 ha to Egyptian government in various parts of the country for growing maize and wheat in 2008. Wilmar International, Singapore, has acquired 40,000 ha of land through a joint effort between the government, The International Fund for Agricultural Development, the World Bank, and Wilmar's subsidiary Oil Palm Uganda Ltd. in three areas in Uganda (GRAIN, 2012). The subsidiary, BIDCO company now holds 10,000 ha of land for palm oil production in Buvuma Islands (Olanya, 2012a). Table 1 below shows the new enclosures in Uganda.

This article is divided into parts preceding introduction, agrarian questions and capital accumulation, and colonial policy of land: protecting or alienating, postindependent land policies, acquisitions of land by Asian Sugar Companies, the quest for primitive accumulation and the new enclosures, discussions, and conclusions.

2. Agrarian questions and capital accumulation

The numerous studies on agrarian questions in Africa originated from colonial legacy, in which settler colonialism created massive land alienation and proleterianization, while indirect rule was used to promote peasant farming for exports (Amin, 1972). For example, in the Democratic Republic of Congo and Cameroon, the colonial governments promoted indigenous elites alongside the peasantry, usually called the bimodal agrarian of the European merchant capitalists. As argued by Lentz (2006), the colonial theories of landownership had a lot of influence in promoting and guaranteeing security of tenure to the European firms interested in concessions or mining, in which the colonial governments could appropriate land for public use. Uncultivated land had no 'owner' and could therefore be legitimately appropriated by the colonial governments for private usages. In the case of Uganda, the British colonial government declared all lands 'Crown land' except those under the *mailo*, freehold and leasehold ownerships.

In the wave of promoting peasantry accumulation, for instance, statutory and customary were encouraged to coexist. In South Africa, statutory and customary tenures featured prominently. Statutory land tenure system is governed by modern land law, while customary law prevented land from alienation in favor of community trust (Mzumara, 2003). In Abure region, among the Burkinabe, one can sell or lease out the land; however, the sale of the land is entangled among political game on the discourse of Ivorian origin (Kouame, 2009). However, as for the case of Zimbabwe, Chimhowu and Woodhouse (2006) examined the historical aspects of land acquisitions. They found that the colonial policies stifled the incorporation of peasants into the agricultural commodity market.

Table 1. Land deals in Uganda.

Source	Investor	Country of origin	Sector	Hectares	Production	Status of the deal	Summary
GRAIN (2012)	Nitol-Niloy Group	Bangladesh	Agribusiness	10,000	Crops	In process	In June 2010, the company was reported negotiating with Uganda government to invest around US$12.5 million to zestablished a farm on 10,000 ha where 2500 farmers from Bangladesh will be working in Uganda and 80% of the production will be exported to Bangladesh
GRAIN (2012)	Hebei Company	China	Agribusiness	450	Fruits, livestocks, maize, rice, vegetables, wheat	In process	In October 2009, the Hebei Company intends to grow horticulture and expand its operation to 41,000 ha within 10 years
GRAIN (2012)	Liu Jianju	China	Finance	4000		Done	Liu Jianju in 2008 acquired 4000 ha for 99-year leases at US$1 or per ha of land for farming
GRAIN (2012)	Egypt	Egypt	Government	80,000	Maize and wheat	Done	In August 2008, the Egyptian Agricultural Minister Amin Abaza confirmed to the Egyptian daily *Al-Ahram* that the Government of Uganda had agreed to allocate 800,000 ha in various parts of the country. The Egyptian government will use seven private companies to work on the project immediately
GRAIN (2012)	Iceland	Iceland	Agribusiness	270	Fruit	Done	Iceland, a leading fruit and vegetable supplier to European supermarket, has three farms in the country
Nature Uganda (2012)	Metha Group	India	Agribusiness	7100	Sugar	Halted	In 2007 and 2011, the government allocation of Mabira Forest to Metha Group for sugarcane growing has met increasing opposition under the 'Mabira Crusade' and the proposed project is temporary halted
GRAIN (2012)	Metha Group	India	Agribusiness	14,600	Sugarcane	Done	Originally the Metha Group was allocated in the Mabira Forest. But the heavy opposition brought forward an alternative plan to provide lands of the defunct Sango Bay Sugar Factory in Rakai district
	Wilmar International	Singapore	Agribusiness	40,000	Oil palm	Done	Through a joint venture effort between the government, the International Fund for Agricultural Development, the World Bank, and Wilmar's subsidiary Oil Palm Uganda Ltd., Wilmar has been allocated a total of 40,000 ha for nucleus oil-palm plantations in different areas of Uganda
Olanya (2012b)	Madhvani	India	Agribusiness	40,000	Sugarcane	Done	Out of the 40,000 ha demanded, 10,000 ha has been allocated to Madhvani Group for sugarcane growing. However, the allocation by the District Land Board is being contested legally since the land in question belongs to the community

Amanor (2010) carried out a similar study in Ghana and found that colonial policy restricted access to through the creation of reserves, and local indigenous people were forced to seek alternative wage labor on plantation.

As seen in the above literature, the land acquisitions to nonindigenous population were accumulated through lease, purchase, or entering into sharing agreements with the local indigenous population. However, capital accumulation may also take another detrimental mode within the capitalist mode of production, especially when it separates people from their means of production and transforms them into landless proletariats (Marx, 1858/1974). The detrimental aspects of expanding process of capital accumulation are called primitive accumulation (Marx, 1858/1974), historical process (de Angelis, 1999; Lenin, 1899/1960), and a continuous process necessary for expanding capitalism (Amin, 1974; Luxemburg, 1913/1963). As mentioned by Harvey (2003), the endless quest for more accumulation involves coercive mechanisms in their legal, political and military forms constituting 'accumulation by dispossession,' which involves violence and expulsion of peasants, conversion of property rights, and suppression of communal rights. Dobb (1963) argued that primitive accumulation must first be interpreted as accumulation of capital claims and titles to existing assets which are accumulated for speculative purposes, and accumulation in a historical sense often refers to ownership of assets and to a transfer of ownership (p. 178). In fact, primitive accumulation remains a precondition for accumulation proper, although it has a continuous character. 'Primitive accumulation' and 'accumulation by dispossession' are used interchangeably in this article. This article focuses only on primitive accumulation being instigated by the government to give public and communal lands to Madhvani Group and Metha Group of companies, respectively.

3. Colonial policy of land: protecting or alienating?

Regarding how colonialism protected African interests, the West African case showed that colonial authority prohibited sales of 'communal' land in order to avoid 'spirited opposition to individualization' by Africans as ambitious settlers and corporations increased acquisitions of land (Chanok, 1991, p. 82). In Northern Rhodesia (now Zambia), reserves and trust lands were defined as areas for African use, and the legality of private transactions were not recognized (Colson, 1971, p. 209). However, Lentz (2006) showed how colonialism appropriated land for public use and guaranteed security of tenure to European firms interested in concessions for mining or commercial agriculture, and uncultivated land without owners were legitimately appropriated. In some instances, settler colonies created massive land alienation and proleterianization, while indirect rule was used to promote farming for exports (Amin, 1972).

Unlike settler colonialism (Kenyan Highlands, South Africa), British colonialism government in Uganda promoted smallholder farming in cash growing such as cotton and coffee in the central and western part of the county. The policy of promoting smallholder farming encouraged the farmers to own land under *mailo, freehold*, and *customary* (under Crown land) ownerships to grow cotton and coffee. At the same, they were expected to pay graduated tax as a measure to keep them productive to the economy by working on cash crop plantations. The land policy supported non-alienation of land to non-Africans and provided security of tenure to peasant Africans. Land Transfer Ordinance 1906 authorized commissioner to consent to any land transfer to non-Africans unless the land was less than 1000 acres. Buganda Land Law of 1908 stipulated that *mailo* land granted under the provisions of 1900 Agreement could not be sold to any nonnative without the approval of both the Governor and *Lukiiko* (Ahluwalia, 1995). The colonial government maintained

Table 2. Registered alienation of land in the Uganda Protectorate to enterprising Asian communities, 1934.

Province	District	County	Alienation (in freehold) (acres)	Asians on Crown land leases (acres)	Alienation from native owners (acres)	Number of Asian freeholders (acres)
Buganda	Entebbe	Busiro	1178.89	422.3	209.6	8
		Busujju	61.68	–	–	1
		Butambala	–	–	11	2
		Gomba	1829.99	–	12	4
		Mawokota	1110.5	–	21	6
	Masaka	Buddu	640	17	845.27	17
	Mengo	Bulemezi	490.72	–	197.3	18
		Buruli	–	–	25	1
		Kyadondo	1599.95	–	998.3	25
		Kyagwe	11,8876.33 (1)[a]	744.32 (1)[a]	4778.65 (1)[a]	3
	Mubende	Dugangadzi	–	6	15	3
		Buwekula	–	5	–	1
		Buyaga	–	–	10	–
		Singo	386.51	–	251	17
Eastern	Budama		–	29	–	4
	Bugishu		–	18	–	3
	Busoga		8783.73 (2)[b]	6231.42 (2)[b]	–	22
	Karamoja		–	–	–	–
	Teso		16	176.58	–	10
Northern	Bunyoro		106.45	581 (3)[c]	–	3
	Chua		–	13	–	2
	Gulu		–	25	–	3
	Lango		–	83	–	2
	West Nile		–	–	–	6
West	Ankole		–	–	–	–
	Kigezi		–	–	–	–
	Toro		584.7	9	–	–

Source: Uganda Protectorate, Office of the Ministry of Local Government, Entebbe, 4891, communication from Land Officer to Chief Secretary, 6 January 1934, cited in Ahluwalia (1995, p. 56). 1, land owned to Metha; 2, land owned to Madhvani; 3, land owned for cotton and sisal crop production.
[a] 5176.7, 744.32, and 3649.96 acres held under ownership of Lugazi Sugar Factory.
[b] 5050.6 and 6095.42 acres held by owners of Uganda (Kakira) Sugar Works (formerly Vithaldas Haridas and Co.).
[c] 5000 acres held by Hoima Cotton Co. Ltd., at Masindi; Pontas Sisal Plantation.

balanced power relations with the *Buganda* government because most of those who were in authority were landowners. As a result, through Crown system and freehold systems, the non-Africans were able to apply for lease on Crown land which was under the control of colonial government, while others were able to buy directly from private owners such *mailo* owners and defunct white farmers as shown on Table 2.

The degree of those acquisitions was minimal and did not raise a big concern to the general population. British colonialism handled land alienation with caution as evidenced by the position of Secretary of State for the Colonies memorandum submitted to the parliament on the native policy in East Africa that:

As the alienation of land to non-natives must, in its bearing on future native needs, assume increasing importance, His Majesty's Government considers that an annual return should be furnished to the Secretary of State showing what land included within Native reserves has been expropriated for other native occupation or use, and which land outside reserves has been alienated, under what terms such alienation has been effected and to whom, and what stipulations have been made in case with a view to prevent purchase by mere speculators, and for ensuring reasonably early and adequate development by purchasers themselves.[1]

For instance, out of the total 80,371 square miles of land, less than 300 square miles had been alienated to non-Africans, and 155 square miles of freehold and 61 square miles of leasehold accounted for the purchases from local indigenous Africans by non-Africans in Buganda after the 1900 Agreement by 1950 (Ahluwalia, 1995). This illustrated how the colonial government was not encouraging massive land speculation despite the increasing demand for land by non-Africans. As stated by the Chief Secretary:

> Had it not been for the Protectorate Government which took over the ownership of all land for which no title could be produced, and passed legislation as far as 1906 prohibiting the transfer of land occupied by or held by any African to a person not of the Protectorate without the consent in writing of the Governor, there is little doubt that many Africans would have sold land to non-Africans.[2]

The colonial government since 1906 introduced an official policy to minimize land alienation to non-Africans, introducing a policy cap of 10,000 ha to be owned by non-Africans. However, the sugar companies demonstrated their abilities to acquire additional land from the *Lukiiko* and colonial authorities. They illicitly acquired *mailo* land indirectly from *mailo* owners, converted them into Crown land and then to leasehold, entered into yearly agreements with local indigenous population and then applied for legal transfer to the colonial government, and also purchased from freehold from defunct white farmers.

4. Postindependence land policies

As always for most African countries, the postindependence governments treated leasehold and freehold as superior to customary ownership that later became the focus of land reform initiatives. This was also the same for Metha and Madhvani Sugar Companies that remained as the pillar for economic transformation in Uganda. In fact, the sugar giants were not affected by the desired goals of introducing the local population into agricultural transformation. It was only in trade and civil servants that were affected by the postindependence policy of promoting Africans role in the growth process (Ahluwalia, 1995, p. 222). For example, while Amin's regime was very hostile to the people of Asian descent, his government revisited the 60% takeover during Obote's regime of May 1970 to 49% in 1972 (Becker & Madhvani, 1973). Yet, Amin was not in support of Asian businesses except the sugar industry.

In general, it should be noted that the postindependence government did not removed restriction despite the instrumental role of the sugar industry in Uganda. This was evidenced when the World Bank's field report to the country had advised the government to remove restriction on the amount of land to owned by sugar companies since such restrictions was hindering capital inflows to the agricultural production and expansion (International Bank for Reconstruction and Development, 1962). Instead, the government retained land tenure systems introduced by the colonial government except the Crown land, which was converted into public land. The Crown Act of 1962 converted Crown land into public land, under the control of Uganda Land Commission. Leaseholds were granted for 99 years and a viable rent was paid. Under the 1969 Public Lands Act, lands that did not fall under either as freehold or leasehold were held under customary Law. The 1975 Land Reform Decree (No. 3) declared all land in Uganda as public land under the control of Uganda Land Commission in accordance with the provisions of Public Land Act (1969). The 1975 Land Degree abolished freehold interests in land except those where interest was vested in the state through Uganda Land commission. The 1975 Land Decree gave the state control over all lands in Uganda. As a result, several areas originally gazetted for protection (especially forest and wildlife reserves) were degazetted after the 1975 Land Decree (MLHUD, 2007b). Amin's regime (1969–1979) was interesting in seeing state's control over land in which all lands were placed under lease and the state was to hold land in trust for the people of Uganda and to be administered by the Land Commission. This was the beginning for peasantry's accumulation of land in Uganda, especially in Northern Uganda where land was not developed during colonial and postindependent period, as rapid accumulation took place when the 1975 decree was passed. The decree dispossessed the customary owners in Northern Uganda as productive land was grabbed, in this case Lakang Land in Amuru. The 1975 was aimed at ending peasant's ownership of big undeveloped land, distributing land use for development projects.

The 1995 constitution of Uganda and subsequently the 1998 Land Act, however, repealed the decree and restored the land tenure systems based on customary, *mailo*, freehold, and leasehold. Article 237 of the 1995 constitution stipulates that land belongs to citizens of Uganda and shall be vested in them in accordance with the customary, freehold, *mailo*, and leasehold. While article 237 of the 1995 constitution stipulates that land belongs to citizens of Uganda and shall be vested in them in accordance with the customary, freehold, *mailo*, and leasehold, the New National Land Policy March 2011 now suggests a number of changes to be made in the current legislation including article 237 (1) of the constitution which grants radical title to citizens not the state to exercise sovereignty over all land on behalf of its citizens. The land tenure shall be categorized as private, public, and government land. Customary tenure shall be recognized along other tenure categories, but state shall establish a customary land registry for registration of customary tenure in its own form (MLHUD, 2011).

5. Acquisitions of land by Asian sugar companies

Asians arrived in Uganda as causal laborers and commercial workers during the construction of the railway in East Africa. After the completion of the railway, those who remained behind began petty trade, mostly middlemen in cotton business, buying cotton from remote places. Through cotton shop 'dukawallas,' they gradually came to control the marketing of cotton to the Europeans. When the shipping route to Lancaster was closed, India became the alternative market for Ugandan cotton. By 1925, there were 100 ginneries owned by Indians out of 114 ginneries (Ahluwalia, 1995). Nanji Kalidas Metha and Muljjibhai Madhvani were all petty traders who gradually changed to cotton ginning, and when the European planters became bankrupt, they had the opportunity to purchase land, and Metha became the first Asian to buy 5000 acres of defunct coffee and rubber plantations in Kyagwe district and 2000 acres at Kawolo Hill from an African chief for 36,000 rupees.

In general, the land acquisition was through an incremental process by both Metha and Madhvani: (1) purchasing freehold land from other non-Africans, (2) leasing untenanted Crown land directly from the British authority, (3) acquiring *mailo* land indirectly from African landowners, a practice where *mailo* land was surrendered as Crown land, and when Governor's consent, the land was regranted leasehold Crown land, (4) exchanging freehold for *mailo* land with the consent of colonial government and Buganda authority, and (5) entering into yearly agreements with African landowners as shown Table 3.

Table 3. Land holding by type.

Type of land	Total number of acres
Madhvani (originally Vithaldas Haridas and Company in 1930)	
Freehold	5551.59
Leasehold	2129.75
Total	7681.34
Nanji Kalidas Metha (Lugazi-based sugar company) 1923–1933	
Freehold	4321.33
Leasehold	4401.14
Total	8722.47

Source: Adapted from Ahluwalia (1995, pp. 61, 77).

5.1. The Metha Group

Established in 1923, the sugar company today controls assets in excess of US$400 million and employees more than 15,000 people in Asia, Europe, North America, and Africa.[3] Nanji Kalidas Metha, born in Gorana, India, 1888, first came to Madagascar at the age of 14 years and then made his second journey with only 50 rupees to Mombasa, Zanzibar, and finally settled in Uganda. He started his own shop with an initial capital of 240 rupees, buying commodities from rural areas, and set up his own ginneries in Kamuli and Busembatia in 1916, and additional two in 1918 (Ahluwalia, 1995). Metha obtained more in various ways: entering into yearly agreements with the African landowners and then seeking a long term of 49 years from the colonial authority. Such land was then regranted as Crown land and then leased to Metha. As stated:

> This is investigation has disclosed a gap in the effectiveness of my control over leasing of native land to non-natives. It has shown that, by collusion between a native landowner and a non-native planter, the latter can, if he cares to take the risk of occupying land without an enforceable registration title, enter upon the native's land (paying him of course the agreed rent) and create conditions for any native tenants of the former which may leave them with no option but to accept the offered compensation and to move. Thus, when in due course my consent to the lease is sought, there is no longer an opportunity of investigating the propriety of removing any tenants from the land, and I am confronted with the accomplished fact that the land is unoccupied.[4]

When a limit of 12,400 was imposed on Metha, approved by Secretary of State to be absolutely final, Metha again in 1934 proposed to surrender 3900 acres of leasehold in exchange for 2600 acres of Crown land adjoining the factory. This was approved by the Governor and the Buganda on the ground that there were no tenants on the land.

5.2. The Madhvani Group

Once again, the Madhvani Group is featured in this study so as to illustrate the Company's quest for communal land in Acholi subregion of Northern Uganda, Lakang, in Amuru district, at a zero-sum cost from the local community, but using the office of the President to acquire free land without following the national laws on acquisitions and compensations to the affected community.

The Kakira Sugar Works was established in 1930 by Vithaldas Haridas and Company Ltd. in Busoga region. At the beginning, Madhvani acquired land through freehold and leasehold from white settlers. He then started applying for additional lease of 1500 acres in 1931which was granted easily. When the Sugar Company sought for additional 3500 acres, it was not accepted since it was beyond the maximum cap of 10,000 acres. However, he continued buying freehold as well as gaining minimum concession from the colonial authority. The Sugar Company also requested 5000 additional acres of uninhibited infected area. This came due to good demand for sugar after World War II and the neighboring countries such as Sudan, Kenya, Zanzibar, Palestine, and India. By 1945, the company had acquired 22,750 acres of land, and 18,320 acres were under sugar plantation. Land issue in Busoga region was not as critical as in Buganda that was highly populated and left little room for expansion (Ahluwalia, 1995, p. 94).

Kakira Sugar Works (KSW) provided resources for the Madhvani group. When his son Jayant Madhvani took control of the business from his father in 1958, there were only five companies. He then acquired Nile Breweries (1958), Emco Glass Works Ltd. (1959), Chande Industries Ltd., Steel Corporation of East Africa Ltd., Kenya Glass Works Ltd., Kilimanjaro Breweries Ltd., Rasha Rasha Estates Ltd., the Sweet Factory, and the Soap Factory in Arusha. The number of industrial and commercial units increased up to 70 in 1970 (Becker & Madhvani, 1973, p. 55), employing about 22,000 employees with the turnover GBP 30 million per year, becoming the leading company in the country. The company turnover also increased from GBP 2 million in 1958 to GBP 26 million in 1970. Capital investment jumped from GBP 1,876,000 to GBP 16,682, 962 (Becker & Madhvani, 1973, p. 12).

While progress was retarded during Amin's regime (1971–1979), in 1985, the company repossessed KSW (1985) Ltd. through a joint venture company, in which government had 51% of the share holding. In 1992, the Government of Uganda reduced its shareholding to 30%. Today, KSW (1985) Ltd. is owned 100% by the Madhvani group, employing more than 7500 persons. It also generates 22 MW of electric power on 24 h per day basis – of which 12 MW is supplied to Uganda's national grid.[5]

5.3. The emergence of out-grower scheme: an alternative to land alienation

One of the alternatives to land grabbing is the introduction of out-grower scheme. This is the approach used by the colonial government to avoid land alienation from the local indigenous population, a discourse that is rarely considered by foreign investors and host governments in Africa. The colonial government introduced the out-grower scheme in 1928, which later became successful in the 1940s and 1950s when it became very difficult for Metha and Madhvani to amass more land (Ahluwalia, 1995). It was when the British approved only 12,400 acres instead of 15,000 acres in consideration of African peasants adjacent to the factory that Metha adopted the scheme. The number of acres under out-grower scheme increased from 7 acres in 1942 to 36 acres in 1943 after massive support by the colonial authority. There were only 149 out-growers by 1972 and the whole program was abandoned by 1974 due to the economic crisis. As per now there are 1,169,268 out-growers at KSW.

In 1958, KSW started developing under Jayant Madhvani. The out-growers increased from 4 out-growers to 1462 out-growers in 1970, assisted by out-growers department created in 1963. Unlike Metha, Kakira was more organized when it comes to assisting out-growers. They registered farmers and also provided them with the necessary transport for cane to be transported to the factory. However, in the mid-1970s, the out-grower scheme at Kakira was also abandoned because of the political instability, economic recession, and political isolation during Amin's regime (1971–1979). Today, Kakira Nucleus Estate has almost 10,000 ha under cane cultivation and provides 35% of the factory's cane requirements, with more than 7000 out-grower farmers cultivating additional 19,000 ha as shown in Table 4.

Table 4. KSW cane supply – tonnes per annum (TPA).

	1990–1991	1995–1996	2000–2001	2005–2006	2009–2010
Estate cane	80,771	459,727	392,490	582,311	492,078
Percent	86	71	62	59	30
Out-growers cane	13,448	187,357	244,672	407,456	1,169,268
Percent	14	29	38	41	70

Source: KSW 2012 (www.kakirasugar.com/content/agriculture, accessed 4 December 2012).

The out-grower scheme promotes African interests and supports smallholder farmers. This case review shows that when land alienation from local indigenous became politically unsustainable, out-grower scheme was then adopted officially and the colonial government influenced the Kakira Sugar Works to start developing out-grower scheme, although local indigenous population had no capital, security to secure credit, and support in terms of labor and transport costs.

6. The quest for primitive accumulation and the new enclosures

This subsection concentrates on two cases of the quest for primitive accumulation and the implications. As mentioned earlier, the colonial government had put a policy cap of 10,000 ha of land to be acquired by Asian investors. Unlike the current demand in which the government supports acquisitions without subjecting such acquisitions to how much can be acquired and the performance standard to meet before additional land is added.

6.1. Mabira Central Forest Reserve

Established in 1932 as a nature reserve, the government since has planned to give away 7100 ha of Mabira Forest to the Metha Group for sugar growing (World Rainforest Movement, 2007). The rationale is that giving the additional 7100 ha for sugarcane growing increases the sugar production in the country to meet the increasing sugar demand, both domestically and in the regional market. The government believes that the benefits of converting *Mabira* Forest outweigh costs since the country will benefit from the project spillovers such as jobs creation and development. *Mabira* Forest makes up to 30,000 ha of land and home to 312 species of tree, 287 species of bird, and 199 species of butterfly. It receives more than 62% of all tourists visiting forest reserves in the country. It is a vital water catchment area for the Lake Victoria and rivers, a cultural heritage, and a source of livelihoods to 200,000 surrounding communities. It contains carbon sink worth US$212 million (Nature Uganda). This has attracted outright opposition and resistance such as the 'Mabira demonstration' in 2007 in which peoples of Asian origin were the target during the demonstration in Kampala.

As a result, the project is temporarily halted as pressure mounts on the government. The pressure from the concerned citizens, Members of Parliament such as Kitgum Women Member of Parliament Hon. Beatrice Anywar, the Shadow Minister of Environment for opposition political parties in Parliament, civil society organizations such Nature Uganda, conservationists/environmentalists, and donor communities such as the European Union Delegation in Uganda was against the project since the Union has invested a lot funding in conservation projects in Mabira Forest. In 2011 again, the government made another renewed interest to give away the Mabira to Metha as sugar prices escalated in the country. This move is interpreted as primitive accumulation; it was the same government that in the early 1990s took a step of evicting settlers who encroached on Mabira Forest in 1970s– 1980s with the intention of preserving the forest. Alternative, the government has given 14,600 ha of defunct Sango Bay factory in Rakai district (GRAIN, 2012). This was a compensation for the failed deal in Mabira Forest giveaway to KSW since the project received national demonstration and discontent under the 'Mabira Crusade.'

6.2. *The Amuru Sugar Project in Northern Uganda*

The British colonial government forcefully evicted the Acholi (Luo) people from Lakang, Amuru district, in 1911. The forceful evicted was conducted on the following grounds: (1) Lakang was infected with small pox and tsetse flies, (2) British colonialism had a strategic policy of bringing people closer to each other for administrative purposes, and (3) the practice of eviction as divide and rule to contain Lamogi rebellion (Uma-Owiny, 2012). This eviction was a harbinger of accumulation by dispossession in the areas owned communally by the people of Lamogi, Pagak, Boro, Parabongo, Pabbo, and Pagak that were converted into a game reserve, covering the areas of Lakang, Kinene, Appa, Anaka, and Lamogi. The game reserve was later rebranded as Kilak Hunting Area in 1936. However, the Legal Order 364 of 1963 gazetted the former game reserve to Kilak Hunting Area, preventing the communities from returning to their customary and ancestral lands.

During Amin's regime, the Statutory Instrument No. 55 decreed that the Game (Kilak) Reserve Order be revoked. The Game Preservation and Control Ordinance No. 14 of 1959 was revoked paving way for the degazetting of Kilak Hunting Area and Aswa/Lorim Game Reserve. The decree allowed the communities to return to their lands. The 1975 Land Decree declared that all land became public land and vested it in the state on behalf of its people. This was the time when large tracts of land were dispossessed in Lakang since those on customary ownership must get leased by the Uganda Land Commission to become the owner of customary, otherwise Lakang land became a public land. This was the time when ministers, government officials, the military, and Amin's tribesmen acquired land in Lakang. In fact, during Amin's regime, Uganda Land Commission issued many land titles: 20 in Koch Goma, 22 in Amuru, and 50 in Purongo since it is located on Pakwach highways, totaling to 23,838 ha (Rugadya & Kamusiime, 2010). In fact, the 1995 Land Decree deprived customary owners to own land, instead political elites and foreign investors from Saudi Arabia got land for cattle ranch (Akena, 2010).

After a long history of 21 years of displacement in concentrated camps, Lakang became vacant. Without consultation with the local people, Amuru District Land Board fraudulently allocated 10,000 ha of land out of the 40,000 to the Madhvani Group, 10,000 ha to General Julius Oketta, and 1000 ha to Aber Harriet, the wife to Salim Saleh.[6] Lakang is now being claimed by many people: Acholi clans as an ancestral land, Uganda Wild Life Authority that the area was a game reserve, those who got the land under the 1975 Land Decree, individuals who fraudulently acquired the land during resettlement process after civic wars, and the Madhvani Group who were illicitly allocated 10,000 ha out 40,000 ha. Uganda Wildlife Authority is claiming Apaa as a game reserve and about 20,000 ha of land, violating the rights of local population.

The Amuru project is a joint venture between the government and the Madhvani Group (Madhvani, 2012). Out of 40,000 ha of land, 10,000 ha of the land has already been fraudulently given away by the government through Amuru District Land Board to the Madhvani Group. Then 20,000 ha will be used for nuclease estate of the factory and the remaining land will be leased to the communities under the out-grower scheme. The Madhvani Group will then be given the title deed to the tune of 40,000 ha to secure additional funding of US$50 million from the African Development Bank (Rugadya & Kamusiime, 2010). While it is a joint venture, the puzzling issue is that 40,000 ha of land is supposed to be given at a no cost. This is where the issue of primitive accumulation comes in. The contested land was set aside by various clans for community activities such as hunting and grazing of animals, honey collection and medicinal purposes. In this sense, areas used for grazing and hunting were owned collectively and access was automatic for all the chiefdoms.

Although the market can take place between the willing seller and willing buyer, this is not case for Amuru Sugar Project. The state through arms such as the Ministries and the Office of the President is actively backing the Sugar Company to acquire land in Lakang at zero cost given the fact that the land is owned communally. Key government officials have been seen publicly negotiating with the affected communities to let their land to the Sugar Company, promising better infrastructure such as health and educational services, nuclear faming, as well as employment. Therefore, the state has become the official facilitator of this primitive accumulation, providing the necessary legal and physical infrastructure, offering fiscal exemption and the land at no cost. The project is believed to create more than 7000–8000 employment to local population as well as creating additional 7000–10,000 sources of livelihood to the local population (Madhvani, 2012). The Madhvani would supply farm inputs to clear, plough, arrow, and furrow the land, as well as distribute 'treated cane seeds' and give technical advice. The model would be similar to KSW in Busoga region.

7. Discussions

While a maximum cap policy of 10,000 acres was instituted by British colonialism in 1906 to protect African land interests from land alienation so as to promote smallholder farmers in cotton and coffee growing, 'waste and uncultivated land' was allocated as Crown land that was either leased or sold to incoming non-Africans. Within this context, what are the implications on Metha's demands of 7100 ha of Mabira Forest and Madhvani's demand of 40,000 ha of land in Amuru? The 40,000 ha demanded right now could be 100,000 ha in 50 years or more to come since there is no intention of establishing a policy cap. Because capitalism is very mercurial in sourcing for additional wealth, the peasantry economy becomes the target for the expanding capitalism. Historically, both Metha and Madhvani initially started with 8722.47 acres and 7681.34 acres, respectively. However, as discussed earlier, they illicitly managed to amass more land by purchasing freehold land from other non-Africans, leasing untenanted Crown land directly from the Protectorate Government, acquiring *mailo* land indirectly from landowners, exchanging freehold land for *mailo* land, and entering into exploitative yearly agreements with the African landowners. This could be the possibility in Lakang, the 40,000 ha is just the initial demand; the people of Amuru must be expecting more dispossession in the coming years. Moreover, the lands in question are being given at zero-sum cost by the government.

In addition, the idea of open resource (land) is an obsolete proposition. Large-scale plantation does not really need massive displacement and dispossession. Both Metha and Madhvani started on a small scale but got additional land as opposed to the orthodoxy thinking that investment needs huge tract of land. When land becomes politically unacceptable, out-grower scheme was induced as the only viable option. While Madhvani was located low-density populated area in Busoga, Metha was located in a highly populated and politically active region of Buganda. Metha was located in a high population density and politically active region of Buganda.

Whenever British colonialism tried to control massive land alienating from indigenous local population, the Metha and Madhvani Sugar Companies had to demonstrate that they were economically productive enterprises before being given additional acres, both to the traditional institutions – the *Lukiiko* – and the British authorities. While the colonial government's official position was that land should not be alienated to non-Africans, in practice the colonial government had considerations for the sugarcane companies to amassed land. The historical policy contractions is similar the current government position that land belongs to citizens, but in practice supports land alienation of local population in the name of promoting development. The constitution of Uganda (1995) article 237 and the Land Act 1998 specify that land belongs to the citizens and shall vest in accordance with the land tenure systems: customary, freehold, *mailo*, and freehold. By recognizing customary tenure, people in Northern Uganda could hold and utilize in a customary form without government dictating what they should do with their land. This causes us to question neoliberal thinking that the land is not currently being utilized; yet the question of marginal land is not applicable in Northern Uganda since the constitution recognizes it. Unfortunately, the state has always not been the protector of proletariat's cause.

The intention of government through Amuru district to allocate 40,000 of communal land to the Madhvani Group for sugar industry without prior, free, and informed consent and consultation, and compensation constitutes accumulation by dispossession. As noted above, land in Lakang, Amuru district, belongs to the communities. The gist of the matter is that the District Land Board owns no land, but can only confirm transfer of ownership from the community to the company only when the company and the community had reached an agreement to transact on the principle of willing buyer and willing seller. Despite the resistance from the peasants, the state is determined to make sure the project succeeds. In the name of development, violence is being sponsored through its sister institutions such as the Uganda Wild Life Authority, the military, the police, and Resident District Commission to dispossess peasants from their land.

The common narratives from both the company and the government that the project will create more than 7000–8000 employment opportunities to local population, accommodate 7000 out-growers, and the company will supply farm inputs to clear, plough, arrow, and furrow the land, as well as distribute 'treated cane seeds' and give technical advice are just mere promises that replicate the model similar to KSW in Busoga region (Madhvani, 2012). However, the group's Sugar Works at Kakira is yet to develop its modest conditions for work environment as the company had witnessed worker's strikes in the recent years. In fact, increasing population is not taken into consideration nor those already employed in the agricultural sector. The majority of peasants depend on environmental services and many may not be employed by the investors. The implementation of sugar project could displace around 20,000 peasants, either from displacement and dispossession, denying the peasants their production labor power. It is unfair now to judge the outcome of the project without impact assessment analysis on the socioeconomic benefits. As mentioned earlier, the case of Amuru is a state-sponsored dispossession; the land in question is being guarded by the military, the police, and Uganda Wildlife Authority. Educational centers are being used to house security personnel instead of being used for education. The civil war caused displacement and deaths, as well as low population density. It became very easy for the government through the inefficient and corrupt Amuru District Land Board to fraudulently allocate 10,000 ha to the Madhvani Group. During the court proceedings, the judge based his ruling on the principle of terra nullius, that the land given was vacant, not considering the deployment of military that guard these areas. The concept terra nullius has been used to justify communal/customary systems as 'empty,' 'idle,' and/or 'unutilized.'

8. Conclusions

The study has also shown that colonial government could support accumulation by dispossession to those with access to power by introducing the landed class in terms of *mailo* and *native freeholds* owners. This heralded the process of primitive accumulation as peasants became the target for rent extraction as they were converted into tenants and were demanded to pay rents for land usage. The *mailo* and freehold ownerships were created to accommodate the interests of the ruling elites and maintain the loyalty to the British colonial authorities. For the colonial authorities, the Buganda Agreement of 1900 provided a detailed land settlement whereby uncultivated land was vested in the Crown land and the remainder were divided into private and official estates. Through the Crown land, the accumulation to non-African was done through leasing to institutions such as the churches, plantations, and private individuals. The non-Africans were able to apply for lease on Crown land which was under the colonial government, while other accumulated through directly buying from private owners such as *mailo* owners and defunct white farmers.

This article reviewed the historical economic cases of capital accumulation by Asian investors of Indian origin in Uganda. The Asian capitalism in the country arose from the failure of settler class and peasantry classes. The Metha and Madhvani Groups then embarked on acquisitions of more land despite the existence of unfavorable policy environment to foreigners of non-colonial root in Uganda. In general, both Metha and Madhvani incrementally acquired land through (1) purchasing freehold land from other non-Africans, (2) leasing untenanted Crown land directly from the British authority, (3) acquiring *mailo* land indirectly from African landowners, a practice where *mailo* land was surrendered as Crown land, and when Governor's consent, the land was regranted leasehold Crown land, (4) exchanging freehold for *mailo* land with the consent of colonial government and Buganda authority, and (5) entering into yearly agreements with African landowners.

This study also suggests that one of the alternatives to land grabbing is the introduction of out-grower scheme. This is the approach used by the colonial government to avoid land alienation from the local indigenous population, a discourse that is rarely considered by foreign investors and host governments in Africa. This model was successfully in Uganda during the earlier 1940s and has managed to survive up to today. The colonial government used to approve additional land subject to accommodation of the interests of out-growers. In KSW, for example, 70% of the cane supply comes from the out-grower scheme.

The presence of relatively balanced power relations could be very helpful in countries experiencing land grab to reduce massive displacement and dispossession. The Metha and Madhvani cases reviewed in Uganda showed that while the colonial policy was encouraging investments in farmlands from both local indigenous population and foreign companies, a maximum cap of 10,000 ha was institutionalized to regulate land acquisitions by foreign investors, although the Metha Group and the Madhvani Group, beyond the national legal requirements, circumvented the national laws to acquire more than 10,000 ha of land for sugarcane production. However, the application of the limitation on acquisitions by foreign investors has not received adequate attention within the land grab discourses. When the policy was introduced in 1906 by the British colonial authorities, putting a maximum of 10,000 ha for foreign investors, both Metha and Madhvani Group of companies have managed to acquire only 15,000 ha and 22,000 ha, respectively.

The presence of land policies protecting African interests, promoting smallholder farmers besides the existence of foreign companies, may not guarantee the protection of land rights. As observed in the cases from Uganda, states are always driven by the need to derive more rents from the land under their domains, regardless of the tenure types, by shifting policy in favor of productive owners since it is cognizant with the interests of accumulation and rent extraction. Therefore, the recognition of land right – whether *mailo*, customary, or freehold – may not guarantee the future of land security.

The new enclosure policies in Uganda are manifested through violence expulsion of peasants, conversion of property rights, and the suppression of communal property rights to support private accumulation process, as seen in the demand for 40,000 ha of communal land in Amuru to the Madhvani Group and 7100 ha of Mabira Forest to the Metha Group. For the case of Amuru, the military is used to scare the local population, given the timing of the investment project after a two decades of wars and displacement people from their ancestral places.

As shown, customary land rights is only a political strategy being used by the ruling elites to mobilize short-term tenure security, but such recognition does not guarantee long-term security both in the current form and in the future since changes in development will be targeting communal land. Commonly shared in the strategies to dispossess land by both companies is the use of state institutions to free land at zero-sum cost of communal land through leases, yet historically Madhvani first acquired land through freehold and leasing from the white farmers and then resorted to acquire more by gaining minimum concession from the colonial government. It takes long for those in a particular political geography to realize how much their land has been alienated until the alienation becomes politically unviable. When such land alienation becomes politically unsustainable, companies polished their image by adopting out-grower schemes as evidenced in the case of Metha and Madhavani, an issue often ignored by host governments and land-grabbers in Africa because of perception that land in Africa is abundant. The presence of unused land makes it very easy for companies to enter into a concession, but may not be the same all the time. The popular codes of conduct proposed by the international development agencies such as the World Bank are not useful in preventing the ongoing process of primitive accumulation. The emphasis on transparency, good governance, consultation, and participation featured well in democratic society, but capitalism and democracy are not compatible in weak governance.

Notes

1. His Majesty's Government, Memorandum on Native Policy in East Africa, cmd, 3573, presented by the Secretary of State for the colonies to Parliament by Command of His Majesty, June, 1930 (London: His Majesty's Stationery Office).
2. Uganda Protectorate, The Uganda Gazette, Vol. XLIII, No. 30, 11 July 1950 (Entebbe: Government Printer).
3. www.mehtagroup.com/index.html (accessed 4 December 2012).
4. Uganda Protectorate, Secretariat Minute Paper No. 11774, Minute 160, Confidential Memorandum, 4 November 1940.
5. http://www.kakirasugar.com/content/agriculture (accessed 4 December 2012).
6. http://www.ugandaradionetwork.com/a/story.php?s=17147 (accessed on 30 December 2012).

Notes on contributor

D.R. Olanya is a researcher and lectures at the Department of Public Administration and Management, Gulu University, Uganda. His research interests currently focus on the politics of agrarian transformation and resource governance, globalization, and sustainability politics.

References

Ahluwalia, D. P. S. (1995). *Politics of sugar in Uganda*. Kampala: Fountain.

Akena, P. (2010). *Amuru Sugar Works investment by Madhvani Group*. Response 2: Stakeholder Briefing KKA/01/04/001.

Amanor, K. J. (2010). Family values, land sales and agricultural commoditization in South-Eastern Ghana. *Africa, 80*(1), 104–121.

Amin, S. (1972). *Neocolonialism in West Africa*. Harmondsworth: Penguin.

Amin, S. (1974). *Accumulation on a world scale: A critique of the theory of underdevelopment*. New York: Monthly Review Press.

Becker, R., & Madhvani, N. J. (Eds.). (1973). *Yayant Madhvani*. London: Muljibhai Madhvani.

Carswell, G. (2007). *Cultivating success in Uganda: Kigezi farmers and colonial policies*. London: The British Institute in Eastern Africa.

Chanok, M. (1991). Paradigms, policies and property: A review of the customary law of land tenure. In Kristin Mann & Richard Roberts (Eds.), *Law in Colonial Africa* (pp. 61–84). Portsmouth, NH: Heinemann Educational Books.

Chimhowu, A., & Woodhouse, P. (2006). *Officially forbidden but not suppressed: Vernacular land markets on communal lands in Zimbabwe. A case study of Svosve communal land in Zimbabwe*. Manchester: Institute for Development Policy and Management.

Colson, E. (1971). The impact of the colonial period on the definition of right. In Victor Turner (Ed.), *The Impact of Colonialism* (pp. 193–215). Cambridge: Cambridge University Press.

de Angelis, M. (1999). *Marx's theory of primitive accumulation: A suggested reinterpretation*. London: University of East London.

Dobb, M. (1963). *Studies in the development of capitalism*. London: Routledge.

Friend of the Earth Uganda/National Association of Professional Environmentalists. (2012). Land, life and justice: How land grabbing in Uganda is affecting the environment, livelihoods and food sovereignty of communities.

GRAIN. (2012). Land deals. Retrieved January 25, 2013, from http://www.grain.org/article/entries/4479-grain-releases-data-set-with-over-400-global-land-grabs

Harvey, D. (2003). *The new imperialism*. Oxford: Oxford University Press.

International Bank for Reconstruction and Development. (1962). *The economic development of Uganda*. Baltimore, MD: John Hopkins Press.

Juma, A. O. (2006). The Land Act (1998) and Land Tenure Reform in Uganda. *African Development, XXXI*(I), 1–26.

Kouame, G. (2009). Infrafamily and socio-political dimension of land markets and land conflicts: The case of Abure. Cote D'Ivore. *Africa, 80*(1), 126–132.

Lenin, V. I. (1899/1960). The development of capitalism in Russia. In *Collected Works* (Vol. 3. London: Lawrence and Wishartt.

Lentz, C. (2006). *Is land inalienable? Historical and current debates on land transfers in Northern Ghana*. Colloque International 'Les Frontieres dela Question fronciere – At the Frontier of Land Issues', Montpellier, pp. 1–8.

Luxemburg, R. (1913/1963). *The accumulation of capital*. London: Routledge.

Madhvani, M. (2012, February). Amuru sugar project will bring development to northern Uganda. *The Monitor*, Thursday. Retrieved January 12, 2013, from http://www.mobile.monitor.co.ug/Oped/-/691272/1322852/-/format/xhtml/-/5dl0mtz/-/index.html

Marx, K. (1858/1974). *Grundrisse*. New York: Penguin.

MLHUD. (2007a). *Drafting the national land policy*. Working Draft 3 Kampala: MLHUD.

MLHUD. (2007b). *The national land use policy*. Kampala: MLHUD.

MLHUD. (2011). *The Uganda national land policy*. Final Draft March 2011, Kampala, Uganda.

Mugambwa, J. T. (2002). *Source book of Uganda's land law*. Kampala: Fountain.

Mzumara, D. (2003). *Land tenure systems and sustainable development in Southern Africa*. ECA/SA/EGM/Land/2003/2 Economic Commission for Africa, Southern Africa Office, Lusaka, Zambia.

Nature Uganda. (n.d.). Say no to Mabira give away. Retrieved December 20, 2012, from http://www.natureuganda.org/save_mabira_campaign.php

Nkioki, A. (2006). *Land policies in Sub-Saharan Africa*. Nairobi: Center for Land, Economy and Rights of Women.

Ofcansky, T. M. (1996). *Uganda: Tarnished pearl of Africa*. Boulder, CO: Westview Press.

Olanya, D. R. (2012a, July). Our common future and climatic change policy: Whose security? OIDA International Journal of Sustainable Development, *4*, 109–124.

Olanya, D. R. (2012b). *From global land grabbing for bio-fuels expansion to acquisitions of African water for commercial agriculture.* Current African Issues No. 50 Uppsala: Nordic African Institute.

Rugadya, M., & Kamusiime, H. (2010). *Property rights assessment in Amuru district: Supporting seasonal migration of wildlife between Murchison Falls National Park and East Madi Game Reserve/Zoka Forest.* Kampala: Wild Programme Wildlife Conservation Society Uganda.

World Rainforest Movement. (2007, May). *Uganda: Fighting for the Mabira Forest and final success.* Bulletin 118. Retrieved November 30, 2012, from, http://www.wrm.org.uy

Land grab in new garb: Chinese special economic zones in Africa
The case of Mauritius

Honita Cowaloosur

International Relations Department, University of St Andrews, Fife, UK

At the 2006 Forum on China–Africa Cooperation, President Hu Jintao announced the establishment of Chinese Special Economic Zones in Africa (CSEZAs) in the spirit of mutual development and cooperation. The Chinese government launched seven such projects across Nigeria, Ethiopia, Egypt, Zambia and Mauritius. In most of these countries, there was social outcry over land expropriation for the construction of the CSEZAs and the resultant displacement of existing settlers. Seven years since their launch, the delayed CSEZA development only exacerbate the frustration of the host African communities as they contemplate whether the land they appropriated for the zone, at the expense of rural livelihoods, is getting an appropriate usage. The case of Mauritius is particularly salient considering its size, location and outward economic dependence.

Introduction

In May 2012, the United Nations Committee on World Food Security established a policy framework in order to regulate instances of land-based investment which entail the displacement of local communities. This demarche aims to address the malpractices that developing countries engage in when putting local land at the disposition of foreign investors. These deliberations followed from a report of the Food and Agricultural Organisation (FAO; Lorenzo, Vermulen, Leonard, & Keeley, 2009) which investigated large-scale land appropriation by foreign investors in Africa, Latin America, Central Asia and Southeast Asia. Following this, several studies were conducted on land deals, with the majority focusing on Africa and examining one-off investment projects by foreign governments and private companies in either agriculture or biofuels (see, e.g. Kugelman & Levenstein, 2009).[1] However, the advent of Chinese Special Economic Zones in Africa (CSEZAs) altered the exclusivity of African land grab through singular agro-investment projects. Based on China's own Special Economic Zone (SEZ) model, CSEZAs have been transposed into five African countries. Based on fieldwork carried out in China and Mauritius, this paper discusses how CSEZAs – which were initially launched as diplomatic development initiatives – get eclipsed by the land expropriation they entail. The first sections of this paper investigate the proliferation of this problem in the patron country itself, and in India, which has also adopted this experiment. The second section outlines the involvement of the Chinese government in the CSEZAs and contemplates the extent to which land appropriation through CSEZAs can be equated to Chinese state land grab in Africa. As data from the seven CSEZAs increasingly support this hypothesis, the presentation of the Mauritian case defines the symbiotic role the African state plays in this exploitative game. After an evaluation of the impact of the CSEZA-initiated land grab on Mauritius, this paper concludes on a note that resonates with Gopalakrishnan's observation that SEZs' only purpose is spatial presence. CSEZAs seem to head down the same path.

SEZs and land acquisition

The SEZ is China's interpretation of earlier forms of territorially bounded economic practices such as custom-bonded warehouses, free trade zones (FTZs) and export processing zones (EPZs), which function on similar preferential fiscal treatments. In the 1970s, Deng Xiaoping resorted to SEZs because China needed capital in order to fund its Four Modernization programme, and only foreign direct investment (FDI) could bring in that money.[2] But inevitably, an inflow of FDI could only be secured if a competitive market-based economic base was established. So, in an attempt to reconcile China's needs and its reservations, Xiaoping opted for the construction of zones to contain these FDI in profit-conducive, yet restricted, fiscal environments. Since then, the SEZ model has proliferated across China. Today, China counts 330 SEZs which are divided into seven types, i.e. Economic and Technological Development Zones, High-Tech Industrial Development Zones, FTZs, Border Economic Zones, EPZs, Provincial Development Zones and others. However, these zones come at a cost.

On 6 August 2011, *Caixin* newspaper reported that local county officers had illegally requisitioned 267 hectares to make space for real estate development in Hebei (Shen & Yishi, 2011). Farmers who occupied the land were threatened and their crops were destroyed when they resisted. Three months later, on 24 November 2011, *South China Morning Post* wrote about riots in Lufeng city (Guangdong province) over the acquisition of 323.7 hectares of land by the local government in order to build an industrial park and residential areas (Chi-yuk & Pinghui, 2011). A total of 12,000 resident farmers claimed to have been poorly compensated. These two cases are only glimpses of the innumerable similar occurrences, which generally prelude the construction of SEZs in China. A Chinese civilian-led voluntary project called 'The Blood Stained Housing Map' which uses *Google Maps* to locate tragic land and property grab in China enlists such macabre cases. This initiative was publicised by *The Wall Street Journal*'s *China Real Time Report* on 29 October 2010 (Chin, 2010). Cognisant of exploitative activities carried out in the light of SEZs, Gopalakrishnan (2007) remarks that land tenure of farmers situated near SEZs are threatened as the Chinese government favours large-scale development projects. He refers to figures from Huang and Yang:

> ... between January 1992 and July 1993, rights over 1,27,000 hectares of land were granted to real estate developers across China but only 46.5 per cent of this land to developers was actually developed. (Huang and Yang as quoted in Gopalakrishnan, 2007, p. 1493)

This is not to say that the Chinese constitution is devoid of legal provisions regulating land acquisition.

Until 2002, only the Land Administration Law addressed grievances regarding SEZs in China. While Article 2 of the Land Administration Law accounted for the authority of the state to requisition land owned by collectives in order to serve national interest, Article 31 transfers the onus of pursuing the compensation upon the evacuated farmers. Nonetheless, Article 37 of the same accommodates prospects of having the requisitioned arable land to be reconverted to arable land if construction of the scheduled project fails to start within two years. In 2002, China introduced the Land Contract in Rural Areas Law, which seeks to safeguard the hold of farmers on the land they have been contracted for cultivation through the collective. Its Article 16 (2) commits to providing adequate compensation to the displaced farmers. The latest relevant legal development came in the form of the 2004 Amendment to the Land Administration Law whereby issues pertaining to the conversion of requisitioned agricultural land into construction land were comprehensively addressed under Chapter 6. Under this amendment, People's Republic of China (PRC) displayed more consideration for compensation towards the displaced farmers; nevertheless, the power of the state to requisition land at its will reigned supreme. Therefore, with power vested in the state's ability to retrieve land deemed essential for national development, and a growing fondness for SEZs, land acquisition at the expense of rural livelihoods only proliferates. This mass requisition of land for SEZs has also affected Chinese national food security. In an article by *China Daily (2012)*, it is informed that according to the Ministry of Land and Resources, PRC, China needs to maintain at least 120 million hectares of agricultural land. However, in 2009, the total expanse of land under cultivation had already fallen to 121.7 million hectares. Thus, while the patron nation of SEZs itself experiences inflictions of land grab through SEZs, little respite can be expected for those countries who adopt the model.

Introduced as a spatial economic initiative in 2000 and framed within the relevant legislations in 2005, there are currently 158 operational SEZs in India (Indian Ministry of Commerce and Industry, 2006). The government has approved 588 more. Indian SEZs can be developed by the government (central or state), private sector or by both, under a joint venture. Instances whereby farmers have struggled against land acquisition for SEZs abound across India. Raigad farmers' protest against SEZ land acquisition by Reliance Industries since 2006 and the Barnala farmers' protest against Trident SEZ in Punjab are only two examples. However, the worst case was that of the protest against the 2007 Nandigram SEZ project in West Bengal, which threatened the livelihood of 30 villages. Villagers were killed and numerous women were raped during the protest.

If we contemplate the legal provisions framing SEZ land acquisition in India, there are obvious lacunas and these nurture unwarranted land grab through SEZs. First, the responsibility to acquire the land for the SEZ is the developer's. Left to their own resources, developers are free to resort to ill means to acquire the land. Second, the Land Acquisition Act 1894 does not take land acquisition for the purpose of SEZs under its purview. Consequently, SEZ land acquisition is not legally bound to provide for adequate compensation, resettlement and rehabilitation to those evacuated. Abuses due to these loopholes pushed the government to review the legislation in 2012. The *Outlook India* (2009) issue of October summarised the draft bill submitted at the Parliament. The bill proposed to make it compulsory for private project developers to receive 80% landowners' consent, and for public–private partnership projects to receive 70% landowners' consent before they can appropriate all land at the SEZ site. It was also suggested that the compensation for displaced farmers be raised. Other anomalies which the Indian government rectified in 2007 were: (1) the introduction of a cap of 5000 hectares to which all SEZs have to adhere and (2) that developers have to ensure that at least 50% of the zone activities should be production. The latter provision was inserted to prevent developers from conducting real estate businesses under the guise of SEZs (Dohrmann, 2008, p. 76).

Despite the emerging political consciousness and new demarches to curb exploitative SEZ land grab in India, the preferential treatment received by Reliance SEZs only reinforce the belief that SEZs are less of a development carrier and more of an excuse for land grab. Starting 2006, Reliance Industries was granted one year – as per rules of the

SEZ Act 2005 – to acquire land for its SEZ in Mumbai. Although legally developers are allowed only one extension (in case the land has not been acquired within the first year), on 15 September 2009, *The Economic Times (2009)* revealed that Reliance has benefited from three extensions. Moreover, on 6 January 2013, *Daily News and Analysis* shed light on negotiations regarding the permission to Reliance's Navi Mumbai SEZ to develop housing and commercial properties over 50–60% of its SEZ territory (Suryavanshi, 2013).[3] As per rules, housing and commercial properties are restricted to 40% of SEZ activities only. Increasingly, it appears that Gopalakrishnan (2011, p. 148) was right when he said that the SEZ is purely a political concept whose true purpose is the 'creation of space rather than any particular activity'.

While China has a legal framework to address SEZ-related land-grab activities, with a priority given to the state's developmental needs at the expense of (albeit compensated) affected rural farmers, India constantly postpones comprehensive regulation of SEZ land-grab activities and even bends existing laws to favour SEZ land acquisition. The Chinese and Indian experiences demonstrate that regardless of the degree of legal framing that SEZ land acquisition processes have, given that land is the key ingredient for this developmental business form, SEZs inevitably equate to condemnable land acquisition activities. If land grab by China within China and by Indian government and private companies within India can derail to such extents, we can only imagine the plight land grab through Chinese SEZs will inflict on host African communities.

Chinese special economic zones in Africa

President Hu Jintao's speech at Forum on China–African Cooperation (FOCAC) 2006 was replete with allusions to mutuality and cooperation between Africa and China. One of the Chinese commitments to the continent was to set up 'three to five trade and economic cooperation zones in Africa in the next three years' (Jintao, 2006). As these are based on China's own SEZ model, they are referred to as the Chinese SEZs in Africa. The seven CSEZAs are:

(1) Nigeria: Lekki Free Trade Zone (LFTZ) and Ogun Guangdong Free Trade Zone (OGFTZ).
(2) Ethiopia: Eastern Industry Zone (EIZ).
(3) Egypt: Egypt TEDA (Tianjin Economic-Technological Development Area) SEZ.
(4) Zambia: Zambia–China Economic and Trade Cooperation Zone (ZCCZ) and Lusaka Multi-Facility Economic Zone (LMFEZ).
(5) Mauritius: JinFei Trade and Economic Cooperation Zone Co Ltd (JFET).

Although they are the Chinese government's commitment to its African counterparts, CSEZAs are implemented through Chinese companies who pass the tender rounds carried out by Ministry of Commerce (MOFCOM), PRC – regardless of whether they are private enterprises or State-Owned Enterprises (SOEs).[4] Nevertheless, the Chinese government retains direct activism in these CSEZAs through the fiscal support it provides. Brautigam and Xiaoyang (2011, pp. 82–83) list the benefits received by the CSEZA developers:

(1) Upto USD 44 million grant from MOFCOM.
(2) Upto USD 294 million long-term loans from MOFCOM.
(3) A total of 30% subsidies on the cost of feasibility studies, travelling, market studies, initial land rent from the Trade and Economic Cooperation Zone Fund of MOFCOM.

The Chinese government also supports the Chinese companies, which settle within these CSEZAs. They are granted:

(1) Reimbursement of half of their moving expenses.
(2) Export and import tax rebates on materials sent for construction.
(3) Ease of access to foreign exchange.
(4) Eligibility to apply to MOFCOM's Special Fund for Economic and Technological Cooperation, which grants a rebate of up to 100% on interest paid on Chinese bank loans for five years.

Brautigam and Xiaoyang (2011, pp. 82–83) also mention funding from provincial governments, such as Jiangsu province's and Suzhou municipality's to the EIZ. China–Africa Development Fund (CADFund) and the Export–Import Bank of China (EXIM) too, respectively, extend partnership opportunities and loans to CSEZAs. Currently, CADFund supports LFTZ and Egypt TEDA SEZs, while EXIM Bank has granted a concessional loan of USD 208 million to ZCCZ in order to finance the construction of its mining plant.

Two observations can be made from the above exposé:

(1) Regardless of whether the CSEZA developing companies are private or state-owned, Chinese government retains the reigns of the CSEZAs through its authority to select the developer, provide the funds and also because CSEZAs are essentially bilateral state ventures between China and the African countries. Therefore, it is imperative that the Chinese government closely monitors the unfolding of these zones.
(2) China contributes to the CSEZAs in the form of 'capital'. Though China's history of successful SEZs should posit its 'SEZ experience' as the main input in CSEZAs, it is more appropriate to exclude the 'expertise' element from this account because an investigation of the background of the companies entrusted the responsibility of developing these CSEZAs reveal that most of them have no previous experience in SEZ management. Only TEDA of Egypt TEDA SEZ and Nanjing Jiangning Economic and Technological Development Corporation of LFTZ have prior SEZ experience.[5]

Therefore, while China's input in the CSEZAs is money, it is its lands that Africa put at the disposition of the developers – with the aim to create the developmental synergy sought at FOCAC 2006.[6] Table 1 holds details of the relevant land aspects each of the CSEZAs.

Regardless of their unequal stage of advancement, all the CSEZAs (except for ZCCZ which is situated on land which can have no purpose other than for mining) face land-related difficulties. As the website of the Social and Economic Rights Action Center, Lekki, writes, LFTZ is the result of the uncompensated displacement of 26 rural communities from their ancestral land and source of living (Social and Economic Rights Action Center n.d.). OGFTZ implicated forced acquisition of the land of settlers who were not granted full compensation (Ogun State Government n.d.). EIZ is based upon two occurrences of land abuse – first, in its displacement of hundreds of farmers occupying the site and, second, in the acquisition of an additional 320 hectares near Addis Ababa by Hujian who wants to expand its already functional production plant situated within the EIZ (Ethio News 24, n.d.). Interviews with Egyptian diplomats reveal that as it plans Phase 2, Egypt TEDA – strategically located by the Suez Canal – wants ownership of the SEZ land instead of renting it (Commercial Secretaries, 2011). Moreover, the developer has

Table 1. Details of the land aspects of the CSEZAs.

CSEZA	Land size	Lease period	Location	Status	Land-related issues
LFTZ, Nigeria	16,500 hectares excluding seaport and airport area[a]	99 years	Access to Atlantic Ocean and Gulf of Guinea	Started in 2004 Phase 1 under construction	(1) Displaced settlers and farmers[b] (2) Greater portion of residential spaces (3) Toll-road on Lekki/Epe Axis to reach LFTZ
OGFTZ, Nigeria	10,000 hectares	99 years	Near Ikeja and Appa airport	Started in 2004 Phase 1 under construction	(1) Displaced farmers
EIZ, Ethiopia	500 hectares	N/A	35 km from Addis Ababa, Oromia	Started in 2006 Phase 1 under construction	(1) Zone rumoured to have a 1000 hectares extra land reservation (2) Displaced farmers (3) Overspilling[c]
Egypt TEDA SEZ, Egypt	703.2 hectares Within the 2000 hectares North West Suez SEZ	N/A	North West Suez SEZ, near South entrance of Suez canal, Sokhna port	Started in 1998 and then in 2009 Phase 1 completed Operational	New demands for Phase 2: (1) Land ownership rather than rental. (2) Residential development
ZCCZ, Zambia	1158 hectares within the 4100 hectares owned by non-ferrous company, Africa	99 years	Copperbelt	Started in 2003 Operational	N/A
LMFEZ, Zambia	570 hectares	79 years	Near Kenneth Kaunda International Airport	Started as a sub-zone to ZCCZ Off-site infrastructure under construction	N/A
JFET, Mauritius	211 hectares	99 years	Near harbour and Port Louis	Started in 2006 Phase 1 yet to start	(1) Displaced farmers (2) Seeking to develop real estate (3) Overspilling[d]

Note: CSEZA, Chinese Special Economic Zones in Africa; LFTZ, Lekki Free Trade Zone; OGFTZ, Ogun Guangdong Free Trade Zone; EIZ, Eastern Industry Zone; TEDA, Tianjin Economic-Technological Development Area; SEZ, Special Economic Zone; ZCCZ, Zambia–China Economic and Trade Cooperation Zone; LMFEZ, Lusaka Multi-Facility Economic Zone; JFET, JinFei Trade and Economic Cooperation Zone Co Ltd.

[a] The agreement between Nigeria and China was renegotiated, leaving only 3000 hectares for SEZ development to the Chinese consortium. The rest was to be opened for development by other foreign developers.

[b] Settlers and farmers were displaced from the site prior to the setting up of LFTZ. They present the following grievances: (1) dispossession of their ancestral land and jeopardise their means of livelihood; (2) unconvinced that the land being taken purportedly for the project is not in excess of what it is meant for; (3) not compensated for past land acquisition; and (4) land acquired is being resold by agents to individuals for private use.

[c] Hujian, a Chinese footwear company, who already owns a production plant within the zone, has acquired land outside the zone to expand its production.

[d] JFET set up a subsidiary company named JFET Travel & Tours which functions outside the zone.

expressed interest in constructing residential spaces within the SEZ. ZCCZ, as such, does not entail obvious land-abuse issues – except for the fact that years after having launched its sub-zone, i.e. LMFEZ, the plot remains underdeveloped still. And last, JFET was set up after farmers were displaced and the SEZ blueprint now emphasises real estate development. Thus, as the CSEZAs drag their feet in delivering the development they promised to Africa (in the form of job creation, infrastructural upgrade, export income, backward technological linkages and transferring of skills and know-how), the land acquisition aspect of these ventures only magnifies contempt towards these new development models of China. However, of all the seven cases, JFET is particularly interesting and salient given the macrocosmic economic, political and geographic context within which the CSEZ is located.

Mauritius JinFei Economic and Trade Cooperation Zone Co Ltd

Figure 1 designates the locations that will be discussed in the Mauritian case study.

At the behest of Tianli Spinning (Mauritius) Co. Ltd, a Chinese company based in Mauritius, Mauritian Prime Minister, Ramgoolam, pursued negotiations with the Chinese government for one of the Chinese SEZs in Africa at FOCAC 2006. China relented and the Mauritius Tianli Economic Trade and Cooperation Zone Ltd was set up, with Tianli Group as its patron investor.[7] The location finalised for the zone was Riche Terre. Riche Terre is located at 5 km from the harbour and the capital city, Port-Louis, and the site borders the Baie-du-Tombeau coast. However, at the time the developers made their choice, i.e. October 2006, the 211 hectares sought for the SEZ at Riche Terre was occupied by two groups of farmers:

(1) The Terre Rouge Land Settlement, which covered 160 hectares and comprised of 106 sugarcane planters – of which, 20 members had residential leases. The lease agreement dated back to 1947 and was scheduled to terminate on 30 June 2007.

(2) The Riche Terre Land Settlement, which covered 51 hectares and was occupied by

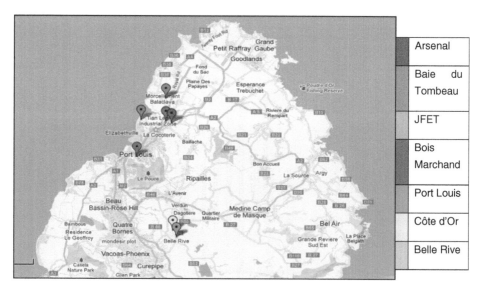

Figure 1. Partial map of Mauritius locating the places discussed in this work.
Source: *Google Maps* edited.

121 vegetable planters. This lease was signed between the individual farmers of the Riche Terre Cooperative Society and the Ministry of Agro-Industry, Fisheries and Natural Resources on 31 July 1985. The plots became available for cultivation only in 1990 and the lease was scheduled to end in September 2015.

Given that the lease period was nearing its end, land under Terre Rouge Land Settlement was easier to reclaim. The 106 sugarcane planters were granted a cash compensation of MUR 509,433 for each one arpent.[8] The 20 residential leases were regularised and the remaining 86 planters were promised to be each relocated upon 10 perches at Côte d'Or so that they could resume their cultivation.

In a strange evolution of events, surveys regarding the displacement of the Riche Terre and Terre Rouge planters started before the 4–6 November 2006 FOCAC meeting, i.e. before the SEZ project was agreed upon by China. On 31 October 2006, a committee consisting of the Chief Government Valuer, the Agricultural Research and Extension Unit (AREU), the Irrigation Authority (IA) and Board of Investment (BOI) was formed by the Mauritian government in order to identify the activities of the planters and to calculate the compensation to be paid to them. Studies reported that only 51 of the 121 Riche Terre planters were regular cultivators. Furthermore, it was concluded that crop-loss compensation would be unnecessary since the planters will be given time to harvest their crops before the displacement. Accordingly, the compensation calculated for the Riche Terre planters was MUR 100,000 per arpent. This calculation was computed keeping the following in mind (Noël & Ramkissoon, 2010):

(1) No compensation for fencing since planters had not applied to Land Use Division, Ministry of Agro Industry and Food Security (MAIFS), for permission to put it up initially.
(2) It is agricultural land.
(3) No compensation for crop loss as planters will be allowed to harvest before displacement.
(4) No compensation for irrigation network as that is provided by the government.
(5) Full market rent of agricultural lands in Mauritius is estimated to be MUR 12,000 per arpent per annum. The rent paid by the Riche Terre lessee is MUR 120 per arpent per annum. Therefore, the profit rent is MUR 11,880. Application of an estimated 4% per annum for capitalisation rate of profit.
(6) Other relocation losses estimated at MUR 8000 per arpent.

The equation resembled the following:

Full market rent p.a.	= MUR 12,000
Less passing rent	= MUR 120
Profit rent	MUR 11,880
Years purchase nine years at 4%	= × 7.73
	MUR 91,832
Other losses	MUR 8000
	MUR 99,832
Rounded to	MUR 100,000

Two and a half weeks after these evaluations, on 15 December 2006, the Riche Terre planters were notified that as from the following year, i.e. 1 July 2007, the rental fee for their plots at Riche Terre would increase from MUR 165 to MUR 4500. This was followed by another letter received on 7 February 2007, informing the planters that instead of MUR 4500, they will be paying MUR 2000 as rental fee from 1 July 2007. Eventually, on 6 March 2007, MAIFS asked the Riche Terre planters to vacate the land by 30 April 2007. Following the vacation orders, the President of the Riche Terre Mixed Farming Cooperative Society wrote to the MAIFS to confirm that the planters will leave the land by the date and that no new cultivation would take place. However, he requested for time until 30 June 2007 to allow the planters to harvest their crops. The Ministry conceded to the request. Nevertheless, a week before the evacuation deadline, a bulldozer started working the land at Riche Terre. In protest against this act, some of the Riche Terre planters did not leave the land by 30 April 2007. Five days afterwards, IA damaged and removed the water pump at the Riche Terre site. Prime Minister Ramgoolam thereafter met the 121 planters and promised to increase the compensation from MUR 100,000 per arpent to MUR 120,000 per arpent. Additionally, he promised that the planters will be permitted to sell their vegetables in the Tianli zone once operational.

By July 2009, 58 planters, who were non-active, had collected their compensation of MUR 120,000 each; six cases remained unresolved due to death or uninterested planters; 34 of the active planters took MUR 120,000 plus one arpent at either Arsenal or Bois Marchand each; and the remaining 23 contested the compensation. They demanded a compensation amount which would account for elements overlooked by the government evaluation exercise (Mangar, 2010):

(1) Moral damage/loss of livelihood.
(2) Loss of investment in crops.
(3) Terre Rouge Land Settlement sugarcane planters received cash plus land ownership compensation for foregone revenue, while Riche Terre vegetable planters could have derived three harvests from their existent crops compared to one harvest from sugarcane plantation.

The total compensation they sought was a sum of the following items:

MUR 100,000 per arpent/planter × nine years	= MUR 900,000
Moral damages per planter	= MUR 500,000
10 perches for settlement per planter +	MUR 1.4 m

On 19 February 2010, the 23 Riche Terre planters started a 30-day-long hunger strike, requesting the government to reconsider their case. Government appointed Alain Noël and Jairaj Ramkissoon to form a Comité de Mediation in order to investigate the grounds for considering the case of the 23 planters. On 27 April 2010, the committee submitted its report and recommendations – which the government refused to release until in November 2010. The committee noted the following essential points (Noël & Ramkissoon, 2010):

(1) In comparison to relevant UK legislations, Mauritius lacks the regulatory framework to manage retrieval of leased lands and the appropriate assessment of compensation.

(2) Although 14 are genuine planters and 9 are not eligible for relocation, the report recommends that in the light of the problems encountered throughout this case, all 23 planters should receive similar compensation.

The committee proposed that the 23 planters be granted:

(1) Basic/displacement compensation of MUR 120,000 per arpent adjusted for accrued interest for the period 23–24 May 2007 to the end of June 2010.
(2) Either: (A) Relocation to Arsenal and Bois Marchand with a land lease starting from July 2010 to August 2018, with additional financial support of approximately MUR 120,000 from the Food Security Fund (FSF) for land preparation, and technical support from AREU.[9] FSF may also consider additional support for activities like waterlogging and access roads. Their loans from IA and the Central Electricity Board (CEB) be written off, while their loans from the Development Bank of Mauritius (DBM) rescheduled. Or: (B) Cash compensation in lieu of option A, computed for net revenue forgone from July 2007 to August 2015, estimated at MUR 35,650 per arpent per annum. The resultant amount is to be adjusted to MUR 276,760 per arpent, in line of present value.

By the end of June 2010, the government had still not released the report submitted by the Comité de Mediation. In the meantime, one of the 23 planters opted for land and cash compensation and abandoned the group, leaving 22 plaintiff planters.

On 7 November 2010, the 22 contesting planters staged a second hunger strike. After the latter refused to terminate the strike, the government established a ministerial committee to solve the problem. On the 17th day of the strike, government announced that it will reach a decision only after three days. Ministers still refused to bring out the report submitted by Ramkissoon and Noël. Eventually, on 26 November 2010 (19th day of the strike), a press conference was organised to officially communicate the final decision of the ministerial committee regarding the case of the 22 Riche Terre planters. The measures put forth were as follows:

(1) There is a distinction to be made between the 13 planters who were cultivating their plots at the time of AREU's survey and the nine planters who were not.
(2) Noel and Ramkissoon's recommendation for an equal treatment of the 22 planters will not be accepted.
(3) The 13 active planters will be offered: MUR 120,000 + accrued interest + MUR 276,760 as in option B of Noel and Ramkissoon's recommendations.
(4) Cabinet has approved to: write off their debts to CEB and IA, reschedule their DBM loans and extend AREU and FSF support.
(5) The remaining nine planters will receive: MUR 120,000 per arpent + accrued interest. However, if they want to pursue agricultural activities, they may request for land, which will be considered on a case-to-case basis.

The 22 planters decided that it was wise to take their cash compensation. Thus, the active planters of Riche Terre received *either* MUR 120,000 plus a relocation plot *or* MUR 396,760 with accrued interest of MUR 25,000, totalling to MUR 421,760.

Since, the displaced farmers underwent numerous problems. In an interview carried out in August 2012, the Riche Terre farmers who had opted for relocation at Bois Marchand and Arsenal revealed that their harvest was stolen. The fencing and facilities on their land had also been damaged.[10] Those active farmers who have not opted for relocation presently find themselves without a permanent source of income. Most of them have undertaken odd jobs as gardener, painter and other manual tasks. Moreover, contrary to what was promised to them, DBM had not suspended the loans they had taken for their agricultural activities. In February and June 2011, President of the Riche Terre Mixed Farming Cooperative Society wrote to DBM and to MAIFS requesting them to look into the matter – but to no avail. During an interview(Mooloo, Manager, Development Bank of Mauritius, September 4, 2012), the Manager at DBM declared that the loans of the displaced Riche Terre planters have not been written off because there has been no formal request from the government to do so. Therefore, the planters have had to repay their loans, leaving them with little or no money from the compensation amount. Also, most of the Terre Rouge Land Settlement farmers are yet to receive their 10 perches each at Côte d'Or. In the light of this unruly treatment, the Riche Terre planters are contemplating reviving their case vis-à-vis the state, and maybe even conducting a third hunger strike. They feel deceived by the government and, in the light of the now-accessible Ramkissoon and Noël report, they explain why the money they were given is not enough:

(1) Although the crops were harvested, plants like chilli and brinjal have a life exceeding one year during which they can repeatedly yield fruits. Moreover, newly sowed crops could not be harvested within the one-month leeway government gave them.

(2) As the Noël and Ramkissoon report acknowledges in its calculation, the sum of MUR 120,000 is the basic/displacement compensation, one which has been granted to non-active planters whose lands were uncultivated. Therefore, MUR 120,000 excludes compensation for the type of crop loss mentioned above. The planters estimate compensation for crop loss to be MUR 250,000. They also point out that MUR 120,000 excludes all extra expenditures that active planters have borne in relation to their lands, e.g. purchase of machinery for land preparation (MUR 120,000), pesticides and fertilisers (MUR 10,000), and labour (MUR 150,000). Another element discounted in the computed compensation is severance payment, which the planters estimate to be MUR 10,000.

The planters see their contestation as justified especially given that JFET has hardly developed since they were evacuated. Since its inception in 2006, the master plan for the zone has constantly been revised. From the initial plan comprising of light assembly, manufacturing, food processing, souvenirs manufacture, home appliances, garment, residential headquarters for expatriate workers, support services, logistics, warehousing facilities, shopping facilities, exhibition halls, business centre and staff dormitory, L'Express (2008) reported that the SEZ developers wanted access to the beach in order to construct hotels. There were talks about an Oriental Entertainment City, factories, a custom-built plant, two hotels and a commercial boulevard, amongst others. By March 2008, it was no more to be an industrial zone, but an integrated industrial city. Tianli SEZ project stagnated until the February 2009 visit of President Hu Jintao to Mauritius. Following this, a new set of stakeholders joined Tianli Group in the project: Taiyuan Iron and Steel Group Co Ltd and Shanxi Coking Coal Group Co Ltd from Shanxi province. A special purpose vehicle called Shanxi Jin Fei Investment Co. Ltd was set up in China which would invest USD 80 million in a new company to be incorporated in Mauritius, called the Mauritius Jin Fei Economic and Trade Cooperation Zone Co. Ltd. These were accompanied by contractual changes. The developers were thereon allowed to pledge their leasehold rights to banks outside Mauritius when raising money for the development and construction phase, and to pledge their leasehold rights, buildings and properties to banks both inside and outside Mauritius when raising loan for business operations.

Meanwhile, the off-site infrastructural provisions of which the Mauritian government was responsible were already in place: new access roads, upgrade of existing road connections, upgrade of reservoirs which would supply water to the zone, upgrade of existing sewerage networks in the surrounding, and the installation of water and electricity networks and exchange centres within the zone. Nevertheless, the SEZ remained dormant. In March 2012, a warehouse was under construction and was to be completed by June 2012. Plans for a residential and a business complex had been finalised. Four months later, JFET promoters communicated that they are seeking to rent out the site to local Mauritian and foreign firms. However, a special condition is attached to renting out to local Mauritian firms: the directors of the local Mauritian firm looking to rent the land at Jin Fei should be of foreign origins (Earally, 2012). By September 2012, only the carcass of a warehouse was erected. But the entire perimeter of the site had already been fenced with iron rods, making the zone-local community segregation inescapable to the eye.

Impact of JFET on Mauritius

At first glance, a dormant 211 hectares of land does not appear of much consequence, even less so if we contemplate it in comparison to China's own expansive ghost towns. Nor should the displacement of 57 erstwhile active planters who have been compensated – though inadequately – be a matter of national distress. But the fact is that, it is the *context* within which these evolve that do make these issues of national distress. Allusion is here being made to the geographical, political and economic contexts.

Geography:

(1) The total surface area of Mauritius is 186,475 hectares, of which 41.5% is covered by sugar cane, livestock and other crops. Of the 41.5%, maps reveal that less than 1% is dedicated to 'other crops', i.e. fruits and vegetables (Mauritius Sugar Industry Research Institute, 2010). Riche Terre (whose English translation is 'fertile soil') is one of the regions which cultivated a large share of these vegetables and fruits. Eric Mangar (2011), head of Mouvement pour l'Autosuffisance Alimentaire, Mauritius, comments in an interview to *L'Express* on 3 April 2011[11]:

> The farmers of Riche-Terre produced and supplied at least 20 tonnes of vegetables to the Port-Louis market weekly. They contributed to the country's food security in a very significant way before they were displaced because of the Tianli/JinFei project in 2006. The JinFei project, if completed, will cover the most fertile soil of the island with concrete in order to respond to the economic imperatives of the leaders of the country.[12]

However, even as it remains undeveloped, the fact remains that the island has lost one of its most productive vegetable cultivations.

(2) Situated in the middle of the Indian Ocean, the location of Mauritius – if exploited well – can be a boon to the country. In fact, that is indeed the intention of the Mauritian leaders who incessantly repeat that the establishment of JFET in Mauritius is in line with positioning Mauritius as a stepping stone for Asia into Africa. Nevertheless, by welcoming JFET in its particular format and lengthiness, the island finds its strategic geographical position used to its disadvantage. As an externally oriented economy, the harbour is one of Mauritius' key assets. But by giving away the plot adjacent to the port to JFET for 99 years under the exclusive management of the Chinese developers, the leaders have compromised the opportunity to expand this point of sea access in favour of the Mauritian economy.

Politics:

(1) The substantial and assured benefits Mauritius could have derived from the leasing of the Riche Terre site to the Chinese are the land conversion tax and rent. But due to the political context within which this land agreement was signed, the impact of JFET has become markedly negative. Although the 211 hectares was agricultural before it was suddenly granted industrial and commercial status under JFET, the Sugar Industry Efficiency Act 1988, Part IV, Section 5, 7 (ix) exempts the case from payment of land conversion tax. Moreover, as per the State Lands Act 1945 (http://attorneygeneral.gov.mu/English/Documents/A-Z%20Acts/S/Page%204/STATELANDS1.pdf; accessed 30 July 2013), the location of the Riche Terre site sets it to pay an industrial lease fee of MUR 270,000 per arpent per year.[13] But on 30 July 2009, the government strategically made changes to the State Lands Act 1945 which reduced the rent payable by the JFET developers. It now reads:

> Notwithstanding subsection (1C), where a large investment project is deemed by the Minister, subject to approval of Cabinet, to be in the economic interest of Mauritius, the annual rent determined in accordance with that subsection shall be reduced by such amount as may be determined by the Minister and any lease may be granted for a period not exceeding 99 years, with the approval of the Minister, subject to the approval of Cabinet.

According to the contract, the rent is MUR 270,000 per arpent per year for the first five years. Hence, at the very outset, a foregone rent of MUR 125,915 per arpent per year is borne by Mauritius.

Economy:

(1) In 2002, Mauritius introduced the Integrated Resort Scheme (IRS), 'a project for the development and sale of luxurious residential units to foreigners' (BOI, 2009). These projects are developed on freehold land exceeding 10 hectares and each unit is priced to a minimum of USD 500,000 (BOI, 2009). IRS was followed by the Real Estate Scheme (RES) in 2007. RES allows small landowners to develop and sell residences to non-citizens. It is developed on freehold land sized between 0.34 and 10 hectares. Presently, there are 12 IRS projects, 10 of which cover a total of 860.85 hectares, and 50 RES projects of a minimum of 0.34 hectare each (BOI, 2013). This has led to the privatisation of a large part of the Mauritian coastline. The two schemes also caused land prices to increase, and consequently a lot of these villas have not attracted clientele. In a survey by newspaper *Le Défi* on the 19 January 2013, Mauritian real estate and construction businesses agree that there is a saturation of real estate activity in Mauritius and that this might cause the economic bubble to burst (Vilbrin, 2013). Referring to the recent liquidation of Port Chambly RES, they warn of potential appearances of ghost towns in Mauritius – a prospect which an island of the size of Mauritius cannot afford.

It is when evaluated within these frameworks that the weight of JFET's impact is felt upon Mauritius. By acquiring the land at Riche Terre at the expense of the farmers, not only has the SEZ contributed to unemployment, but also has aggravated the food security situation, compromised prospects of port development, initiated disadvantageous and opaque policy changes, and added to the pressure on land on the island. Based on its comparative grandeur, JFET can be described as representative of the culmination of land-based economic mismanagement in Mauritius.

Conclusion

In an attempt to upgrade China's national wealth creation by investing in high-value goods and services, Chinese economic players now seek to claim the space held by rural agrarian communities for the construction of SEZs. This is contested by rural communities, who only receive rhetorical support from the government in the form of taciturn legislations. India's SEZ challenges though similar have a more magnified nature: while China's central, provincial and local government levels engage with every stage of the SEZ establishment – from the land acquisition to assuming the role of the SEZ developer – India transfers the responsibility of land acquisition to the developer itself, who often is an entirely private entity. Thus, the SEZ's development objective is ignored and profit-making or even the mere pride of land ownership takes forth. However, through CSEZAs, these non-developmental ends assume a new dimension. CSEZAs, under a diplomatic aura, impose an equation of cooperation within which the African host country has to expropriate strategically located land from its own electorate, only following which the Chinese developers will take over the land to develop the zone. As it is apparent from the representative experience of Mauritius, there is no guarantee of upcoming developmental goods. Seven years since the launch of these CSEZAs, Africa muses whether it was wise to expropriate land for these zones at the expense of lives, livelihoods and domestic political goodwill. Nevertheless, the willingness with which Africa sacrificed existing national development at the altar of distant and unsecured promises of development and profit is all to the credit of China's nearly whimsical CSEZAs.

Notes

1. The FAO report equated land grab to three specific purposes: (1) food security, (2) biofuels and (3) rising rates of return in agricultural businesses.
2. The Four Modernization programme aimed to develop the four main areas of the Chinese economy: agriculture, defence, industry and technology.
3. Given the strategic location of the SEZ – near Navi Mumbai International Airport and Mumbai Trans-harbour Sea Link – it is obvious that real estate and housing investment in that area can be highly priced, and will attract a wealthy clientele.
4. Although the general understanding is that the Chinese government did not favour SOEs as developers of the pilot CSEZAs, a glance at all the developers involved across the seven zones reveal that all the main developers of the SEZs in Africa are SOEs – with the exception of the Jiangsu Qiyuan Group in the EIZ Ethiopia, and Tianli Group in JFET – who, nevertheless, partner with SOEs in their respective SEZs.
5. Besides, contribution in terms of expertise derived from previous SEZ management experience also cannot be counted as an input if we consider the case of TEDA in Egypt. The Egyptian SEZ started in 1998. The contract for its development was assigned to TEDA, who by that time was running the successful Tianjin Economic-Technological Development Area in China. Nonetheless, TEDA had a disappointing launch in Egypt, which pushed it to revisit the project in 2000. It adopted a new partnership pattern and reduced the size of the SEZ project to only 100 hectares. Egypt TEDA SEZ was relaunched in 2007, with TEDA again revising the partnership pattern it adopted in 2000. This indicates that even though China has experience in SEZ management, the transposing of this expertise onto CSEZs in Africa is of no value as it fails to deliver (Brautigam & Xiaoyang, 2011, p. 75).
6. Here, we are referring to land not only for the construction of the CSEZ but also for the roads and other infrastructural networks like water, sewerage, telecommunications and electricity, essential to service the zone. The construction of service plants, exchange centres, reservoirs and so on are also accounted for. By land, we also allude to the location of the land, which, if strategically situated, elevates the value of the African input in the CSEZAs.
7. Tianli Spinning (Mauritius) Co Ltd is a subsidiary of Tianli Group.

8. Throughout the discussion of the case of the displaced planters of Riche Terre and Terre Rouge, this work will apply the currency and land-measuring units used in Mauritius, i.e. Mauritian Rupee (MUR), and arpent and perches, respectively. These are the units on basis of which the compensation was worked out.

    The exchange rate of the MUR to US dollars is as follows:

    MUR 1 = USD 0.0326/MUR100 = USD 3.26

    The land unit conversion ratios are as follows:

    One arpent = 0.34 hectare/one perche = 0.0025 hectare.

9. The report calculated the per arpent additional support cost coming from FSF in terms of: land preparation (MUR 25,000), upgrade of irrigation network (MUR 25,000), fertilisers and seeds (MUR 10,000) and fencing (MUR 60,000).

10. Bois Marchand is one of the pockets of poverty in Mauritius. It was the recent beneficiary of a corporate social responsibility housing project by Mauritius Telecom.

11. Translated as Movement for Self-sustaining Food Security.

12. Original: 'Les agriculteurs de Riche-Terre produisaient et fournissaient au marché en gros de Port-Louis au moins 20 tonnes de légumes par semaine et contribuaient d'une façon très significative à la sécurité alimentaire du pays avant d'être déplacés dans le cadre du projet Tianli/JinFei à partir de 2006. Le projet JinFei, s'il se réalise, va couvrir de béton les terres les plus riches de l'île afin de répondre aux perspectives et aux impératifs économiques de nos dirigeants et du pays'.

13. With reference to the second schedule of State Lands Act 1945: Calculation is done on basis that JFET site is beyond 81.21 m from the high water mark of Zone D. Therefore, it would have benefited from a 25% rebate of the prescribed rent of MUR 38, 259 per arpent per year.

Notes on contributor

Honita Cowaloosur is a doctoral research candidate at the University of St. Andrews, UK. She currently works as an economic reporter at L'Express (Mauritius) and has been a member of the Knowledge and Capacity Building Department of the Ministry of Finance (Mauritius). She has a Master of Science in International Relations from the London School of Economics and Political Science, and a Master of Arts in Politics from the University of Iceland.

References

BOI (Board of Investment, Mauritius). (2009). The integrated resort scheme. Retrieved January 15, 2013, from https://pams.investmauritius.com/docs/Guidelines-p-IRS.pdf

Brautigam, D., & Xiaoyang, T. (2011). China's investment in special economic zones in Africa. In T. Farole & G. Akinci (Eds.), *Special economic zones: Progress, emerging challenges and future directions* (pp. 69–100). Washington, DC: World Bank. Retrieved March 16, 2013, from https://openknowledge.worldbank.org/handle/10986/2341

Chin, J. (2010, October 29). China's blood stained property map. *China Real Time Report*. Retrieved May 30, 2013, from http://blogs.wsj.com/chinarealtime/2010/10/29/chinas-blood-stained-property-map/

China Daily. (2012, December 25). Pressure mounts over arable land resources. Retrieved January 6, 2013, from http://www.chinadaily.com.cn/china/2012-12/25/content_16054495.htm

Chi-yuk, C., & Pinghui, Z. (2011, November 24). Vow of land-grab probe silences Lufeng uprising. *South China Morning Post*. Retrieved January 12, 2013, from http://www.scmp.com/article/980156/vow-land-grab-probe-silences-lufeng-uprising

Commercial Secretaries (2011). Embassy of the A.R. of Egypt, Commercial Bureau, interviewed on 8 December, Beijing.

Dohrmann, J. A. (2008). Special economic zones in India: An introduction. *ASIEN: The German Journal on Contemporary Asia, 106*(January), 60–80. Retrieved January 17, 2013, from http://www.asienkunde.de/articles/a106_asien_aktuell_dohrmann.pdf

Earally, A. (2012, July 2). Jin Feiveut sous-louersesterres, *L'Express*. p.1.

Ethio News 24. (n.d.). Hujian receives 320 hct in Addis. Retrieved June 6, 2013, from http://www.ethionews24.com/hujian-receives-320-hct-in-addis

Gopalakrishnan, S. (2007). Negative aspects of special economic zones in China. *Economic and Political Weekly*, *42*, 1492–1494. Retrieved January 17, 2013, from http://www.jstor.org/stable/4419511

Gopalakrishnan, S. (2011). SEZs in India: An economic policy or a political intervention. In C. Carter & A. Harding (Eds.), *Special economic zones in Asian market economies* (pp. 139–155). New York: Routledge.

Indian Ministry of Commerce and Industry. (2006). The special economic zones rules, 2006, India. Retrieved September 15, 2011, from http://sezindia.nic.in/writereaddata/rules/SEZ_Rules_July_2010.pdf

Jintao, H. (2006, November 4). Address by Hu Jintao President of the People's Republic of China at the opening ceremony of the Beijing Summit of the Forum on China-Africa Cooperation. *FOCAC.org*. Retrieved July 12, 2011, from http://english.focacsummit.org/2006-11/04/content_4978.htm

Kugelman, M., & Levenstein, S. (2009). *Land grab? The race for the world's farmland*. Washington, DC: The Woodrow Wilson International Center for Scholars. Retrieved January 15, 2013, from http://www.wilsoncenter.org/publication/land-grab-the-race-for-the-worlds-farmland-0

L'Express. (2008, January). Jin Fei: Chronique. Retrieved September 15, 2012, from http://www.lexpress.mu/services/epaper-61207-Jin Fei--chronique-d-un.html

Lorenzo, C., Vermulen, S., Leonard, R., & Keeley, J. (2009). Land grab or development opportunity? Agricultural investment and international land deals in Africa. Food and Agricultural Organisation (FAO), Corporate Document Repository. Retrieved January 15, 2013, from http://www.fao.org/docrep/011/ak241e/ak241e00.htm

Mangar, E. (2010). Report of the Forced Displacement of Planters of the Riche-Terre Mixed Farming Cooperative Society in the Wake of the Mauritius JinFei Economic Trade and Cooperation Zone Project at Riche-Terre. Mauritius, MAA.

Mangar, E. (2011, April 3). Eric Mangar (MAA): Avec le projet Jin Fei, nos décideurs n'ont pas vu assez loin: Interview with Eric Mangar. Interviewed by Iqbal Kalla for *L'Express*. Retrieved April 13, 2013, from http://www.lexpress.mu/node/108179

Mauritius Sugar Industry Research Institute. (2010). 2010 Land use map of Mauritius. Retrieved January 25, 2013, from http://www.msiri.mu/Userfiles/file/2010_Land_use_of_Mauritius.pdf

Noël, A., & Ramkissoon, J. (2010, April 27). Report of the Committee on ex-planters of Riche-Terre Land Settlement.

Ogun State Government. (n.d.). Views and decisions of the Ogun State Government (White Paper) on the Second and Final Report of the Judicial Commission of Inquiry into all land allocations, acquisitions, sales and concessions of government properties and administration of land policies, rules and regulations between January 2004 and May 29, 2011, and other matters connected therewith. Retrieved January 20, 2013, from http://www.ogunstate.gov.ng/LANDSWHITEPAPER.pdf

Outlook India. (2009, October 29). Fresh changes in land acquisition bill draft. Retrieved June 24, 2013, from http://news.outlookindia.com/items.aspx?artid=779442

Shen, L., & Yishi, Z. (2011, August 6). Grubby land grab. *Caixin Online*. Retrieved May 30, 2013, from http://english.caixin.com/2011-06-08/100267231.html

Social and Economic Rights Action Center. (n.d.). Lekki free trade zone. Retrieved February 12, 2012, from http://www.serac.org/lekkiFreeTradeZone.html

Suryavanshi, S. (2013, January 6). Govt to gift Ambani SEZ with separate policy, *Daily News and Analysis*. Retrieved January 12, 2013, from http://www.dnaindia.com/mumbai/1786062/report-govt-to-gift-ambani-sez-with-separate-policy

The Economic Times. (2009, September 15). Mukesh Ambani-promoted Mumbai seeks third extension. Retrieved April 24, 2012, from http://articles.economictimes.indiatimes.com/2009-09-15/news/28436778_1_mumbai-sez-third-extension-land-acquisition

Vilbrin, C. (2013, January 19). UttumSanmukhiya (Directeur de V5 IMMOBILIER): "Attention à l'éclatement de la bulledansl'immobilier". *Le Defi*. Retrieved January 20, 2013, from http://www.defimedia.info/defi-plus/dp-interview/item/25385-uttum-sanmukhiya-directeur-de-v5-immobilier-attention-à-l'éclatement-de-la-bulle-dans-l'immobilier.html

Fixity, the discourse of efficiency, and enclosure in the Sahelian land 'reserve'

Erin Kitchell

Department of Geography, University of Wisconsin-Madison

The spate of foreign investments in land in developing countries in recent years has sparked speculation about trends in agriculture in developing countries, including the nature of land consolidation and the tradeoffs between food sovereignty and export-oriented growth. Consistent with policy favoring mechanization, irrigation, and chemical inputs, the economy of scale and access to infrastructure provided by large concessions is viewed as a means to overcome biophysical production constraints. Domestic officials legitimize large concessions through references to stores of available 'idle' and 'marginal' land. However, this raises important questions about the historical track records of modern management techniques as well as existing claims on these lands. Low productivity areas are heavily used by pastoralists as extensive grazing tracts, but these lands have historically been viewed as an agricultural reserve. In the Sahel, policy discourse around large-scale leases has a long history that can be traced back to *mise en valeur* clauses that defined productivity solely in terms of agricultural output. This represents a consistent undervaluing of the economic and ecological contributions of pastoral production, prompting agricultural expansion and fragmentation of rangelands. Land reforms and land-use policies are underpinned by particular narratives of efficiency and long-held assumptions of degradation through overgrazing. Strategies promoting irrigation, mechanization, and large-scale farming have weakened symbiotic links between rangelands and croplands. Increased privatization and commodification of land will exacerbate the problem. Cases from Sudan and Mali reveal an increasingly rigid enforcement of fixed boundaries around the leases disrupting local livelihoods' use of movement and secondary claims on land to cope with climatic variability.

Introduction

Global attention is increasingly attuned to the scope of foreign investment in farmland across the African continent. The growth of investment in agricultural land is driven by concerns about domestic food security in Middle Eastern and Southeast Asian countries following the 2007–2008 food crisis, policies promoting development of biofuel alternatives in Europe and the USA, and the desire of private equity firms following the financial crash to find new portfolio options that are both stable and likely to bring high returns. Welcoming investment in the hopes of securing long-term benefits through the building of infrastructure, the governments of many leasing nations have begun to catalogue the extent of land available for lease and to streamline the bureaucratic process for obtaining title. Large-scale concessions are likely to result in increased production through mechanization and inputs as well as the expansion of infrastructure including roads and irrigation systems. However, they also often ignore long-standing informal claims and can lead to appropriation and dispossession of small-scale resource users. The scope of the transfer of capital and territory is a new feature of globalization; underwritten by emergent conceptions of efficient ecological zoning, the current phenomenon of large-scale foreign investment in farmland also echoes some of the assumptions of colonial agricultural policy. An analysis of the definitions of 'available' land and the discourse used by domestic governments to legitimate foreign acquisitions of territory reveals a narrow underlying vision of economic efficiency that has a particular history. This represents a consistent undervaluing of the economic and ecological contributions of pastoral production, prompting agricultural expansion and fragmentation of rangelands.

In order to meet the demands of a growing global population for food, feed, and fuel, some have argued that increased resource scarcity necessitates the reevaluation of production priorities and the efficient allocation of land use through a globally integrated production system. However, the Sahelian region highlights some of the complexities that can be obscured in coarse-scale land use planning. If regional assessments do not sufficiently incorporate local ambiguities, their formulations will likely result in significant difficulties for maximizing the productive potential of this unique agroecological system. Fixed and rigid boundaries work against natural ecological flux and have historically increased the exclusion of multiples uses and poorer resources users. Fluctuations in rainfall, soil quality, and vegetative cover handicap firm planning and boundary delineation. Of even greater importance than subregional landscape variation is the significance of temporal variability. In consequence, extreme flexibility and a depth of knowledge are required of successful land users. For the Sahelian region, intensification of production through integrated crop–livestock farming systems balanced with the maintenance of significant pasture lands offer the greatest potential for balancing increased production and efficient land use with resilient livelihoods. In order to encourage these trends, policies are needed to support pastoral mobility and access to grazing lands, to secure smallholders' property rights, and to deter land speculation.

Historical context of agricultural expansion

The Sahel is the transition belt between the hyper-arid Sahara Desert and the subtropical forests and grasslands along the southern coast of West Africa. As an ecological zone, it stretches across over 4500 km, spanning the west to east coasts. Since 1973, nine Sahelian countries have formed a geopolitical entity under the Permanent Interstates Committee for Drought Control in the Sahel (CILSS); the total area of the CILSS is roughly 5.7 million square kilometers and includes parts of Mauritania, Senegal, the Gambia, Mali, Burkina Faso, Niger, and Chad. Although not part of the CILSS, significant portions of Sudan and Ethiopia are in the same ecozone and have socioeconomic and production characteristics similar to other Sahelian countries. These lands are dominated by grasslands and wooded savannas, with rainfall ranging from 200 mm per year in the north to nearly 600 mm per year in the south (Kandji, Verchot, & Mackensen, 2006; Mortimore 2001). Since the 1980s the Sahel has been undergoing rapid population growth of around 3.2% per year (United Nations Conference on Trade and Development [UNCTAD], 2000). The pace of growth and the rate of urbanization are unprecedented, exceeding rates in Asia and other regions of the world. There is increasing demand for food due to both population growth and changing consumption patterns among the expanding urban class. Alongside these demands, agricultural production has also been growing since the 1970s. Increases in production have been largely achieved through extensification, with an estimated 47% of the increase from 1960 to 1990 directly resulting from new lands being brought under cultivation (UNCTAD, 2000).

Following a shift in policy focus from domestic food production to export-oriented production in response to structural adjustment in the 1980s, production continued to increase at the rate of 4% per annum in Mali, Niger, Burkina Faso, and Nigeria, 3–4% in Chad, and 1–2% in Mauritania and Senegal from 1985 to 1995 (UNCTAD, 2000). These numbers reflect a clear variation in growth patterns between countries. Furthermore, the positive growth rates for production must be contextualized by the dramatic decline in returns per unit labor as well as a much shallower growth in output per hectare (Bolwig 2001; Mortimore 2001). Sub-Saharan Africa, and the Sahel in particular, has followed a very different pattern of agricultural growth than Latin America and Asia. There has been much more limited use of inorganic fertilizer and lower adoption of mechanization due to lack of infrastructure, prohibitive initial investments, lower value crops, and lower returns on yields (UNCTAD, 2000). All of these patterns point to the historical primacy of extensification in increasing agricultural output.

Given the limited area of optimal farmland, agricultural expansion in the Sahel was already leading to pressure on marginal lands with low yields by the 1960s. The transition from land abundance to land scarcity has been accelerated by climate patterns. Climatic shifts in combination with social and economic changes are transforming occupancy and land use. Over the past four decades the Sahel has experienced a marked downward shift in rainfall regimes with higher relative temporal variability in rainfall than in the past (Boko et al., 2007; Lucio, Molion, Conde, & de Melo, 2012; McIntosh 2000). While fluctuation of the supply of ecosystem services is normal in drylands, the increased frequency of rainfall perturbations puts greater climate stress on local livelihoods. In many areas, people have responded to reduced production by expanding cultivation of marginal lands, often involving the conversion of rangelands to cropland, followed by migration to other areas (Galvin 2009; Millennium Ecosystem Assessment [MEA], 2005). Pastoralists, in turn, are moving further south within the Sahel and into the Sudano-Guinean farmbelt (Bassett & Turner, 2007); the timing of migration patterns is also being altered, with significant implications for farmer–herder conflict. Although analysts agree that the region will continue to be particularly impacted by climate change in the future, there is considerable uncertainty as to the probable outcomes (Boko et al., 2007). Climatic change will increase temperatures and variability of rainfall, but effects on biodiversity and species composition are more difficult to predict. Regionally, rainfall may increase in some areas, while decreasing in others; however, evidence unambiguously points to a dramatic increase in climatic variability across the region (Kandji et al., 2006; MEA, 2005).

Significant challenges exist to determining the thresholds beyond which regions of the dryland Sahel would reach irreversible change. This is related to the difficulty of understanding interactions between biophysical, social, and economic factors; analyses of resilience and thresholds must be long-term in order to capture slow and stochastic processes (Dong et al., 2011; MEA, 2005). Within the Sahel, understandings of degradation have been problematic. Declines in productivity are not easily identified through short-term inspection, yet short-term visual measures have led to a history of conflating the poor current condition of a resource with land degradation (Turner 2003). Simplistic models of degradation have often been the basis of political decisions to reallocate land use, frequently stressing agricultural expansion and marginalizing pastoral production with little attention to the nature of the resource base (Homewood 2004; Reenberg 2001; Sullivan & Rohde, 2002). Widespread spatial and temporal heterogeneity in resource quality is characteristic of the Sahel. Soil, elevation, and topography create patches of heterogeneous vegetation; heterogeneity is also increased by local patches or large-scale gradients in rainfall. Fluctuations in rainfall and variation in soil qualities mean that vegetative production in a given location can vary on a daily, seasonal, and annual basis (Ellis 1995; International Institute for Environment and Development [IIED], 2010; Turner 2004). Movement is critical to access forage and water unevenly distributed in space and varying across time. Pastoralist systems based on high mobility successfully maximize returns from highly variable production (Reid, Galvin, & Kruska, 2008).

The integration of livestock and agricultural systems has been historically important. Inadequate rainfall is a constraint on cultivation in areas with less than 250 mm annual rainfall, but in other areas soil nutrients are the limiting factor (Powell, Fernandez-Rivera, Hiernaux, & Turner, 1996). Soil fertility is inherently low, and livestock have been the principal vector of nutrient transfer. The seasonality of rain-fed agriculture allows for mutually beneficial exchanges between transhumant herds and croplands. During the rainy season herds graze in the northern areas of the Sahel, usually moving south to dry-season pastures in the farm belt following harvest. Crop residues provide important dry-season forage for herds and livestock grazing on postharvest fields return nutrients to the soil in the form of manure and urine (de Leeuw, Reynolds, & Rey, 1995). This effectively represents a nutrient transfer from rangelands to croplands via the cycling of biomass through livestock, an exchange vital to maintaining soil fertility over time (Powell et al., 1996). Traditional systems of land administration fostered this exchange and relied on reciprocal arrangements between farmers and pastoralists.

Under current conditions, 46% of land in sub-Saharan Africa is unsuited to rain-fed agriculture due to aridity. Despite the rapid expansion of agriculture in the past decades, the fraction of cultivated land remains quite low (UNCTAD, 2000). Currently, the land reserve in the Sahel and Sudano-Sahel is roughly equal to the area under cultivation. However, the majority of these lands are marginal, defined as yielding 20–40% of the production of the same crop on optimal farmland, and nearly 75% of the reserve area is located in Sudan (UNCTAD, 2000). Looking more closely at the case of Sudan can illustrate some trends across the region. Nearly 49% of Sudan's total area is classified as desert and semidesert; although there is some cultivation in these regions, it is largely irrigated agriculture concentrated around the banks of the Nile and Atbara rivers with some additional lands cultivated with dryland farming and water harvesting techniques. Table 1 shows FAO land use figures from 1995 and Ministry of Agriculture targets for 2001, and figures on grazing lands from a 1991 ILO-UNDP mission.[1]

With a total land area of 237 million hectares, Sudan has roughly 84 million hectares of arable land. Of these lands, 1.63, 8.21, and 7.93 million hectares were under irrigated agriculture, rain-fed traditional agriculture, and mechanized farming, respectively, in 1995 with an additional 24 million hectares of pastures and 64 million hectares in forest and

Table 1.   Cropland and land cover figures from Sudan, ranging from 1991 to 2001.

	Total area	Arable land	Area under irrigated agriculture	Traditional rain-fed agriculture	Mechanized farming	Pastures	Forested
ILO-UNDP, 1991[a]	237	40	–	–	–	120–150	–
FAO, 1995[b]	237	84	1.63	8.21	7.93	24	64
Ministry of Agriculture targets for 2001[a]	237	84	3.78	9.12	12.6	–	–

Note: All areas are given in millions of hectares.
Source: [a] Library of Congress; [b] FAO Country Profiles.

woodlands. Ministry of Agriculture plans aimed to dramatically expand all cropland, more than doubling irrigated land and nearly doubling land under mechanized cultivation to 3.78 and 12.6 millions hectares, respectively, by 2001 (FAO 2006). In a five-year period, this goal would mean the expansion of cultivated lands by a total of nearly 8 million hectares. It should also be noted that considerable uncertainty exists in these measures; in 2009, the FAO listed arable land at 20 million hectares (FAOSTAT) and the ILO-UNDP have estimated pasture land at between 120 and 150 million hectares. The ILO-UNDP mission also estimated that of all lands potentially suitable for grazing, at least two-thirds were already in use (Library of Congress 1991). These figures reflect the lack of a standardized method for determining available cultivable lands, indicating that presumably large reserves of arable land likely require significant qualification.

Current pressures on land resources

Strategies of increasing production through extensification of agriculture have been dominant, with a pronounced emphasis even in recent policies. Policymakers' perceptions of the availability of wide tracts suitable for expanded cultivation have been brought to the fore in recent years due to increased foreign acquisition of large areas for agricultural investment. Prioritizing the increase of irrigated lands is common, and in some countries, officials are clearly articulating a development policy of growth led by the sale or lease of large-scale land concessions to foreign investors. Mali, Ethiopia, Sudan, and, to a lesser extent, Senegal, seek to capitalize on their large landmasses by encouraging foreign direct investment in agriculture and associated infrastructure. Since 2008, a series of acquisitions termed 'land grabs' by the media were fueled by spikes in food prices, assessments of future booms in agrofuels, and the crash of the financial market and devaluation of other investment opportunities; the spate of investments have sparked speculation about future trends in agriculture in developing countries, including the role of consolidation and the tradeoffs between food sovereignty and export-oriented growth (Borras & Franco, 2009; Borras, McMichael, & Scoones, 2010; GRAIN 2008). Domestic officials have frequently attempted to legitimize large-scale concessions through references to stores of idle and marginal land available for expansion. While debate on the extent of these stores and nature of existing claims to the land is ongoing, many receiving governments have begun cataloguing land banks to facilitate investment (Cotula, Vermeulen, Mathieu, & Toulmin, 2011; Global Land Project 2010).

Potential for increasing production on marginal lands seems to offer a win-win solution to the problem of land scarcity and growing demands for agricultural products. Consistent with policy trends favoring mechanization, irrigation, and chemical inputs, the economy of scale and access to infrastructure provided by large concessions is viewed as a means to overcome biophysical production constraints. However, this raises important questions of historical track records of modern management techniques as well as existing claims on these lands. Throughout the Sahel, marginal lands are heavily used by pastoralists as extensive grazing tracts. Although the dominant land uses include wide areas of temporary crops and pasture, there is relatively little idle or unused arable land in the region (Galvin 2009). Extensive pastures have historically been viewed as a land reserve for agriculture. *Mise en valeur* clauses that make ownership claims contingent on productive use are defined implicitly and in practice in terms of agricultural use (Thébaud & Batterbury, 2001). Government policy has often operated on the assumption that pastoral landscapes represent 'underutilized' lands. Misunderstanding the spatial requirements of extensive production systems under the French colonial system for legal purposes, all uncultivated lands, including pastures, were labeled 'abandoned land' (Kirk 2000).

Somewhat paradoxically, the state has also held the view that pastoral lands were easily subject to degradation from overgrazing. This view of the landscape has been reinforced by a perception of pastoral livelihoods as chronically prone to crisis, necessitating outside aid in times of drought (Reid et al., 2008). Together, these views facilitated the nationalization of pastoral lands by the state. State-led agricultural development through irrigation programs spurred the expropriation of communally administered pastoral lands, nationalization, and the allocation of formal usage rights to irrigated areas in the form of individual leaseholds (Kirk 2000). Since the 1980s, irrigation schemes and consolidation of land for mechanized agriculture have been important drivers of conversion and enclosure of rangelands. In Sudan, the conversion to large mechanized farms has been so pronounced and conducive to localized conflict that in recent years the UNEP called for a moratorium on large-scale concessions (IIED, 2010).

Policy favoring agricultural production over livestock husbandry has shifted land use and had distinct impacts on local balances of power between farmers and herders. Livelihoods in the Sahel have historically depended on negotiated, nonexclusive access to water and reciprocal land agreements between pastoralists and agriculturalists (Dong et al., 2011). Thus, the traditional system was flexible and able to respond to environmental changes. In contrast, policy frameworks have been shaped by the assumption that formalization of boundaries around individual property rights would facilitate investment and the adoption of technology, ultimately driving a shift to cash cropping and higher levels of production (Chimhowu & Woodhouse, 2006). Reliance on this linear model of agricultural change informed policies of land reform and agricultural development. Reforms emphasizing privatization and modern land tenure systems in Africa have virtually universally resulted in the fragmentation of grazing lands (Reid et al., 2008). This process often occurs as cropland encroaches onto pasture land, a trend likely to accelerate in the future due to both climate change and policy pushing for increased production (Galvin 2009; Homewood et al., 2001). Along with extension of cropland, privatization and increased market access have been driving enclosure of rangelands by both pastoralists and nonpastoralists. Poverty sometimes drives pastoralists to begin fencing off pastures for sedentary rain-fed farming, while a perception of increased incursion of charcoal production has lead some to enclose rangelands to protect them for grazing (IIED, 2010). Charcoal production and the investment in livestock production by urban-based business interests are both important drivers of enclosure. However, in addition to the total area of pastures enclosed or converted, subtler mechanisms of exclusion exist even in zoning schemes that may nominally protect both cropland and pasture land.

Two examples are particularly relevant. The first concerns ecologically strategic areas (wetlands, riverine beds, and other water points) that act as buffers allowing livestock to survive the harsh dry season. Because of their higher productive potential, these strategic points are often the first to be privatized. Although they may represent insignificant losses in terms of area, loss of access can undermine the resiliency of the entire transhumant system (IIED, 2010; Reid et al., 2008). A second example is the implementation of village-based zoning, *gestion des terroirs villageois*, under decentralization. Noting the poor condition of soils, development policy misdiagnosed the poor resource base as evidence of institutional failure; village zoning aimed to fix this supposed failure by clearly delineating areas for discrete land uses by individual communities (Bassett, Blanc-Pamard, & Boutrais, 2007; Turner 2011). On the one hand, the establishment of hard boundaries tended to disrupt traditional integration of cropping and transhumant systems; on the other, as participatory plans were made based on village communities, it increased the vulnerability of the rural poor, notably pastoralists, whose action space was larger than a single village territory (Bassett et al., 2007; Turner 2004).

The impetus behind formalization was partly due to shifting perspectives on communal land tenure produced by the complex relationships between colonial authorities and traditional officials. Increasing infrastructure and market access have also led to the commodification of land, further disrupting traditional tenure systems. Because land has historically served social and political as well as economic functions, the transition from reciprocity (land or access given as socially embedded gifts) to increasing influence of market forces (land as an exchange value) has far-reaching effects on social and ecological exchange between user groups (Chimhowu & Woodhouse, 2006). In recent decades, the commodification of livestock has arisen as a further factor in land use change. The marketing of livestock as a primary livelihood strategy and increasing investment in the livestock sector in response to growing livestock consumption are reshaping landscapes and ownership. Contract herding arrangements are increasing and the commodification of livestock results in intensified production, land concentration, or both (Reid et al., 2008). The history of agricultural development in the region highlights the fact that policy interventions aimed at increasing production have embodied a particular politics with significant consequences for local livelihoods and environmental sustainability.

Evaluating the impacts of large-scale concessions

On the macro-level, past agricultural policies privilege concentration of agricultural land and marginalize the livestock sector. This focus has the potential to generate investment in infrastructure and increase yields in the short term. However, important criticisms lie in the increased vulnerability of the entire social-ecological system due to foreseeable biophysical constraints and impacts on livelihoods. Rain-fed arable soils in the Sahel are low in carbon ($<0.5\%$), nitrogen ($<0.05\%$), phosphorus (<30 ppm), and potassium ($<0.2\%$) as well as some micronutrients (Mortimore 2001). High sand fractions lower water retention and heighten the effects of evapotranspiration in an arid environment. Lowland areas with greater accessibility of groundwater and potential for irrigation do differ from this characterization of general bioproductivity, but such areas are scarce; for this reason, irrigation does not offer a general solution to low productivity in the Sahel (Mortimore 2001). Irrigation also requires extensive public capital investment and can have important consequences, including waterlogging, salinization, eutrophication, and unsustainable exploitation of groundwater aquifers (MEA, 2005).

Concentrating nutrients through organic and inorganic fertilizers is required to maintain crop production. However, uptake of inorganic fertilizer on poor soils is limited and often requires organic fertilizer as a complement (Powell et al., 1996). Scarcity of supplies and the cost of fertilizer use are prohibitive; returns are marginal for low-value crops and external inputs remain profitable only in the case of high-value cash crops (Mortimore 2001). Variability of rainfall means that any such investments carry risks for both small-scale and large producers, albeit risks with much different stakes. High frequency of crop failures mean that agricultural investments require a long period of time in order to bring benefits; as small-scale producers are more vulnerable to short-term shocks, policies subsidizing high input agriculture may result in shifts toward consolidation (Mortimore 2001). Globalization is strengthening links between local, national, regional, and global factors related to degradation and desertification. Trade liberalization, macroeconomic reforms, and an emphasis on raising production for export markets can boost productivity, but may either amplify or attenuate drivers of resource degradation. To date, impacts in the Sahel have been mixed with significant evidence that current processes are likely to increase degradation; in addition, although improved access to inputs and export markets has increased output, international food markets have driven down prices and undermined the livelihoods of food producers in developing countries (MEA, 2005).

A further difficulty posed by the dominant processes of tenure reform and agricultural expansion requires returning to the issue of variability of the resource base. As the severity of climatic shifts in the Sahel increase, likelihood of periodic crop failure will also increase. For large-scale producers this means a lowered margin of returns, but for small-scale producers climatic shocks could trigger severe vulnerability and periods punctuated by dependence on outside food aid. Coping with risk is at the fore for both pastoralists and subsistence farmers; strategies that enhance adaptability to change have been historically successful and individuals often choose production strategies that minimize risk rather than maximizing production (Anderson 2003; Reenberg, Nielsen, & Rasmussen 1998). For smallholders, expanding production has been one important response to climate stress. However, rather than a simple extension to less suitable land, expansion has been a more refined adaptation strategy that also served as a reallocation of land from one soil type to another as climatic variations influenced farmers' perceptions of suitability (Reenberg et al., 1998). This clarifies difficulties with the concept of marginal land in the Sahel; classification of land as marginal and nonmarginal presupposes that one type of land is unambiguously more suitable than another. Soil maps and agroecological zones do not clearly demarcate marginal land since productivity varies with rainfall, which is itself increasingly variable. There is little fixity in resource quality, increasing the need for flexible strategies that spread risk (Reenberg et al., 1998; Swift 1995). Thus, neither biophysical conditions nor human response options are permanent.

Despite challenging conditions for agriculture, the Sahelian savanna is highly productive. Grasslands and the wooded savanna can reproduce up to 150% of their weight in biomass per year and contain high ratios of edible plant matter relative to other biomes (Reid et al., 2008). The potential for carbon sequestration on rangelands in sub-Saharan Africa has attracted increased attention. Globally, grasslands store 34% of the carbon stock, an ecosystem service worth $7 per hectare; over 13 million square kilometers of grassland pastures are currently found in sub-Saharan Africa (IIED, 2010). Degradation of rangelands, frequently occurring through conversion to cropland, significantly reduces the sequestration value.

Land policies focused on agriculture have also insufficiently recognized the role pastoralism plays in national economies. In many Sahelian countries, livestock contributes over 40% of the GDP; as this figure is based on the value of final products (meat, milk, and hides), it does not reflect the additional social and ecological benefits pastoralism adds to domestic economies (IIED, 2009, 2010). While the cost of intensifying agricultural production is high in terms of inputs and investment required in an arid and low-fertility zone, Sahelian countries have a comparative advantage in livestock production. Livestock trading across borders is also vital to food security, as revenues are primarily used to finance imports of grain (IIED, 2010). These factors have been discounted by a narrow focus on increasing agricultural production. Little research has been carried out to examine whether the expected benefits of the new land uses are greater than the economic and environmental benefits lost by displacing pastoralism.

Intensification of pastoralism through sedentarization and zero-graze systems has been proffered by some as a pathway for increasing output per hectare. However, in the context of the Sahel this involves a few problems. The first is the requirement for cultivating forage to supplement natural browse available in fenced areas. Currently, rangelands provide the majority of livestock forage in the region, with the use of purchased feed supplements remaining relatively low. Increased use of crop residues could continue to be used as one source of supplements, but producing the remainder would require significant use of cultivated land. A movement to sedentary livestock production would require extensive use of chemical fertilizers and is dependent on access to sufficient land and labor – all constraints for small-scale producers; labor and external inputs also required prohibitively decrease margins of profitability (Powell & Williams 1993). Second, this pathway for intensification could be successful on a limited individual scale with a small herd, but offers little promise for broader application in the region. Such a model fails to effectively respond to the resource variability in the Sahel, and concentration of livestock ultimately leads to livestock disease and degradation from localized overgrazing (IIED, 2010; Reid et al., 2008).

To date, intensification through consolidation, mechanization, and exclusion of multiple uses and users have produced marginally increasing agricultural returns while exacerbating vulnerability and unlinking traditional systems for maintaining fertility. Commercialization of agriculture also raises issues of food security and sustainable livelihoods in a region where small-scale producers remain prevalent. Exposure to both climatic variability and the fluctuations of the market increase vulnerability to periodic shocks, with potentially disastrous results if pursued as an exclusive strategy (Brown 2011; Eakin 2006; Morton 2007). However, pathways for more equitable, environmentally sound increases in production do exist. They are dominantly low-input, integrated systems that capitalize on labor inputs and maintain sufficient flexibility to adapt to climatic variability. Reinforcement of traditional interchanges between pastoralist and cropping systems, maintenance of transhumant corridors, development and dissemination of drought resistant high yield varieties, and the integration of forage legumes and tree browse all hold promise (Powell et al., 1996).

Typically, conflict between farmers and herders is understood as conflict over land cover; however, resource conflict between groups is much more diffuse than supposed and in conditions of decreasing availability of land tighter integration of pastoralism is both possible and necessary. As land scarcity increases and length of fallows decrease, farmers' demand for manure rises in order to maintain fertility. Although many cultivators also keep livestock, they often have an insufficient herd to replace loss of nutrients (Powell et al., 1996). In areas of expanding cropping pressure, cropping is reducing pasture land and competition between agricultural and pastoral production systems does exist over vegetation, water points, and movement spaces (Turner 2004). In this context, protection of transhumance corridors and creation of flexible systems to ensure access to water points and key buffer areas is vital. Pastoral charters and amendments to national constitutions protecting pastoral tenure and mobility signal growing attention to the production value of pastoralism, but it remains to be seen whether new institutions will be able to respond to the challenges of implementation.

In many regions of the world, informal collective arrangements have compensated for the fragmentation of rangelands resulting from privatization by establishing shared use rights that maintain connectivity between grazing tracts. In the Sahel, customary rules based on social networks held a similar purpose, regulating access to resources and serving as pastoral safety nets in times of drought (Niamir-Fuller 1999; Reid et al., 2008). Formal institutions to protect mobility need to provide sufficient protection of key sites without being prescriptive and rigid. Past efforts at tenure regularization have prioritized rigid classification of resources users and resource rights due to ease of implementation and enforcement (Kirk 2000). Further delineation of fixed boundaries is inappropriate, given the need for both secure access and the flexibility to move in response to climate, politics, and other social factors. New methods for improving security of pastoral tenure should look to informal institutions as a model of flexibility and management of land use based on social capital. Tensions over water points are evidence of the need to integrate land and water management. Securing equitable resource tenure will require considering them as a linked bundle of resources (IIED, 2010; Reid et al., 2008). Finally, negotiation of cross-border agreements is vital to maintaining mobility, facilitating access to markets, and increasing economic returns from the livestock sector. Significant transnational integration is occurring through ECOWAS, a regional economic grouping of 16 West African nations. However, high taxes on transhumant border crossings currently restrict access to transhumant routes and livestock markets. Harmonization of regulatory mechanisms, reduction of barriers, and coordination of land use planning across borders will facilitate increased movement and economic production from pastoralism (IIED, 2010).

Possibilities for intensification within agricultural systems also exist. Recent regreening in areas of Senegal, Niger, and Burkina Faso may signal the potential for labor-intensive mixed agroforestry systems to reclaim degraded lands. Starting in the 1980s, farmers began to spread local innovations to conserve water and increase fertility through grassroots networks. In the past 5–10 years, NDVI satellite measures have shown the regeneration of nearly 5 million hectares in Burkina Faso and Niger (Reij, Tappan, & Smale, 2008). The impact of rainfall patterns on regrowth continues to be questioned, but growing evidence points to the principal role of management techniques. Restoration of productivity and favorable changes to the water table were achieved through the construction of stone contour bunds to harvest rainwater and the digging of planting pits to concentrate nutrients and water for trees as windbreaks and crop alleys (Reij et al., 2008). These were low-cost, low-input initiatives based on traditional practices.

Researchers examining the on-farm impacts of their use in Burkina Faso have found increases in cereal yields ranging from 40% to 100%; similarly, in Niger processes of farmer-managed natural regeneration have increased nitrogen content in fields from 15% to 156%, with linked increases in millet and sorghum yields (Reij et al., 2008, 2009). These two intensification pathways, largely driven by local innovation and diffusion, point to possible avenues for increasing production elsewhere in the Sahel. In addition to new technology, efforts to improve agricultural production must consider local resource availability and the management practices that regularize technology use. Extension and farmer-to-farmer training on labor-intensive innovations as well as training on timing and proper application of inputs can help improve yields for smallholders. These efforts will need to coincide with mechanisms to ensure timely availability of external inputs (Powell et al., 1996).

Available labor is an important constraint for intensification through both integrated crop–livestock systems and extension of agroforestry and other conservation techniques. Currently, crop damage from transhumant livestock results most often from herder inattention, in itself frequently a direct result of decreased labor availability and an accompanying devolution of responsibility for herding to children and the elderly (Turner & Hiernaux, 2008). Emigration is a common livelihood strategy, fueled by what has been termed an 'urban bias' in wages. A large income gap exists between income per capita for agricultural and nonagricultural labor, and the value added per worker is 7–8 times higher in nonagricultural sectors (UNCTAD, 2000). On the one hand, emigration provides flows of cash to rural areas that permit investment in agricultural inputs and livestock (veterinary services, reconstitution of herds). On the other, it is increasingly contributing to a labor shortage that limits the possibility for labor-driven intensification. In order to support these intensification pathways, policies addressing the balance of trade and improving prices for food and primary goods are required. Furthermore, some protective barriers on imports could ensure that domestic farmers are competitive in markets to meet rising urban food demands. However, for both of these measures a balance must be sought with a long-standing emphasis on maintaining low food prices for urban dwellers.

Conclusion

Historically, the concept of a 'land reserve' in the Sahel has implicitly discounted pastoralism in favor of extensification of agricultural production. Since the 1980s, extensification has been driven by an export-oriented strategy with an increasing focus on irrigation, mechanization, and large-scale farming. Efficiency has been loaded with assumptions in favor of both agriculture and land consolidation. Beginning in colonial times and continuing to the present, these assumptions have served to marginalize pastoralists and legitimize the nationalization of pasture lands and other common property resources. They have been retained in development policy and shored up by analyses of soil degradation that rather facilely attributed blame to poor resource management by herders and small-scale producers. In a region marked by a relatively poor resource base and climatic variability, these policy assumptions must be reexamined. Mobile pastoralism is in reality a remarkably efficient use of highly variable resources; its production system is able to adapt to change and is likely to be increasingly competitive as climate change reshapes the Sahel. A singular focus on increasing agricultural production either directly or implicitly dismisses pastoralism, failing to capitalize on its comparative economic advantage, further decoupling historically intertwined agricultural and livestock production systems and contributing to increased livelihood and ecological vulnerability.

On the global scale, demand for land is largely driven by growing demand for agricultural commodities and biofuel feedstocks. This offers opportunities for economic development in low-income countries, but the tradeoffs of shifting land use to these products are likely to be costly. Of even greater concern, demand is currently driving rapid transfer of extensive tracts of arable land to large domestic corporations and foreign investors without adequate consideration of local claims and impacts on linked land uses. Sudan is one example of such shifts producing significant tensions and even violent conflict (Ijaimi 2006), but throughout the region more insidious yet less visible pressures exist at various scales. Suppositions of scarcity have a tendency to create an atmosphere of crisis, driving short-term decisions rather than more nuanced and flexible long-term strategies.

Any attempt to reform land use to make it more efficient requires first a clear discussion of what is meant by efficiency, followed by a clear reckoning of the social, economic, and ecological losses that will be incurred. It must be recognized that a range of goals is being sought. Pursuit of economic growth loses its coherence if it undermines local livelihoods or fails to preserve the resource base that it relies upon. Furthermore, allocation and reallocation are inarguably political; failing to acknowledge this does violence to less-represented groups by pushing forward an agenda under the banner of development or scientific objectivity. Optimistic market-based assertions that efficient solutions can create win-win outcomes of economic development alongside environmental conservation should be carefully examined. Articulation with global markets can enhance insecurity for the poor (Robbins 2004); reducing vulnerability and maintaining protections for small-scale producers is essential to adequately addressing mounting pressures on land resources.

Commitments to economic efficiency should be tempered by commitments to equity. Uncoupling multiple concerns when asking questions about who has access to land and how they are to use it can only be to the detriment of both the resource itself and small-scale resource users. Large-scale land concessions to foreign investors are likely to increase the insecurity of local livelihoods by denying secondary access claims; this will, in turn, have implications for the long-term productivity of land areas as well as for conflict over resource access. In the Sahel, broad-scale delineations of appropriate land uses are particularly challenging because of layered, overlapping land uses and the inappropriateness of fixed boundaries in a landscape dominated by variability. Equitable and ecologically sound intensification of production requires the protection of multiple uses. This poses considerable institutional challenges as it requires both coherence and extensive flexibility.

Note

1. As they were compiled prior to independence in South Sudan in July 2011, all figures represent total land areas for both Sudan and South Sudan.

Notes on contributor

Erin Kitchell has worked in the Sahelian region for seven years in both research and practitioner positions. She has served as a Peace Corps Volunteer in Senegal, the Programs Director for the Mali Health Organizing Project in Mali, and a consultant for an evaluation of World Bank on forest policy in the Sahel. Her current research focuses on the negotiation of local land use agreements at the commune level in West Africa as a means to integrate customary and statutory institutions for resource management.

References

Anderson, J. (2003). Risk in rural development: Challenges for managers and policy makers. *Agricultural Systems, 75*, 161–197.

Bassett, T., Blanc-Pamard, C., & Boutrais, J. (2007). Constructing locality: The *Terroir* approach in West Africa. *Africa, 77*, 104–129.

Bassett, T., & Turner, M. D. (2007). Sudden shift or migratory drift? FulBe herd movements to the Sudano-Guinean region of West Africa. *Human Ecology, 35*, 33–49.

Boko, M., Niang, I., Nyong, A., Vogel, C., Githeko, A., Medany, ... Yanda, P. (2007). Africa. In M. L. Parry, O. F. Canziani, J. P. Palutikof, P. J. van der Linden, & C. E. Hanson (Eds.), *Climate change 2007: Impacts, adaptation and vulnerability. Contribution of Working Group II to the Fourth Assessment Report of the Intergovernmental Panel on Climate Change* (pp. 433–467). Cambridge: Cambridge University Press.

Bolwig, S. (2001). The dynamics of inequality in the Sahel: Agricultural productivity, income diversification, and food security among the Fulani *Rimaibe* in northern Burkina Faso. In T. Benjaminsen & C. Lund (Eds.), *Politics, property, and production in the West African Sahel* (pp. 278–302). Stockholm: Elanders Gotab.

Borras, S., & Franco, J. (2009). *The politics of contemporary (trans)national commercial land deals: Competing views, strategies, and alternatives.* Paper presented at Agrarian Studies Colloquium Series, Yale University, October 30.

Borras, S., McMichael, P., & Scoones, I. (2010). The politics of biofuels, land, and agrarian change: Editors introduction. *Journal of Peasant Studies, 37*, 575–592.

Brown, K. (2011). Sustainable adaptation: An oxymoron? *Climate and Development, 3*, 21–31.

Chimhowu, A., & Woodhouse, P. (2006). Customary vs. private property rights? Dynamics and trajectories of vernacular land markets in sub-Saharan Africa. *Journal of Agrarian Change, 6,* 346–371.

Cotula, L., Vermeulen, S., Mathieu, P., & Toulmin, C. (2011). Agricultural investment and international land deals: Evidence from a multi country study in Africa. *Food Security, 3,* 99–113.

de Leeuw, P. N., Reynolds, L., & Rey, B. (1995). Nutrient transfers from livestock in West African agricultural systems. In J. M. Powell, S. Fernandez-Rivera, T. O. Williams, & C. Renard (Eds.), *Livestock and sustainable nutrient cycling in mixed farming systems of sub-Saharan Africa* (pp. 371–391). Addis Ababa: International Livestock Centre for Africa.

Dong, S., Wen, L., Liu, S., Zhang, X., Lassoie, J., Yi, S., … Li, Y. (2011). Vulnerability of worldwide pastoralism to global changes and interdisciplinary strategies for sustainable pastoralism. *Ecology and Society, 16,* 10. Retrieved from http://www.ecologyandsociety.org/vol16/iss2/art10/

Eakin, H. (2006). *Weathering risk in rural Mexico: Climatic, economic and institutional change.* Tucson: University of Arizona Press.

Ellis, J. (1995). Climate variability and complex ecosystem dynamics: Implications for pastoral development. In I. Scoones (Ed.), *Living with uncertainty: New directions in pastoral development in Africa* (pp. 37–46). London: Intermediate Technology Publications.

FAO. (2006). Sudan. Country pasture/forage resource profiles. Retrieved from http://www.fao.org/ag/AGP/AGPC/doc/Counprof/sudan/sudan.htm

FAOSTAT, *Land use data.* Food and Agricultural Organization of the United Nations. Retrieved November 12, 2011 from http://faostat.fao.org

Galvin, K. (2009). Transitions: Pastoralists living with change. *Annual Reviews of Anthropology, 38,* 185–198.

Global Land Project. (2010). *Land grab in Africa: Emerging land system drivers in a teleconnected world.* Copenhagen: GLP International Project Office.

GRAIN. (2008). Seized: *The 2008 land grab for food and financial security.* GRAIN briefing. Retrieved from http://www.grain.org/article/entries/93-seized-the-2008-landgrab-forfood-and-financial-security

Homewood, K. (2004). Policy, environment and development in African rangelands. *Environmental Science & Policy, 7,* 125–143.

Homewood, K. E. F., Lambin, E., Coast, Kariuki, A., Kivelia, J., Said, M., Serneels, S. & Thompson, M. (2001). Long-term changes in Serengeti-Mara wildebeest: and land cover: Pastoralism, population, or policy? *PNAS, 98,* 12544–12549.

International Institute for Environment and Development. (2009). *Arid waste? Reassessing the value of dryland pastoralism.* London: Briefing Paper, International Institute for Environment and Development.

International Institute for Environment and Development. (2010). *Modern and mobile: The future of livestock production in Africa's drylands.* London: Author.

Ijaimi, A. L. (2006). Mechanized farming and conflict in Sudan. In G. el Din el Tayeb (Ed.), *Land issues and peace in Sudan* (pp. 69–78). Khartoum: UNDP.

Kandji, S. T., Verchot, L., & Mackensen, J. (2006). *Climate change and variability in the Sahel: Impacts and adaptation strategies in the agricultural sector.* Nairobi: UNEP and ICRAF.

Kirk, M. (2000). The context for livestock and crop-livestock development in Africa: The evolving role of the state in influencing property rights over grazing resources in sub-Saharan Africa. In N. McCarthy (Ed.), *Property rights, risk, and livestock development in Africa* (pp. 23–54). Washington, DC: IFPRI.

Library of Congress. (1991). Agriculture in Sudan. U.S. Country Studies. Retrieved from http://countrystudies.us/sudan/55.htm

Lucio, P. S., Molion, L. C. B., Conde, F. C., & de Melo, M. L. D. (2012). A study on the West Sahel rainfall variability: The role of the intertropical convergence zone. *African Journal of Agricultural Research, 7,* 2096–2113.

McIntosh, R. (2000). Social memory in Mande. In R. McIntosh, J. Tainter, & S. McIntosh (Eds.), *The way the wind blows: Climate, history, and human action* (pp. 141–180). New York, NY: Columbia University Press.

Millennium Ecosystem Assessment. (2005). *Ecosystems and human well-being: Desertification synthesis.* Washington, DC: World Resources Institute.

Mortimore, M. (2001). Overcoming variability and productivity constraints in Sahelian agriculture. In T. Benjaminsen & C. Lund (Eds.), *Politics, property, and production in the West African Sahel* (pp. 233–254). Stockholm: Elanders Gotab.

Morton, J. (2007). The impact of climate change on smallholder and subsistence agriculture. *PNAS*, *104*, 19680–19685.

Niamir-Fuller, M. (1999). *Managing mobility in African rangelands: The legitimization of transhumance*. London: Intermediate Technology Publications.

Powell, J. M., & Williams, T. O. (1993). An overview of mixed farming systems in sub-Saharan Africa. In *Livestock and sustainable nutrient cycling dynamics in mixed farming systems of sub-Saharan Africa*. Proceedings of an International Conference held by the International Livestock Centre for Africa. Volume II: Technical Papers, 22–26 November.

Powell, J. M., Fernandez-Rivera, S., Hiernaux, P., & Turner, M. D. (1996). Nutrient cylcing in integrated rangeland/cropland systems of the Sahel. *Agricultural Systems*, *52*, 143–170.

Reenberg, A. (2001). Agricultural land use pattern dynamics in the Sudan-Sahel: Towards an event driven framework. *Land Use Policy*, *18*, 309–319.

Reenberg, A., Nielson, T. L., & Rasmussen, K. (1998). Field expansion and reallocation in the Sahel - Land use pattern dynamics in a fluctuating biophysical and socio-economic environment. *Global Environmental Change*, *8*, 309–327.

Reid, R., Galvin, K., & Kruska, R. (2008). Global significance of extensive grazing systems and pastoral societies: An introduction. In K. A. Galvin (Ed.), *Fragmentation in semi-arid and arid landscapes* (pp. 1–24). Dordrecht, The Netherlands: Springer.

Reij, C., Tappan, G., & Smale, M. (2008). Farmer led innovation in Burkina Faso and Niger. In D. Speilman & R. Pandya-Lorch (Eds.), *Millions fed: Proven successes in agricultural development* (pp. 53–58). Washington, DC: IFPRI.

Reij, C., Tappan, G., & Smale, M. (2009). *Agroenvironmental transformation in the Sahel: Another kind of 'green revolution'*. Washington, DC: IFPRI.

Robbins, P. (2004). *Political ecology: A critical introduction*. Oxford: Blackwell.

Swift, J. (1995). Dynamic ecological systems and the administration of pastoral development. In I. Scoones (Ed.), *Living with uncertainty: New directions in pastoral development in Africa* (pp. 153–173). London: Intermediate Technology.

Sullivan, S., & Rohde, R. (2002). On non-equilibrium in arid and semi-arid grazing systems. *Journal of Biogeography*, *29*, 1595–1618.

Thébaud, B., & Batterbury, S. (2001). Sahel pastoralists: Opportunism, struggle, conflict, and negotiation. A case study from Eastern Niger. *Global Environmental Change*, *11*, 69–78.

Turner, M. D. (2003). Methodological reflections on the use of remote sensing and geographic information science in human ecological research. *Human Ecology*, *31*, 255–279.

Turner, M. D. (2004). Political ecology and the moral dimensions of 'resources conflicts': The case of farmer-herder conflicts in the Sahel. *Political Geography*, *23*, 863–889.

Turner, M. D. (2011). The new pastoral development paradigm: Engaging the realities of property institutions and livestock mobility in dryland Africa. *Society & Natural Resources*, *24*, 469–484.

Turner, M. D., & Hiernaux, P. (2008). Changing access to labor, pastures, and knowledge: The extensification of grazing management in Sudano-Sahelian West Africa. *Human Ecology*, *36*, 59–80.

United Nations Conference on Trade and Development. (2000). *African development in a comparative perspective*. Oxford: First Africa World Press.

Water resources and biofuel production after the fast-track land reform in Zimbabwe

Patience Mutopo[a] and Manase Kudzai Chiweshe[b]

[a]Cologne African Studies Centre, University of Cologne, Cologne, Germany; [b]Department of Sociology, Rhodes University, Grahamstown, South Africa

Discourses on the fast-track land reform programme in Zimbabwe have produced multiple and contested knowledge. Current debates have addressed the increase in biofuel production, which has been pioneered by different state and non-state actors. This has led to debates about understanding who wields more power in terms of the regulation of the agro-based fuel industry at a time of land redistributive reforms in Zimbabwe. Little attention, however, has been given to the issue of water resources in the current biofuel production projects. By examining the large-scale production of *Jatropha* and sugar cane in Chisumbanje and Mwenezi districts in Zimbabwe, we seek to unravel how the new investors have accumulated land and water resources. We analyse how this lead to water competition between the communities, settled in Chisumbanje and Mwenezi, and the new biofuel actors. In the following discussion, we seek to answer the following questions. What is the configuration of the new politics of water and post-land reform in Zimbabwe and how has it been impacted by biofuel production? How has competing water interests impacted principles of Water Act (1998) in Zimbabwe as biofuel production requires the use of large volumes of water? How are water resources creating conflicts over access and use in these communities? What role do water institutions play in these circumstances? How are different smallholder farmers and new conglomerates sharing water in a tense environment especially after fast-track land reform? We use ethnographic fieldwork in Mwenezi district and archival research in the case of Chisumbanje to outline various debates and viewpoints related to these questions.

Introduction

Water and land are important livelihood resources for rural people, which create the basis for their daily sustenance. Water grabbing[1] and land grabbing[2] by foreign investors in biofuel production expand our understanding of intractable link between water and land as they usher in new changes on use and management of the critical livelihood resources. Zimbabwe, like many parts of Africa, is experiencing forms of water grabbing by the large conglomerates that have taken over the Nuanetsi ranch and the Chisumbanje estates as major biofuel production areas. This has led to new water governance structures and competing jurisdictions over limited water sources, which are the mainstay of Zimbabwean farmers for daily use and supplementing rain-fed agriculture due to the erratic rains that have been exacerbated by climate change and variability. In this paper, we seek to answer the following questions. What is the configuration of the new politics of water and post-land reform[3] in Zimbabwe and how has it been impacted by biofuel production? How have competing water interests impacted the Zimbabwe Water Act (1998) principles in Zimbabwe as biofuel production requires the use of large volumes of water? How are water resources creating conflicts over access and use in these communities? What role do water institutions play in these circumstances? How are the different smallholder farmers and the new conglomerates sharing water as communities are primarily agro-based, in a tense environment especially after fast-track land reform?[4] Considering these gaps in understanding and given that water is a medium through which social relations are constructed, this paper shows how access to water is defined and contested in areas affected by large-scale land acquisitions. We demonstrate how contestations for water modify the institutional landscape of water resource management. The implication of every land deal is the loss of access to water by local communities. Water dispossession occurs at the same time with land dispossession.

In commercial farming, not only fertile soils but also water during the dry season are needed. Many land-grabbing contracts also secure water rights to the investor. This has far greater short-term implications on households, especially women. Fencing out water resources by big corporate companies has serious problems. We have long become victims of foreign and local investors under the guise of promoting agriculture and mechanization. Water is an increasingly precious resource used for many critical purposes across Africa. In many areas of Zimbabwe, water resources are already significantly stressed. Communities survive and depend on water for agriculture, livestock, domestic consumption, religious ceremonies, cultural practices and other activities that characterize human and cultural identities. Increased biofuel production highlights a new form of 'fencing out' communities from water resources they have used for generations. Water is a serious commodity that, if not managed well, has a potential to cause conflict. In both Mwenezi and Chisumbanje, communities have lost access to water and thus control of their livelihoods and survival.

Water grabbing: an African experience

Across the continent, rural people are increasingly finding themselves at the mercy of international capital forces as land and water resources are being transferred to mega-farming institutions providing biofuels and food for consumption elsewhere (Cotula 2012; Matondi 2011). The phenomenon of water grabbing has received little attention because scholarship has increasingly concentrated on land deals. Woodhouse and Ganho (2011, p. 10) note that with the exception of some of the large Sahelian projects, relatively little research on these investment deals has addressed the implications for water use. Mann and Smaller (2011, p. 10) note that '... a critical motivation in the current trend towards large-scale land acquisitions is the water factor. Agriculture trade specialists have long recognized the notion of trade in virtual water to account for the water needed to grow different crops'. Today we see investment in water rights in foreign states, through the purchase or lease of land with associated water rights and access, as a critical part of the new process of securing long-term farming investments. Investors often look for lands that have potential high sources of water and are also useful in terms of carrying out irrigation activities. Cotula (2011) notes that:

> many African governments are signing away water rights for decades to large investors. But they are doing so with little regard for how this will impact the millions of other users from fishermen to pastoralists whose livelihoods depend on customary access to water.

The connection between land and water becomes clear-cut, hence the need for the African governments to revisit their understandings of foreign direct investment and how that impacts land-based livelihoods in rural areas.

Speaking in Rome, Ugandan fisherwoman Rehema Bavuma Namaganda from the World Forum of Fish Harvesters and Fish Workers indicated that land grabbing was a serious threat to food security in Africa because both dry lands and water streams are sources of water and therefore food for fishing communities (http://intercontinentalcry. org). As big investments in land and industrial fisheries by large corporations, mining and hydroelectric projects increase, many people are facing uncertainty in future food supplies (Cotula 2011). Those who own land inevitably control water resources. Thus, use and extraction of water in most African countries is not sufficiently regulated to protect local communities from the depletion and pollution of the water resources they rely on, or the regulations that do exist are not enforced. What usually happens is that when large-scale land deals are struck, groundwater and other water resources on these lands become the property of international companies. This leads to dual loss of land and water by local communities because the vast food or biofuel plants require large-scale irrigation, which means diverting water from locals. Usually large companies demand and place clauses in the agreements that allow them first and at times exclusive access to water. An example is how a Libyan company, Malibya, acquired a 50-year lease of 100,000 hectares to grow rice in Mali, in which the government granted the company priority access to water during the dry season. This meant that local producers suffered reduced access to water from the Niger River, the main source of irrigation water in the region (Höring 2011, p. 3).

Practices of large foreign companies, especially those in biofuel production, often lead to depletion and pollution of water resources through clearing of trees and emission of chemicals. Often local communities have little protection against such actions. For example, in Sierra Leone, water from the Rokel River became polluted with herbicides and fertilizers when Addax Bioenergy leased the swamplands and started using the water from the river for irrigation (Höring 2011, p. 2). Woodhouse and Ganho (2011) argue that foreign direct investment projects in Africa's agriculture will involve development of water use and associated infrastructure for storage and distribution of water, which can potentially help small-scale farmers. This benefit is premised on the assumption that investment in water infrastructure will provide new sources of water at times when water may be scarce. On the other hand, new large-scale agricultural projects will have negative impact on existing small-scale water users as 'new owners' fence them out. De Schutter (2011, p. 249) argues that large-scale land deals accelerate the development of a market for land rights with potentially destructive effects on the livelihoods, both of the current land users that will face increased commercial pressure on land and of groups depending on the commons (grazing and fishing grounds, and forests).

Rights-based approach to water dispossession

The process of 'water grabbing', state and non-state, in Zimbabwe has to be understood in the context of international protocols the government signed, which view water as a basic human right. Zimbabwe committed itself to meeting the United Nations Millennium Development Goals, one of which seeks to provide safe drinking water and sanitation to at least two-thirds of its population by 2015. Meeting this target is highly unlikely, and as water becomes more of an individually owned asset, poor communities' access to clean water is reduced. Studies in Zimbabwe (Derman, Hellum, Manzungu, Sithole, & Machiridza, 2007; Hellum & Derman, 2003; Matondi 2001; Nemarundwe 2003) have highlighted how communities in Zimbabwe conceptualize water as a public good for the benefit of all. Fencing out people from safe drinking water is thus an alien concept. In the African cosmology, water does not belong to an individual; thus, all have an equal access to clean water. International Covenant on Economic, Social and Cultural Rights (1996) includes the right to water as a fundamental human right, and Zimbabwe is a signatory to this. Derman *et al.*, (2007) notes that United Nations Educational and Scientific Organization (2003) in a global report titled *Water for People, Water for Life* explicitly emphasize right to water.

Article 24 of the Convention on the Rights of the Child states that a child has a right to clean drinking water, while Article 14.2 h of the Convention on the Elimination of All Forms of Discrimination Against Women states that rural women have a right to 'enjoy adequate living conditions, particularly in relation to housing, sanitation, electricity and water supply, transport and communications' on an equal basis with men (Derman *et al.*, 2007). African governments, including Zimbabwean, also recognize the right to water. Article 15 of the Protocol to the African Charter on Human and Peoples' Rights on the Rights of Women in Africa on the right to food obliges states partly to 'provide women with access to clean drinking water, sources of domestic fuel, land and the means of producing nutritious food' (Derman *et al.*, 2007, p. 250). The link between poverty eradication and access to water is undeniable. In this context, it is clear that the government of Zimbabwe recognizes the right to water as one of the fundamental human rights. Water grabbing thus poses a serious threat to the human rights of smallholder farmers who are increasingly being fenced out of accessible water.

Being near a water source is not sufficient because there are various factors that mediate in people accessing and using the water. Lawrence, Meigh, and Sullivan (2002) note that the water poverty approach seeks to combine measures of water availability and access with measures of people's capacity to access water. Water poverty manifests in various forms. For example, people can be water poor because there is insufficient clean or safe water for their daily use. Water poverty can also be linked to 'income poverty' whereby water may be available but too expensive for the poor (Lawrence, Meigh, & Sullivan 2002). Our understanding of water poverty encompasses water availability, access to water, capacity for sustaining access, the use of water and the environmental factors that impact on water quality and the ecology which water sustains (Sullivan 2002). In the case of Nuanetsi and Chisumbanje, we are witnessing a water poverty induced by marginalization of communities from water sources by large-scale biofuel producers.

Methodological approach and study areas

Nuanetsi ranch is located in Mwenezi East in the southern part of Zimbabwe, in Masvingo Province, 3 km from the Chirundu–Beitbridge R1 highway that connects Zambia, Zimbabwe and South Africa. It is approximately 500 metres from the Mwenezi Rural District Council, where the offices of the district administrator, environmental management agency, the Ministry of Constitutional Affairs and the district agricultural extension services are located. Nuanetsi is situated in ward 13 and covers more than 376,995[5] hectares of land, which constitute more than 1% of Zimbabwe's total land area. Nuanetsi ranch was the biggest cattle ranch in Zimbabwe until 2000, when the land reform process led to the occupation of some parts of the ranch. It was the biggest supplier of beef to the Cold Storage Commission of Zimbabwe, the leading state-run beef marketing company. Nuanetsi is located between agro-ecological regions (iv and v), with a mean annual rainfall of between 450 and 650 mm.[6] It is one of the dry and very hot areas in Zimbabwe.

Ethnographic methodology was used in Mwenezi's Chigwizi village where we resided at the village for a period of six months from February 2010 to August 2010.

By conducting an in-depth study of the village, we wanted to discover the similarities and differences between the two villages since Chigwizi is a fast-track A1 village settlement and Chisumbanje is an old communal irrigated village model based on the 1980 resettlement programme. At Chigwizi, we conducted an in-depth study of 20 households out of 232 households that form part of the whole village. Norms for water management form the backbone of the community system in these villages; we were able to study the dynamics of socio-ecological complexities through the lens of conflicts and cooperation for water. Integrating the two approaches allowed us to investigate the process of cooperation and conflict across time and space. Comparative methods proved especially helpful in probing for information on history and presence of water management. Information generated at one village would serve as a thread for generating information from another village. Using the standard ethnographic methods of participant observation, focused interviews, oral and life histories, water rights were studied at three levels of water management, namely governmental, technological and social configurations.

Participant observation (Bernard 1995; DeWalt & DeWalt, 2002) was the principal method for acquiring information, especially in the initial stage of the field study. We spent the field stay participating and observing a wide range of activities of a general nature such as agricultural activities, village meetings, repair and maintenance of irrigation equipment, celebration of rituals and festivals. As the nature of the research required, we were attentive not to miss daily observational rounds within the village, water and land meetings in Chigwizi. This enabled us to get glimpses into the water conflicts that were affecting the villagers and the investors with regard to irrigation systems and dam facilities. To facilitate the documentation of such observations, we made daily entries in our field diaries to keep track of daily activities.

Semi-structured interviews were held with government officials, rural district officials, multinational companies executives, non-governmental organizations and agricultural extension officers and the people in the communities. These interviews were conducted as a means of finding out important information with regard to land acquisition by the villagers and investors, water use, water sharing and how the investor's coming into these areas was affecting water access and the conflicts that emerged. The interviews were conducted with follow-up sessions and became an iterative process as this helped to bring out new information with regard to water issues in the area. Group interviews were also conducted with a maximum of 12 people and consisted of men and women from the village: this helped in acquiring more information on the hidden notions of water within the village and the community as a whole. Life histories and oral histories were also conducted in each village to get an idea of the process of changes taking place.

Sites

Chisumbanje is a village in the province of Manicaland, Zimbabwe. It is located in the Ndowoyo communal lands on the eastern bank of the Save River. It is about 95 km south of Birchenough Bridge on the Birchenough Bridge–Chiredzi road. The village is in Chipinge district and is bordered by villages such as Chinyamukwakwa and Mashubi. The Chisumbanje case study mainly concentrated on discussions with farmers, desk research and information sought from key informants who included government officials, non-governmental organizations, workers at the biofuel plant and district officials. Use of multiple qualitative methodologies deeply enhanced our comparative narrative decipher-ing various convergences and divergences in water access, practices and values across the two cases. Archival research included going through past studies, official documents, newspaper reports, magazines and official reports. The ethanol plant in Chisumbanje was a US$600 million project commissioned in 2010 and was producing 70,000 litres of fuel a day in August 2011. The plant has over 5000 hectares of land under sugar cane to sustain the production levels. There are also around 400 outgrowers in surrounding communities (http://bulawayo24.com). The project is a joint partnership of the Agricultural and Rural Development Authority (ARDA) with Macdom Rating, Green Fuel Investments and Macdom Investments. Residents of Chisumbanje have gone as far as petitioning Parliament, arguing that they were not properly consulted before the deal was done. The differences in experiences in Mwenezi and Chisumbanje allow for a comparative analysis though the case studies are informed by different methodologies.

Chigwizi shares borders with Mwenezana Estate and Uswaushava, an informal settlement within Nuanetsi on the Chiredzi side. Uswaushava is in the northern sphere of the farm.[7] The ranch is protected by the state (police officers and soldiers and security guards), which guards the animals, livestock, equipment and crops that the Bio Energy Company is involved in. This leads to questions over the ownership structure of the company as a private entity cannot command state security. The security forces also provide protection for the employees because there currently exist hostilities between the Bio Energy Company and the settlers at Chigwizi. To enter the ranch, one is subjected to heavy searching and formal clearing procedures; however, since one of the researchers had been working in Mwenezi for the past three years on her PhD work, entry into the village was negotiated through the social networks she had made in Mwenezi. It is currently being run by the Mwenezi Development Trust of Zimbabwe, an indigenous organization, in conjunction with a consortium of former white commercial farmers and an individual, Billy Rautenbach.[8] These actors have formed the Zimbabwe Bio Energy Company. The biofuel deal involves various high-level political and economic stakeholders in Zimbabwe, whose involvement in the land deal has not really been exposed to the public. The area has savanna vegetation, which is mainly composed of riverine forests, *msasa* and *marula* trees. There is a railway line that connects Nuanetsi with Rutenga and it is currently under construction to enable sugar production in the 2011 harvesting period.

Large-scale land deals in Zimbabwe

In 2000, when the land occupations ignited across Zimbabwe, Nuanetsi ranch by nature of its size became a focal point for land contestations. The ranch became a political hot potato as simmering divisions within ZANU PF became apparent. By virtue of its size and lack of activity over many years, the ranch was an ideal candidate to provide land. Didymus Mutasa, ZANU PF stalwart, argued as much noting: 'we have realized that the Nuanetsi ranch is lying idle and the Masvingo political leadership would want it to be designated for resettlement. It would be unfair to leave such land idle when thousands of Zimbabweans need land'. However, this did not assume former ZAPU leaders within government who could not understand why an indigenous-owned entity was being targeted for forcible resettlement. The land reform was based on the ideology of righting historical injustice of colonization as noted by the late Vice-president Joseph Musika:

> Nuanetsi ranch is owned by DTZ, a black-owned company and if we designate that land, who are we empowering? We cannot take land from a black man and give it to another black man. If there is anyone trying to do something there tell him he is wasting his time because that land was bought and cannot just be given to people without any justification. (Quoted in Mujere & Dombo, 2011, p. 13)

The Masvingo ZANU PF leadership was then instructed not to acquire the ranch for resettlement. Zimbabwe Development Trust (DTZ), however, as a corporate responsibility strategy, offered land for resettlement as Scoones, Marongwe, Mahenehene, Murimbarimba, and Sukume (2010, p. 40) noted:

> The DTZ offered 150000 hectares for official settlement, with 54000 ha going to 120 A2 beneficiaries. About 25 of the A2 farmers went into cattle ranching, with the remaining 100 engaging in crop production under irrigation. About 6500 households were allocated plots ranging in size from 0.5 to 10 hectares under the A1 model. New farmers were allocated grazing blocs by the Trust and there was also substantial lease grazing arrangements with white ranchers whose land had been taken in other areas. No-one is ready to admit the numbers of ranch cattle moved to the Nuanetsi ranch, but they run into the thousands.

There were, however, thousands more who 'illegally settled' within the ranch including the 232 families at our study site, Chigwizi village.

In 2009, construction began on a US$600 million ethanol plant in Chisumbanje by a company known as Green Fuels. The Green Fuel ethanol factory is located at Chisumbanje, Chipinge South, about 500 km from the capital Harare along the Tanganda–Ngundu Road. Checheche is the hosting growth point within the district. The plant is the biggest of its kind in Africa, directly employing 4500 people and creating thousands of jobs in support downstream and upstream services. The project is owned by government through ARDA in partnership with Macdom Rating, Green Fuel Investments and Macdom Investments. Madcom Investments is owned by Billy Rautenbach who also has interests in the Mwenezi biofuel initiative. The exact ownership structure is shrouded in secrecy; however, villagers in Chisumbanje in 2011 petitioned the House of Assembly Committee on Agriculture, Water, Lands and Resettlement claiming the deal does not comply with the country's indigenization laws, which make it compulsory for all companies to have 51% of ownership by locals. The plant is set on 46,000 hectares (10,000 at Middle Sabi and 36,000 at Chisumbanje) of land and, in 2012, 8500 hectares were under sugar cane plantation. Just three months after commissioning, the plant had produced one million litres of fuel.

In Chisumbanje, the plant is built on estates that belong to government through ARDA. From interviews with community leaders it is apparent that communities know the land belonged to ARDA. Even though communities had settled on the land they knew very well, it belonged to the government. Communities are, however, not happy by the way the transaction was done without their knowledge and being removed without alternative settlement and having their crops destroyed. As of June 2012, figures from the Chipinge Rural District Council indicated that out of the 1733 families displaced by the company, only 499 were allocated 0.5 hectares of land each. More families will be displaced if the plant starts to operate at full scale (http://www.zimpdates/news.co.zw).

The nexus between water and land in Zimbabwe

Fast-track land reform introduced a new agrarian structure in Zimbabwe where farms were dissected into small to medium enterprises and a few large-scale farms remained as they were before the land reform process. The fast-track process had not affected areas like Chisumbanje, which already had resettlement models based on irrigation set up in the 1980s and 1990s. Acquisition of land by the communities in Chisumbanje was based on the need to extend farming activities with prime productive lands and hence the people who resided in communal areas wanted to move to the irrigation schemes. The irrigation schemes are mainly smallholder systems, where the farmers were supported by the government during the first five years. After that period, farming became a cooperative effort where the farmers had to maintain irrigation pumps together and pay for the water. In Zimbabwe, individual farm operated irrigation systems also exist with the large-scale farmers and the medium-sized farmers operating with highly mechanized equipment that draws water from even man-made dams on the farms. In 2000, Nuanetsi ranch was occupied by the communities of Lundi, Neshuro, Matibi and Chikombedzi necessitated by the need for more land. However, Nuanetsi ranch had not been gazetted for resettlement because it was owned by an indigenous company, DTZ, having been bought by Joshua Nkomo[9] who wanted to promote indigenous farming (Moyo 2011). As of 2010, however, the families have been served with eviction notices and asked to move out of the ranch because it has now been taken over by a consortium of former Zimbabwean white farmers, DTZ and political elites (Mutopo 2011). This stems from the sociopolitical history of Zimbabwe where land has been a contested resource amongst the whites and blacks. However, there have also been contestations over land access and use amongst various indigenous ethnic groups within the country over scale, geography and use. This has also been exacerbated by the policy processes where the national elites have also been involved in the water- and land-grabbing activities, undermining the local populations whose livelihoods are underpinned by the resources.

The eviction efforts by the government have been resisted by the communities who argue that they have a right to the land and water sources. Politicization of land and water resources has been much heightened with the DTZ enacting irrigation facilities at Nuanetsi, fencing all the dams and increasing security patrols to avoid water harvesting and water usage by the communities of Chigwizi. The water is meant for crocodile farming, sugar cane farming, livestock and game at the farm. Nuanetsi ranch has now become a site of heightened political tension with the district and provincial land committees advocating for the removal of the settlers. Contestation is now over land and water because during the fast-track land reform process the government pointed out that the settlers could use the water resources at the farms, and thus dams and irrigation, but now there has been a shift in policy direction reverting to the pre-fast-track period where large-scale farms could not share their water resources with the communal areas surrounding them. Borras, Fig, and Monsalve (2011) highlight that there is an intractable link between mega-lands and water for biofuel production such that, if biofuel land deals are not properly managed, livelihoods of communities in places such as southern Mozambique will be disrupted as companies such as ProCana grab land and water simultaneously.

In this paper, we have discussed how post-fast-track land reform, in the light of current biofuel frenzy in Zimbabwe, has led to new water user principles and how government had not deciphered how land reform would impact large-scale production of sugar cane and *Jatropha*. One cannot talk of investing in farmland, given that there is a symbiotic connection between crop production and water use as commercial agriculture requires use of irrigation systems that require the availability of underground water. The impact of water grabbing on rural livelihoods is assessed by the perceptions of affected communities with regard to distance to present water sources, use of water sources developed by the multinational companies, villager initiatives for creating water sources and the statutory acts governing water use in Zimbabwe. Perceptions of the investors were also taken into account because they have a greater bearing on the current configuration of livelihoods for communities in Chisumbanje and Mwenezi, particularly over rights to water. This has to be understood with regard to the fact that ownership of land that covers a river has been understood by the communities as meaning that one controls land and not the water: according to the customary norms, water is a God-given resource that anyone can use (Matondi 2001); hence, the villagers have a right to cross into Nuanetsi ranch's protected side where there are streams and rivers where one can acquire water for their multiple uses.

Water dispossession in Mwenezi and Chisumbanje

Water-related conflicts are caused by the way in which water and its uses are governed, which inevitably involves conflicting interests. Water is becoming not only a scarce resource but also a resource that is divided unevenly between regions and states, and within societies. Unevenly divided scarce resources are – as history shows – contentious subjects that can lead to conflict. Conflicts may easily arise if water is, or is perceived as being, (over) used and/or degraded by other actors at a cost to oneself. Water conflicts have emerged at the local level in Chigwizi and Chisumbanje over: reduced access or heightened competition over access; the impact of dams and diversions; and the privatization of water services. In Chisumbanje and Chigwizi village in Mwenezi, conflicts emerged particularly over riparian rights to water that can be understood with regard to the fact that ownership of land that covers a river has been understood by the communities in Zimbabwe as meaning that one controls land and not the water; hence, the villagers have a right to cross into Nuanetsi ranch's protected areas as well as in Chisumbanje where there are dams, streams and rivers to acquire water for their gardens or their livestock. These water use practices were not favourable to the multinational companies who argued that to them the villagers' entry into their premises constituted trespassing and collection of water was viewed by the company officials as stealing because the water was now under their jurisdiction since they owned the land legally. In Chigwizi, the conflict was more pronounced as the villagers argued that when they acquired land during fast-track land reform the government had pointed out that villagers had to share water sources as the government had to embark on increasing water sources for the villagers.

In Chigwizi, the villagers complained that water at the Moriah weir which constituted the Sosonye dam, Injelenga River, Duvi River and Sosonye River is now under the control of the white farmer at Moriah who practises citrus irrigation farming and Nuanetsi ranch which was using it for growing vast tracts of sugar cane, breeding crocodiles and as a water hole for their thousands of beef cattle and game animals such that the villagers had lost direct access to the water sources. Hall (2011) and Woodhouse (2012), points out that rich countries and rich individuals are now buying poor countries' soil fertility, land and water resources at meagre amounts as compared to the livelihoods that can be generated from the land for the indigene communities. The farmer at Moriah and Nuanetsi officials pointed out that they paid for the water service at the Zimbabwe National Water Authority (ZINWA) and so they had exclusive rights of overseeing and controlling their water sources to avoid depletion. Thus, users who did not pay for the water service should not have access, demonstrating how water was now emerging as a commercial product. The farmers pointed out that fences had been erected and patrol game police officers were now protecting Nuanetsi, making it difficult for them to access water within the farm they had settled in. This had created scenarios of 'water fencing' that were meant by the multinational companies to exclude the community of Chigwizi from accessing water. The settlers felt this was a way of pushing them out of the farm because they had no access to domestic use and for their animals. Lack of access to water meant they were, in other words, landless: water and land access has a knit connection where availability of one without the other is not useful.

Conflicts also erupted over irrigation water use particularly in Chisumbanje, where the village was an irrigation entity. The villagers noted that, since 2003, their irrigation pump had not been working but in 2010 the company involved in the biofuel production in the area had repaired their irrigation pump. However, now the irrigation pump has been connected to the company's main water supply and villagers argued that sometimes they were told there was no electricity to pump water when the company wanted to control their water use, ignoring that their livelihood was based on horticultural production, which required water for most of the crops. The company authorities pointed out that they had revamped the whole irrigation system for the village and had a right to control its use as they require huge amounts of water for their sugar cane and *Jatropha* fields. Water control using the legal and economic principles proved to be unimportant to the villagers who argued that the company was now taking over their water user rights and they feared that they could lose their water to the company as the company was indeed the one that required more water use than the villagers. ZINWA has not helped the villagers in creating a common ground with the company, which emphasized the technological aspects of water as being key in land use practices for biofuel production. This leads to water creating dependant relationships amongst farmers and companies that are highly unequal and always leave smallholder farmers at a disadvantaged position. Effective water measurement systems are important with regard to water just like in land management systems where boundaries of land are demarcated amongst the users so that there are no conflicts over trespassing, especially with regard to land and water sources that are interlinked. Measurement here does not translate to the cubic meters used by the farmers but rather to the way water institutions are managed transparently and users have common understanding about water sharing principles.

According to the Water Act of 1998 of Zimbabwe, all water is vested in the president and not private institutions or individuals. However, the two cases under examination reflect how water is becoming an individual good that is privatized by those with the economic muscle as evidenced by the operations of the biofuel companies in Zimbabwe. The villagers are left with little negotiating power over their water rights because they have lost the water sources and land to the investors. These cases of disputes reflect the interplay of local hydrology, politics and people's struggle for legitimizing their claims for water. Chikozho and Latham (2005) argue that it is paramount to note that in the Shona culture which is prevalent in Zimbabwe, where the people are also the land ('the land is the people') and its resources, this worldview embraces a notion of man and his environment in ecological union, which demonstrates the interconnectedness of water and land in Zimbabwean environmental discourses. Agency problems are cropping up in Chigwizi and Dowoyo villages because the actors are not willing to follow the rules governing water access and use as codified in the national laws. Legal pluralism and forum shopping suggest that when such conflicts over water rights arise, people shop around amongst multiple normative frameworks such as customary law, state law and religious law, coexisting in a society, depending on which of the laws they consider would help validate their claim (Bruns & Meinzen-Dick, 2005; Meinzen-Dick & Pradhan, 2002; Pradhan & Meinzen-Dick, 2003; Spiertz, 2000).

The ideas from the theory of forum shopping, (Benda-Beckmann, 1984), although very helpful in analysing and understanding conflicts over water rights, implicitly assume that people have prior information of provisions of different legal frameworks, at least in relation to water rights. The logic of shopping around also assumes that conflict over water rights arises when there is conflict between different legal frameworks. As evidenced by these cases, people's actual water rights are embedded not in certificates, but in the rules governing who can use how much water and for what purposes. A gradual approach allowing clarification of rights in response to specific problems and local conditions can offer one way to efficiently provide an enabling framework for improving water management. For example, within the irrigation sector in Zimbabwe, by 1994 commercial farmers (predominantly white) still used about 84% of the available irrigation water, while small-scale and subsistence farmers (predominantly black) used only 7% (Hellum & Derman, 2003). With the advent of fast-track land reform irrigation, water usage has changed with more black farmers involved in farming but also irrigation systems have been vandalized by the new farmers which have affected the terrain of irrigation farming. The coming into play of large conglomerates involved in biofuel production leads to new irrigation water use at highest levels again, being dominated by the commercial sector as evidenced by the Nuanetsi and Chisumbanje cases, with little involvement of the smallholder farmers in the process. Consequently, water policy and law represent the complex interplay between multiple interests, priorities and approaches that, as Derman, Gonese, Chikozho, Latham, and Sithole (2000) argue, are not always compatible. Hellum and Derman (2003, p. 11) note that 'the reform process is a site of tensions and conflicts between values and principles embedded in liberal economic thinking and more welfarist concerns embedded in both human rights and African customary laws'.

It became evident that in both sites, due to the contestations over water access, women and children were the most affected because they now had the extra burden of fetching water from other villages that were far, especially during the dry period in Mwenezi where most of the rivers and river beds could not provide water for domestic use. In cases where men went to search for water in Chigwizi or Chisumbanje, they used technology-centred mechanisms such as ox/donkey-drawn carts for fetching water and did not affect their physical well-being unlike women and children who used water carrier they had to balance on their heads. The effect of 'fencing out' local communities in both cases is thus gendered. Women in rural Zimbabwe carry the burden for provision of domestic water. As water sources are lost to large farms, it is women who suffer the brunt as they are forced to improvise alternative means to access water. These alternate ways are in many ways detrimental to their health and their families. As noted above, the physical toil of walking long distances to get water is at times coupled with using unsafe water sources that carry the threat of diseases. In Mwenezi and Chisumbanje, there are families who have resorted to shallow uncovered/unprotected wells for domestic water use.

In Chisumbanje, an ethanol plant has been accused of poisoning water sources. In September 2011, the Platform for Youth Development (PYD) noted that there was panic and fear because emissions from the ethanol production plant killed livestock and destroyed the environment (PYD, 2011). Emissions from the plant are alleged to have contaminated water from Jerawachera River, which is the main water source. Jerawachera River serves the greater part of Chisumbanje as the main source of water and is a tributary of Save River, which feeds into Limpopo (PYD, 2011). Groundwater sources, if affected by emissions from the plant, will directly impact the livelihoods of the poor. Death of livestock is a serious blow, especially in a dry region like Chisumbanje where rain-fed agriculture is problematic. *The Herald*, 30 March 2011, reported that one person died, while 70 others were affected by cholera in Chisumbanje because the ethanol plant could not provide adequate water and sanitary facilities to workers. Water issues thus remain topical and important given its importance to livelihood sustainability for small agricultural producers. The loss of land to the ethanol plant is related to the loss of water, whilst fears of pollution have left communities in Chisumbanje with many questions and uncertainties.

Managing water use, institutions and politics

The political nature of water resources in Zimbabwe keeps increasing both in urban and in rural areas. Different water institutions have been created to deal with water issues from the village to the national level but their proper functioning has been affected by political influences and the continual dwindling of water sources due to climate change and climate variability. In the villages under study, there was a water committee at Dowoyo village in Chisumbanje, which managed the irrigation system and the implementation of rules created for effective functioning of the boreholes and dams. However, in Chigwizi village there was no water committee at the village level; instead, the ZINWA officials managed water use in the community. The villagers in Chigwizi Mwenezi argued that ZINWA officials were not forthcoming when it came to the water problems they faced because they tended to prioritize the Nuanetsi ranch issues, such that one villager remarked that, 'ZINWA is just another entity taking water away from us'. This leads to the fact that ZINWA was associated with undermining the villagers' use of water and hence creating suspicion with regard to its role. Lack of faith with the institution existed and the villagers showed resentment towards ZINWA. However, in Dowoyo, Chisumbanje, the water committee was somehow effective because it managed to discuss water use implications with the biofuel plant managers and ZINWA officials; however, the deciding parameters for the water governance came from the biofuel plant officials who paid more money in terms of the water user pay principle that exists in managing water in Zimbabwe.

A critical look at the management of the water reveals that the biofuel actors have now assumed more power over water governance as compared to the ordinary villagers such that in future the role of ZINWA is going to be affected with the large conglomerates taking over both the land and water governance as has happened in Mozambique (Borras *et al.*, 2011). This also negates the Water Act principle of 1998 which emphasize that water resources and water should flow to the marginalized communities. Available empirical evidence spanning more than 10 years of fieldwork in Zimbabwe by Manzungu and Machiridza (2005) suggests that sustainable productive water use in the smallholder agricultural sector in Zimbabwe, in both the short and long term, is not assured. The argument being made here is not that changing water legislation does not lead to productive water use by smallholder farmers. Rather, the argument is that changes in the water law are likely to succeed if they are underpinned by a sound economic ideology, referring to economic fundamental ideals/values that are popularized and translated into practice throughout society (Manzungu & Machiridza, 2005). This will provide a sound platform for appropriate water-related policies.

Nuanetsi ranch belongs to the Mwenezi River basin and Chisumbanje to the Save River basin, putting them under the Save catchment council. However, the functioning of the catchment councils was affected by the fast-track land reform programme and it is difficult to understand their role in present-day Zimbabwe. The new settlers brought their own institutional mandates that they imposed on the catchment councils, creating somehow ad-hoc parallel structures. The association of catchment council duties has also been affected by a lack of finances. Spatial and jurisdictional boundaries of the new water institutions remain a problem (Latham, 2002). Some of the problems have to do with the fact that communities owe allegiance to traditional institutions, district and provincial administrative boundaries, which do not necessarily follow catchment lines. The management of the institutions has also been highly politicized, especially when it comes to the economic functioning such that this has affected policy implementation and execution of duties. Water management in Zimbabwe has been influenced by the Integrated Water Resources Management principle of stakeholder participation but this has more often been resulted in politicization of the processes.

Conclusion

This research has demonstrated how water dispossession and grabbing by large-scale agricultural corporation is adversely affecting livelihoods of smallholder farmers. Water conflicts are increasing and involve a complex matrix that consists of foreign investors, the government, local villages and bureaucrats, leading to new water governing actors.

As evidenced by the case study, Zimbabwe's pre-fast-track land reform water policies have lost credibility in a new era, where communities are now aware of their rights to livelihoods and how they are embedded in water resources. The conflicts demonstrate how land and water are increasingly being politicized and despite the existence of international human rights law to regulate water and land use, rural communities in Africa have their right to access compromised. The gendered implications of water grabbing lead to women and children being more affected because they have always been the ones who have to fetch water, travelling long distances. The annexation of water and water fencing for biofuel production by the large conglomerates will even lead to an increasing burden on women and children, as they have to devise more strategies of water harvesting techniques. This reflects how water is a politicized livelihood source in as much as the concerned actors try to avoid the reality.

Acknowledgements

We are grateful to the anonymous reviewers. Our Post Doctoral funding initiatives, namely, the Volkswagen Foundation, Germany's Social Science Initiative for Patience Mutopo and the Rhodes University's Sociology Post Doctoral Grant for Manase Kudzai Chiweshe, respectively, are greatly appreciated.

Notes

1. We define water grabbing as the rush by foreign and local elites in acquiring water for large-scale use, especially with regard to commercial production of *Jatropha*, maize and sugar cane, which are the major biofuel crops.
2. Land grabbing is the phenomenon where large tracts of land are acquired for the large-scale production of biofuels and food crops, mainly by countries such as UK, Sweden, Norway, Germany, United Arab Emirates, China, Saudi Arabia and South Africa, in the developing world.
3. The land reform in Zimbabwe is highly contested with some authors arguing that it is completed and others arguing that it is still an ongoing process due to the unresolved issues such as tenure security; however, understanding this problematized notion depends on one's analytical lens. We argue in this paper that the process has been completed since a decade has already elapsed and people have settled on the land acquired during the process.
4. This refers to the accelerated land redistribution programme that the government of Zimbabwe embarked on in 2000 as way of dealing with colonial vestiges that saw blacks residing in communal areas with poor impoverished farms. The programme led to the redrawing of history by resettling ordinary black Zimbabweans on white commercial farms.
5. Mwenezi district files, February 2010.
6. Meteorological office files, Rutenga, April 2009.
7. Scoones et al. (2010) have also provided a rich explanation about how the Nuanetsi ranch has been a controversial entity in the southern part of Zimbabwe's land reform.
8. It has always been argued that Billy Rautenbach is the largest shareholder in the Zimbabwe Bio Energy project. He has also acquired land in the Chisumbanje area where he is growing sugar cane for biofuels. This has been done through partnerships with the local communal farmers.
9. Joshua Nkomo was one of the liberation war heroes of Zimbabwe, who eventually passed away more than a decade ago. He led the movement that started the Nuanetsi ranch in the pre-fast-track era in Zimbabwe in the 1980s.

Notes on contributors

Patience Mutopo is a Post Doctoral Researcher with the Cologne African Studies Centre, University of Cologne, Germany, and the Rural Development Sociology Group, University of Wageningen, the Netherlands. She obtained her Ph.D. from the University of Cologne in Germany.

Manase Kudzai Chiweshe is a Post Doctoral Researcher at the Sociology Department, Rhodes University Grahamstown, South Africa. He obtained his Ph.D. from Rhodes University, South Africa.

References

Benda-Beckmann, K. (1984). *The broken staircase to consensus: Village justice and state courts in Minangkabau.* Dordrecht: Foris.

Bernard, H. R. (1995). *Research methods in anthropology.* London: AltaMira.

Borras, M., Figure, D., & Monsalve, S. (2011). The politics of agro fuels and mega land and water deals: Insights from the ProCana case, Mozambique. *Review of African Political Economy, 38,* 215–234.

Bruns, B. R., & Meinzen-Dick, R. (2005). Frameworks for water rights: An overview of institutional options. In B. R. Bruns, C. Ringler, & R. Meinzen-Dick (Eds.), *Water rights reform: Lessons for institutional design* (pp. 1–25). Washington, DC: International Food Policy Research Institute.

Chikozho, C., & Latham, J. (2005). *Shona customary norms in the context of water sector reforms in Zimbabwe.* Paper presented at the International Workshop on African Water Laws: Plural Legislative Rural Frameworks for Rural Water Management in Africa, 26–28 January, Johannesburg.

Cotula, L. (2011). *Are land deals driving water grabs?* Edinburgh, Scotland: International Institute of Environment and Development.

Cotula, L. (2012). The international political economy of the global land rush: A critical appraisal of trends, scale, geography and drivers. *Journal of Peasant Studies, 39,* 649–680.

De Schutter, O. (2011). How not to think of land-grabbing: Three critiques of large-scale investments in farmland. *Journal of Peasant Studies, 38,* 249–279.

Derman, B., Gonese, F., Chikozho, C., Latham, J., & Sithole, P. (2000). *Decentralization, devolution and development: Reflections on the water reform process in Zimbabwe.* Harare: CASS, University of Zimbabwe.

Derman, D., Hellum, A., Manzungu, E., Sithole, P., & Machiridza, R. (2007). Intersections of law, human rights and water management in Zimbabwe: Implications for rural livelihoods. In B. van Koppen, M. Giordano, & J. Butterworth (Eds.), *Community-based water law and water resource management reform in developing countries* (pp. 248–269). Pretoria, South Africa: CAB International and Institute of Integrated Water Resources.

DeWalt, K. M., & DeWalt, B. R. (2002). *Participant observation: A guide for fieldworkers.* Walnut Creek, CA: AltaMira.

Hall, R. (2011). Land grabbing in Southern Africa: The many faces of the investor rush. *Review of African Political Economy, 38,* 193–214.

Hellum, A., & Derman, B. (2003). *Renegotiating water and land rights in Zimbabwe: Some reflections on legal pluralism.* Paper prepared for presentation at the Conference on Remaking Law in Africa: Transnationalism, Persons and Rights, Edinburgh, Scotland.

Höring, U. (2011). *Water and land grabbing.* Ecumenical Water Network (EWN) and Ecumenical Advocacy Alliance (EAA). The Hague: Institute of Social Studies.

Latham, C. J. K. (2002). Manyame Catchment Council: A review of the reform of the water sector in Zimbabwe. *Physics and Chemistry of the Earth, 27,* 907–917.

Lawrence, P., Meigh, J., & Sullivan, C. (2002). Multidimensional Analysis of Water Poverty in the Mena Region: An Empirical Comparison with Physical Indicators. Department of Economics, Keele University, Staffordshire, United Kingdom.

Mann, H., & Smaller, C. (2001). *A thirst for distant lands.* London: International Institute of Development Studies.

Manzungu, E., & Machiridza, R. (2005). *Economic-legal ideology and water management in Zimbabwe: Implications for smallholder farmers.* Paper presented at the International Workshop on African Water Laws: Plural, Legislative Frameworks for Rural Water Management in Africa, 26–28 January, Johannesburg, South Africa.

Matondi, P. (2001). *The struggle for access to land and water resources in Zimbabwe: The case of Shamva district.* (Doctoral thesis). Swedish University of Agricultural Sciences, Uppsala, Sweden.

Matondi, P. B. (2011). Agro investments at a time of redistributive reform in Zimbabwe. In P. B. Matondi, K. Havnevik, & A. Beyene (Eds.), *Bio fuels, land grabbing and food security in Africa* (pp. 85–89). London: Zed Books.

Meinzen-Dick, R. S., & Pradhan, R. (2002). *Legal pluralism and dynamic property rights*, CAPRi Working Paper No. 22.

Mujere, J., & Dombo, S. (2011). Large scale investment projects and land grabs in Zimbabwe: The case of Nuanetsi, Ranch Bio-Diesel Project. Land Deal Politics Initiative, The Institute of Development Studies, University of Sussex, Sussex.

Moyo, S. (2011). Land concentration and accumulation after redistributive reform in post settler Zimbabwe. *Review of African Political Economy, 38*, 257–276.

Mutopo, P. (2011). *Gendered dimensions of land and rural livelihoods: The case of new settler farmer displacement at Nuanetsi ranch, Mwenezi district, Zimbabwe*. The Land Deal Politics Initiative Programme, Institute for Poverty, Land and Agrarian Studies, University of Western Cape, Cape Town. Retrieved from http://www.plaas/Researchpapers/The-Land-Deal-Politics-Initiative-LDPI/LDPI-Research-Network/

Nemarundwe, N. (2003). *Negotiating resource access: Institutional arrangements for woodlands and water use in southern Zimbabwe*. (Doctoral thesis). Swedish University of Agricultural Sciences, Uppsala, Sweden.

Platform for Youth Development. (2011). *Panic in Chisumbanje as poisonous disposal from ethanol plant kills livestock - PYD press release*. Retrieved October 15, 2011, from http://www.crisis-zimbabwe.org/index.php?option=com_content&view=article&id=381:panic-in-chisumbanje-as-poisonous-disposal-from-ethanol-plant-kills-livestock-pyd-press-release&catid=47:news

Pradhan, R., & Meinzen-Dick, R. (2003). Which rights are rights? Water rights, culture, and underlying values. *Water Nepal, 9/10*, 37–61.

Scoones, I., Marongwe, N., Mahenehene, J., Murimbarimba, F., & Sukume, C. (2010). *Myths and realities of Zimbabwe's fast track land reform programme*. London: James Currey.

Spiertz, H. L. J. (2000). Water rights and legal pluralism: Some concepts of a legal anthropological approach. In B. R. Bruns & R. S. Meinzen-Dick (Eds.), *Negotiating water rights* (pp. 162–199). New Delhi: International Food Policy Research Institute.

Sullivan, C. (2002). Calculating a water poverty index. *World Development, 30*, 1195–1211.

Woodhouse, P. (2012). New investment, old challenges: Land deals and water constraint in African agriculture. *Journal of Peasant Studies, 39*, 777–794.

Woodhouse, P., & Ganho, A. S. (2011). *Is water the hidden agenda of agricultural land acquisition in sub-Saharan Africa?* Paper presented at the International Conference on Global Land Grabbing, April 6–8, 2011, Land Deals Politics Initiative (LDPI), Institute of Development Studies, University of Sussex, United Kingdom.

Index

Note: Page references in **bold** refer to tables
Page numbers in *italic* type refer to tables
Page numbers followed by 'n' refer to notes

INDEX